THINKING ABOUT THE ENVIRONMENT

Readings on Politics, Property, and the Physical World

THINKING ABOUT THE ENVIRONMENT

Readings on Politics, Property, and the Physical World

Matthew Alan Cahn and Rory O'Brien

M.E. Sharpe
Armonk, New York
London, England

Library of Congress Cataloging-in-Publication Data

Thinking about the environment : readings on politics, property, and the physical world /
edited by Matthew Alan Cahn and Rory O'Brien.
p. cm.
Includes bibliographical references and index.
ISBN 1-56324-795-X (cloth : alk. paper).—ISBN 1-56324-796-8 (pbk. : alk. paper)
1. Environmentalism.
2. Man—Influence on nature.
3. Philosophy of nature.
4. Social ecology.
I. Cahn, Matthew Alan, 1961–
II. O'Brien, Rory, 1955–
GE195.T45 1996
304.2—dc20
96-10749
CIP

Printed in the United States of America

The paper used in this publication meets the minimum requirements of the
American National Standard for Information Sciences—
Permanence of Paper for Printed Library Materials,
ANSI Z 39.48-1984.

∞

BM (c) 10 9 8 7 6 5 4 3 2 1
BM (p) 10 9 8 7 6 5 4 3 2 1

For Diane, Jonah, and Andrea

Contents

Acknowledgments xi

1 Thinking About the Environment: What's Theory Got to Do With It?
Rory O'Brien and Matthew Cahn 3

Part I: The Physical World

2 On the Physical World: An Introduction
Rory O'Brien 11

3 The Creation of the World
Genesis 18

4 The Purpose of Nature
Aristotle 20

5 The City of God
St. Augustine 25

6 Creation in Light of Luiseño Religion
Sam Gill 29

7 The Hopi Myth of Creation
Frank Waters 40

Part II: Law and Property

8 Law, Property, and the Environment: An Introduction
Rory O'Brien 57

9 The Nature of Private Property
Jean-Jacques Rousseau 64

10 Of Property
John Locke 76

11 The Commodity
Karl Marx 87

12 The Categorical Imperative
Immanuel Kant 96

13 The Problem of Justice Between Generations
John Rawls 104

14 The New Forms of Control
Herbert Marcuse 112

15 Liberalism and Environmental Quality
Matthew Cahn 120

Part III: The Green Critique

16 The Green Critique: An Introduction
Matthew Cahn 131

17 Higher Laws
Henry David Thoreau 139

18 Nature
Ralph Waldo Emerson 147

19 Silent Spring
Rachel Carson 150

20 The Population Bomb
Paul Ehrlich 156

21 The Closing Circle: Nature, Man, and Technology
Barry Commoner 161

22 Ecology: The Shallow and the Deep
Arne Naess 167

23 The Tragedy of the Commons
Garrett Hardin 173

24 Feminism and the Revolt of Nature
Ynestra King 179

25 The Concept of Social Ecology
Murray Bookchin 185

26 The Diversity of Life
Edward O. Wilson 193

27 Environmental Racism and the Environmental Justice Movement
Robert D. Bullard 196

Part IV: Accommodating the Future

28 Accommodating the Future: Strategies for Resolving the Environmental Quagmire
Matthew Cahn 207

29 Environmental Justice
Peter Wenz 214

30 Should Trees Have Standing?
Christopher Stone 221

31 Ecological Literacy
David W. Orr 227

32 Envisioning a Sustainable Society: Learning Our Way Out
Lester Milbrath 235

33 Free Market Environmentalism
Terry L. Anderson and Donald R. Leal 242

34 Steady-State Economics
Herman E. Daly 250

35 Environmentalism and the Future of Progressive Politics
Robert C. Paehlke 256

36 Normative Theory and Public Policy
Rory O'Brien 261

37 Democratic Dilemmas in the Age of Ecology
Daniel Press 265

38 Rights and the Further Future
James L. Hudson 273

39 Thinking About Sustainable Development: What's Theory Got to Do With It?
Robert O. Vos 281

Index 293

About the Editors 299

Acknowledgments

This project evolved during a series of conversations sparked by the Northridge earthquake. As we watched our classrooms and offices being replaced by trailers and porta-potties, we began to think more practically about the relationship between nature and our lives. The earthquake, in its devastating power, clearly reminded us of the primacy of the natural environment. Similarly, our inability to carry on mundane day-to-day tasks such as scheduling classes and giving lectures reminded us of our need to—at least in part—subdue aspects of the natural environment.

In essence, our response to this natural disaster highlights a question that plagues industrial societies as we look toward the future: To what extent do we limit our development in order to preserve nature? Although we have entered a phase of accelerated growth over the last two hundred years, the drive to find a balance between development and preservation has gone on for centuries. Thinkers from across the Western tradition have struggled with how human civilization fits in the physical world. Certainly the preparation of this book has helped us to integrate our thoughts on thinking about nature. We hope it will help our students as well.

It is therefore fitting that we acknowledge the contributions of our students, and of our teachers. Several people have made contributions to this project over time, including Andrea Nguyen, Diane Berger, Sheldon Kamieniecki, Thomas Greene, Mark Kann, Robert Vos, and Daniel Press. Research assistance was tirelessly provided by Nimrod Cohen. Manuscript preparation was provided enthusiastically by Cynthia Harris. Editorial assistance was provided by Patricia Kolb and Elizabeth Granda. Responsibility for any and all shortcomings, of course, lies squarely with us.

Matthew A. Cahn
Rory O'Brien

Northridge, California

THINKING ABOUT THE ENVIRONMENT

Readings on Politics, Property, and the Physical World

1

RORY O'BRIEN AND MATTHEW CAHN

Thinking About the Environment: What's Theory Got to Do With It?

Over the last 300 years environmental degradation has moved from challenge to quagmire. The difficulty of changing behavior patterns, the interests associated with our complex international economic structure, different notions of how development and nature should be balanced, and conflicting assessments of the risks posed by chemicals in the environment all converge to make environmental challenges extremely difficult to solve. Why should we concern ourselves with ideas about nature? Whether our concern is the development of a greater awareness of the natural world, or the creation of public policies that work to protect the natural world, thinking about nature can help us gain a greater understanding of the physical environment and how we, as humans, fit into the larger drama of ecological diversity and interdependence.

Two Paths Toward the Same Goal

Philosophy and normative theory may provide conceptual tools and methodologies for assessing environmental challenges. When philosophers or theorists consider an issue, they strive to go beyond the most obvious level of inquiry. Philosophers look for causes in an effort to understand the underlying nature of things. In this sense philosophy is a quest for knowledge. This pursuit depends not so much on information gathered through research as it does on speculation about a given question. Philosophy is sometimes referred to as the most general science, in that its project is to discover underlying truths. All science seeks to find answers. In this manner, philosophy can be viewed as both the pursuit of wisdom and the knowledge itself that is gained through philosophical inquiry.

Political theorists, on the other hand, work to develop a view of the political order in society. This view is intended to be as far-reaching as possible, so theorists seek to create a comprehensive picture of how the whole of a political system operates. A political theory, then, is a view or model of society constructed in order to be prescriptive as well as descriptive. Said differently, the model of society that the theorist creates allows for prescription, or recommendations, to either change or correct the ills of a particular social order.

John Rawls distinguishes three roles that political philosophy may play. The first of these is a practical role in which political philosophy serves to focus discussions about particular disputes on the possibility that beneath disagreements there may be some fundamental principles upon which differing groups can agree. If reference can be made to these principles, the implication is that specific conflicts may be settled when the separate parties involved can be made to understand their underlying agreement. If people consider the unifying principles that form the foundation of their society, they may be able to understand that their differences are not as great as they might have imagined. When we think about environmental issues not on the level of specifics, but more on the level of principles and values, we can see these issues in a different light.

The second role that Rawls sees political philosophy playing is one he refers to as "orientation." Political philosophy helps individuals orient themselves, in terms of their rights and obligations, toward others and toward the institutions of society. This orientation leads eventually to an appreciation for the fact that we have obligations not only to the current members of our social group, but even to those who have not yet been born. Additionally, political philosophy may function to reconcile individuals to the society in which they live. Members of society may be convinced of the rational nature in which institutions operate through discussions and arguments made clear by works of political philosophy. In this way political thinking might help people to better understand how environmental protection as a function of government regulation can be made to work better.

Two important distinctions to be made between political philosophy and political theory are in the areas of methodology and applicability. To achieve its goals, normative theory must involve a practicality that goes beyond the boundaries of Rawls's conception. This sort of practicality ideally would produce fruitful and specific prescriptions that can be directly applied to policy. In other words, to have any value beyond the purely speculative, political theory must be able to speak directly to issues that affect society. The challenge to the normative theorist is to go forward from the stage of discussion and logical argumentation, which is the hallmark of political philosophy, and make prescriptive statements based on those arguments. The methodological distinction here should be clear. Whereas philosophy seeks to develop the basic concepts and arguments underlying social relations, political theory—in order to make a dynamic contribution—must offer cogent arguments that may influence policy makers in ways that may have practical applications. Although political philosophy and political theory may follow different paths, they ultimately seek the same goal: discovering the underlying precepts of society and then creating plans or prescriptions that help to improve social life.

Thinking About the Environment: Three Assumptions

The selections in this collection have been gathered and organized with a certain set of assumptions. The first is that *it matters how we think about the environment.* In a very real sense, how we conceptualize the physical world is an important factor in determining how we treat nature. For this reason the study of nature, and the relationship between human civilization and the environment, have always held a prominent position in social and political inquiry. Humans have long been interested in discovering our place in the hierarchy of nature.

This leads to the second assumption: *There is a proper relationship between humans and their environment.* We may not agree on, or even know, the proper relationship, but conceptually it exists. Early in our history this question was based on the desire to understand the physical world. The mystery of the forces of nature prompted human civilization to look for ways to explain what went on around them. As a result, the earliest preoccupation we had with the environment was in finding ways to fit into the natural order. Later, we became fascinated with understanding the order of the world so that we could conquer nature. Contemporary human civilization has been built on the notion that our knowledge of nature leads to an ever-increasing ability on our part to control the physical to our advantage.

A third assumption that we make is that *our notions of how society is organized affect the way we treat nature.* Ultimately, the *way* society is organized contributes to the policies we make. Two important considerations here are how a society views property rights and how it conceptualizes justice. When property is a function of the utility of "things" (as it is in liberal capitalist societies), then nature in its unspoiled state is viewed as unproductive. If our notion of justice, on the other hand, compels us to preserve at least a large portion of the natural world, it is because we find nature itself to be a value.

Shallow Truths vs. Deep Truths

Many theorists make a distinction between shallow and deep truths. Shallow truths are either right or wrong. The weather, for example, can easily be measured and reported. Wind velocity, barometric pressure, precipitation, temperature all can be measured at any single point in time, resulting in a common truth. Few would challenge a thermometer's reading. Deep truths, on the other hand, are neither right nor wrong, in that they are not dependent upon absolute measures. While a temperature for a specific time and place may be a simple truth, the implication of that temperature is much more complex.

Seventy-two degrees Fahrenheit may be comfortable, or it may be unbearable. It depends on the context. As humans we may enjoy a sunny day in the mid-seventies, and we may not mind a variance in temperature of ten or twenty degrees. But many species cannot tolerate temperatures this high, or with such a range. An increase of even a few degrees in critical riparian habitats, for example, disrupts spawning behaviors in a variety of fish. *Context* matters.

What this suggests is that there are often deeper implications to apparently simple dynamics. The physical world, while enormously powerful, is actually quite delicate. The balance of ecological diversity is only now coming to be recognized. Thus, the history of human attempts to know, control, and conquer nature is rife with unanticipated outcomes and unintended consequences. As civilization has become larger and more complex, the impact of human actions has resulted in ever-increasing degradation of the natural environment. It has only been over time that we have begun to realize the deleterious results of our actions.

Deep Truths and Critical Thinking

Thinking about nature and the environment requires a critical thought process—a systematic thought process. In order to address the concerns of current environmental dilemmas, and to avoid harmful results from our future actions, we must work to organize, and systematize, our thinking about the environment. In the way of the political theorist, we can create models of the social order that help us explore options that may bring benefits environmentally, aesthetically, and economically. Thinking critically about the environment and our relationship to it will aid us in discovering ways to sustain our material well-being while simultaneously minimizing our reliance on precious resources. That is the goal of this book.

About What Follows

The book is organized in four sections, plus a concluding chapter which provides a retrospective on the evolving thinking on nature and the physical world. Each section explores an important epoch of thought on the environment. In this sense, the book provides an intellectual history of Western thought on the natural world. Part I—The Physical World—explores early thinking on the role of humanity in the physical world. The selections assess creation myths and the purpose of nature. Part II—Law and Property—explores the evolving role of property rights in the nature discourse. Selections reflect evolving liberalism and the commodification of the physical world. Part III—The Green Critique—presents the literature of naturalist critique on commodification and development. Selections include the classic writings of the ecology and environmental movement. Part IV—Accommodating the Future—evaluates where the discourse is headed. Selections include the more innovative approaches to rethinking the environmental problematic.

The readings appear in a logical order, reflecting the intellectual evolution of environmental thought. But the reader may wish to skip about, focusing on those selections that are most relevant for the reader's purpose. To get a sense of how the material fits together, the reader may want to start with chapter 39. Robert Vos's piece integrates the various themes of the book in a useful retrospective. It is our hope that the excerpts provided will inspire the reader to pursue further research—further thinking—on nature and the physical world.

Questions for a Journey

As you explore the selections within the text—as you develop *your* thoughts on nature and the environment—keep the following questions in mind. They provide conceptual tools that, as Rawls suggests, may assist us in assessing complex environmental challenges.

What Is Humankind's Place in the Natural Order of the World?

As we explore ways of working within the confines of our environment, we must understand how we fit into the larger picture. What role does humanity have to play in the greater context? Are we here to use nature, or are we willing to act as caretakers of the natural world while preparing to pass it on to the next generation?

Does Nature Itself Have a Value Aside from Its Potential to Provide Commodities?

Is it possible for us to conceptualize nature not as a set of resources ripe for our taking, but instead as a valuable asset in and of itself? Certainly many, even in an advanced industrialized society like ours, understand that nature without human intervention represents a value. So, we must assess how we view nature and how we estimate value.

How Does the Way a Society Conceives Property Rights Affect the Way It Looks at Nature?

Even John Locke argues that ownership of property, although a natural right of humans, does not supersede the value of the environment itself. If property owners destroy or seriously damage nature, are they acting responsibly within the context of natural law?

What Are We Willing to Give Up?

Assuming that we realize the deleterious effect we are having on the environment, we might begin to grapple with the fact that industrialized societies cannot continue as they have historically. How far will modern civilization go in the direction of using less? Can we discover ways to continue to grow and develop without relying on the destruction of the environment to serve our needs?

What Is Environmental Justice?

If justice is relative, then decisions that affect the environment can be made solely on the basis of convenience or expediency. In the modern context this often means that the environment is sacrificed in order to maximize profit. If, on the other hand, justice is based on absolute values or truths, then protection of the environment can take the form of a categorical imperative demanding that we act in the best interest of nature. Furthermore, our notion of justice can be extended to include future generations. In this sense, it is both selfish and irresponsible for any current generation to rob the future of the bounty of a rich and healthy environment.

Part I
The Physical World

2

Rory O'Brien

On the Physical World: An Introduction

As the twentieth century comes to a close, modern industrial society finds itself in a challenging position. We stand now at the intersection between what we know we are capable of and what is prudential for us to do. Over the course of the last five centuries, human society has been focused on developing the ability to control and transform nature. We have found ways to integrate our intellectual and physical abilities and to truly change the world. The great accomplishments of the modern era are the culmination of all the scientific and materialistic progress that humans have made throughout time.

Humankind has been able to extract and refine the elements of nature and put them to work for our own purposes in ways that we might never have dreamed possible. Now, however, we have begun to temper our enthusiasm over our success with the realization that productive and industrial gains often come at a price that is dangerous to the environment. As we face the future, we must discover ways to reconcile our desire to continually progress with the balance of nature. Actually, the Western tradition can be viewed on the basis of three major paradigms, or ways of looking at the world, in terms of our physical environment. A paradigm is actually a cluster of ideas that form a sort of mental template that humans use to interpret reality.

In the first of these world views, humankind struggled to gain knowledge of the world so as to create order, to create stable societies, and to understand some of the mysterious forces of nature. Under the second paradigm, humans have strived to control the physical world for our own purposes. In the next paradigm, the dimensions of which we are only beginning to discover, we must find ways to live not only within but also as part of the natural world.

Mind over Matter

What humans have always been concerned about is finding out how the world works so as to construct a rational view of reality. By understanding the world around us, we have tried to make sense out of the seemingly chaotic environment in which we find ourselves. If only we could understand reality, it seems to the human mind, our intellectual talents would allow us to get a firmer grasp on what is going on around us. Here a clear distinction is made between mind and matter. Even without having much of an understanding of the mind, we know of it because this truly is where, and how, our world occurs. The mind is not only closest to us, it is through the mind's activity that we know about the world. The environment outside of us is different, however, it reacts and behaves differently than does the mind leading to our questions about how the world really works.

Early humans theorized about the forces that controlled the natural world, and first came up with a schema that held that each aspect of nature itself was animated. A further sophistication of this concept over time led to the creation of a dizzying array of gods and goddesses who operated the various aspects of nature effecting the phenomena we encounter. Humankind has invented stories in order to explain natural phenomena, in the form of either science or religion, since the dawn of our existence. Obviously, to our ancestors the world was a mysterious and frightening place. So the development of strategies through which they might not only understand, but also control the world, was a reasonable response. What is perhaps not quite as obvious to us living in the modern age is that we have continued to develop new strategies and theories as old ones are discarded toward the same end. The world is still a frighteningly mysterious place to us, and as yet we have a very dim view of reality.

Ultimately this concern with understanding the forces of nature is an integral part of the development of a social order. Without some idea of what the physical world is, and where we fit into it, it would be impossible to imagine creating stable and manageable societies. So a foundational aspect of any philosophy that deals with how humans live and work together in a social framework must be humankind's relationship to the environment. As human societies have evolved over time, we have see the importance our place in the physical world holds for us. Once content with advancing and developing, humanity has finally started to focus on an understanding of our impact on our environment.

From Creation to Chaos

We struggled for thousands of years utilizing the paradigm that helped us to gain some understanding of our surroundings and to develop a stable social order by asking questions about the nature of reality. Eventually we discovered that there were other, more tangible, things to which these ideas could be applied. As the Christian view of the world began breaking down in the fifteenth century in Europe, this paradigm shifted radically. No longer was humankind's inquiry into nature predicated on the notion that developing a sense of the world would allow us to better understand ourselves and our position in relationship to the environment. For the first time, human endeavor became oriented toward scientific development as a means of furthering our ability to conquer nature itself.

For hundreds of years now, we have been on a path toward ever greater growth and development, using a new paradigm that has as its central tenet the primary good of progress. Whether in the fields of industrial development and the creation of machines and equipment to help satisfy the needs of people, in resource extraction and refinement, or in the areas of weaponry and sophisticated devices for mass destruction, human effort during the past five hundred years has been focused on manipulating nature to our will. It is only as one millennium ends and another begins that we have started to see some of the unintended consequences of our overwhelming success.

While we were concerned for such a long time with the effectiveness of our technologies, we lost sight of the fact that our paradigm of progress was leading inextricably toward the destruction of our environment. As progress, and especially industrialization, was a slow process, it certainly did not appear as if human endeavor could permanently harm the earth, air, or seas. But the pace of modern industrialization during the past two hundred years, along with tremendous increases in human population during this period, have exacerbated the problematic nature of growth.

In the long run this second paradigm, which is a strategy to control or harness nature (forcing the physical world into the shapes and forms that we have deemed appropriate, rather than what is natural), functions as a way for us to get what we want while casually taking away what the world has to offer. When the rate of development increases along with out-of-control population growth, we begin to remove or ruin more elements than nature is able to replace. The third paradigm is based on a sensitivity to, and appreciation of, the environment. Rather than viewing the physical world as available for the sole purposes of humankind's needs and wishes, we have recently become much more aware of the need for protection and preservation of our environment, along with conservation of the precious resources nature has to offer.

Over the span of the last few thousand years, then, as we have moved through these three paradigmatic views of nature, we have gone from myths of creation, which explain the environment and our place in it, back to a chaotic world full of uncertainties and dangers.

The World as Our Birthright

Thinking about the environment dates back to some of the earliest works in the Western tradition. Many of the ideas our predecessors had about the environment have been handed down to us embedded in religious writings. When we explore our place in the world, we call into question many of our most fundamental concepts. In order to understand where humans fit into the bigger picture of the universe, we must already assume that we have the ability to gain knowledge about a larger reality. The nature of the universe must certainly transcend the nature of mere mortals!

Furthermore, to get an idea of that bigger picture we must also assume that we have already learned quite a bit about how the universe operates, and that in having a sense of that larger reality we are also able to catch a glimpse of our place in the structure of nature. At least as far back as the Bible we find references not only to the nature of the world, but also to man's position in it. As the crowning achievement of God's creation in Genesis, humanity's preeminent place in the hierarchy of the physical world is assured. In dramatic fashion, not only are humans given dominion over other animals, but, indeed, over the rest of creation in its entirety. In Genesis, God says, "Let us make man in our image and likeness to rule the fish in the sea, the birds of heaven, the cattle, all wild animals on earth, and all reptiles that crawl upon the earth." The Creator then blesses humankind, admonishing them to "Be fruitful and increase, fill the earth and subdue it, rule over the fish in the sea, the birds of heaven, and every living thing that moves upon the earth." In this view, human beings are seen as distinct from the rest of the physical world.

The Biblical definition of our place in the world is an important touchstone in terms of the development of western civilization. From the fourth century C.E. (with the ascendancy of the Catholic Church) until the Reformation, the world view of the Bible held sway throughout Europe. Even as the works of Plato and Aristotle were returned to the West through contact with the Islamic world, these philosophers' ideas were filtered by the standards of the Christian Church. Throughout this period nothing challenged the philosophical notion that humans held a special place in the world. Although subservient to God and to Church doctrine, humankind was perceived as a unique feature in the physical world; we were the only ones capable of understanding the divine message of Christianity.

The City of God

In order to understand the philosophy of St. Augustine, we must first have some idea about Greek thought. By the time St. Augustine wrote in the late fourth and early fifth centuries, Christianity had been confronted with the return of earlier Greek philosophy as mentioned above. Influenced by the Platonic notion of perfection as transcendent to the physical world, Augustine's work represents a synthesis of Greek and Christian ideas. Plato had described the world we know as a mere reflection of the real world, which was comprised of what he referred to as *forms.* The forms were the real essence of things in that they were perfect or ultimate. The physical objects that we are able to have knowledge of through our senses are nothing more than rough approximations of these eternal essences and, therefore, cannot themselves be perfect. The sensual world that we live in, then, is not a world made up of essences, but rather of objects that, in varying degree, reflect the reality of the forms.

The Greek philosophers did not explore ideas of man's place in the hierarchy of nature in the same way that the Bible or other creation myths do. Speculation about the gods and their powers was left to the religion of their day. Philosophy was instead concerned with the causes of phenomena or the true nature of things, which the Greeks believed could be comprehended through the faculty of human reason.

Aristotle (384–322 B.C.) was a student of Plato's and, although only a fraction of his work has been recovered, is one of the best known of the Greek philosophers. In the *Physics,* Aristotle suggests that nature must have some sort of purpose. Aristotle argues that the course of nature corresponds to the course of action. In other words, nature's direction is one of action or activity, and as actions have a purpose, so must nature. For Aristotle, the most important element of anything is its end, or purpose. All things, regardless of what they are, are developing toward some end. This philosophical idea is called *teleology* and it is a fundamental notion of modern Western thinking. Everything in nature has some purpose and is moving toward its own end. As Aristotle puts it, "Natural things are things that are continuously moved by some principle within themselves and attain some end." But nature itself goes beyond merely having a purpose in that "nature is a cause, and is a cause in the sense of being a purpose."

St. Augustine (354–430) was a Roman who converted to Christianity and who eventually became an important member of the church hierarchy. As one of the most influential of the early Christian philosophers, Augustine's thought has had an impact on how the modern world considers nature. When St. Augustine speaks of the city he is referring to the community of humankind and the way that humans live with one another. In modern terms we might substitute "nation" or "country" for the word "city," understanding that this is meant to represent a political unit. The *City of God* is an allegorical reference made to a perfect community, and as Augustine's overriding concern is with virtue he is interested in discovering the most virtuous form of society.

Bringing together the disparate ideas of Platonic and Aristotelian philosophy with Christian thought and Church teaching, St. Augustine seeks to reconcile these ideas through human virtue. A civil society is predicated upon an understanding of the weakness of human nature, which, in Augustine's view, is only mitigated through the observation of scriptural doctrine. In the earthly city (not the City of God), decisions are made on the basis of human desires and natural impulses. Augustine has replaced the teleological notion in Aristotelian thinking of nature as a cause in itself with the more narrow Christian doctrine of God's will as the organizing feature of the universe. The City of God would operate on the dictates of God's ideas of virtue as revealed through Scripture and the church's teaching. But the human city remains corrupted in its application of human, not Christian, principles.

The "Other" Western Tradition

Western thinking is not limited to the philosophical and religious works of Europeans and Eurasians. The creation myths of Native Americans stand in stark contrast with the dominant Judeo-Christian view. Whereas the Biblical view of creation culminates with God's giving to humans power over the rest of creation, the Native American views provide a more integrated approach to the hierarchy of nature. Both the Hopi Indians of the Southwest and the Luiseño of California have well developed stories of how the world began, including the place that humankind holds in nature.

The Luiseño believe that the world was created when Mother Earth is raped by her own brother. The Earth and her brother the Night get into an argument and in the ensuing power struggle the brother wins, finally impregnating his sister. The Earth's brother the Night, shamed by his act, goes up to become the sky. As the tradition has it, the Mother Earth then gives birth, or creates a small piece of land. Thus the Luiseño hold that the world was created through this violent act, not made by the forces of nature. The world is formed, then, through the dominance of one element of nature over another. The created world is subsequently ordered into a hierarchy of dominance. Many of the themes presented in the Luiseño religion involve violence, dominance, and death. For the Luiseño, death, although not desirable, is necessary because it brings order into the world.

The Hopi trace the travels of humans through four different worlds. Each successive world is destroyed before the next is created. And it is human greed and less than virtuous behavior outside the laws of nature that lead to the destruction of the worlds. Throughout their sojourn the people described in the Hopi myth of creation learn how to better coexist with nature. At each level the people are made more and more aware of the fact that it is only through cooperation with nature and the natural order that they will be successful in being part of the world's hierarchical order.

These Native American views of creation and the Judeo-Christian story are at once similar and strikingly different. The Bible is full of stories similar to the Hopi version of creation and destruction. God becomes angry with the lack of virtue demonstrated by the people he has created and rains destruction on the earth in the form of floods or fire. And although the violence of the Luiseño view of the physical creation of the world is rarely equaled in the Bible, there certainly are plenty of references to acts that are nearly as traumatic. Where the Native American accounts of nature and humankind's place in it are unique is in terms of our perspective toward how we live within the environment itself. Far from finding the natural world to be our birthright, this other Western tradition suggests that humankind's greatest challenge is to discover where we fit into the hierarchy of nature.

The Third Paradigm

As discussed earlier, the third paradigm focuses our attention not just on what we find ourselves capable of doing, but also on the effects our actions have on the environment. As the modern world has developed, fueled in part by ideas drawn from both the Biblical and the philosophical traditions, we have reached the limits of our ability for unchecked growth. In retrospect it appears that the point of view of Native Americans may more accurately reflect this new way of looking at the world than any of the more traditional Western sources considered here.

This chapter has reviewed some of the major ideas and explanations of how the world was created and where humankind fits into the larger scheme of things. We have also looked at the paradigms that helped us first understand our world and then find ways to conquer it. As our modern industrialized society looks forward into the next millennium, we find ourselves beginning to ask the questions that will help us come to grips with living and prospering without destroying our world.

3

Genesis

The Creation of the World

In the beginning of creation, when God made heaven and earth, the earth was without form and void, with darkness over the face of the abyss, and a mighty wind that swept over the surface of the waters. God said, "Let there be light," and there was light; and God saw that the light was good, and he separated light from darkness. He called the light day, and the darkness night. So evening came, and morning came, the first day.

God said, "Let there be a vault between the waters, to separate water from water." So God made the vault, and separated the water under the vault from the water above it, and so it was; and God called the vault heaven. Evening came, and morning came, a second day.

God said, "Let the waters under heaven be gathered into one place, so that dry land may appear"; and so it was. God called the dry land earth, and the gathering of the waters he called seas; and God saw that it was good. Then God said, "Let the earth produce fresh growth, let there be on the earth plants bearing seed, fruit-trees bearing fruit each with seed according to its kind." So it was; the earth yielded fresh growth, plants bearing seed according to their kind and trees bearing fruit each with seed according to its kind; and God saw that it was good. Evening came, and morning came, a third day.

God said, "Let there be lights in the vault of heaven to separate day from night, and let them serve as signs both for festivals and for seasons and years. Let them also shine in the vault of heaven to give light on earth." So it was; God made the two great lights, the greater to govern the day and the lesser to govern the night; and with them he made the stars. God put these lights in the vault of heaven to give light on earth, to govern day and night, and to separate light from darkness; and God saw that it was good. Evening came, and morning came, a fourth day.

God said, "Let the waters teem with countless living creatures, and let birds fly above the earth across the vault of heaven." God then created the great sea-monsters and all living creatures that move and swarm in the waters, according to their kind, and every kind of bird; and God saw that it was good. So he blessed them and said, "Be fruitful and increase, fill the waters of the seas; and let the birds increase on land." Evening came, and morning came, a fifth day.

God said, "Let the earth bring forth living creatures, according to their kind: cattle, reptiles, and wild animals, all according to their kind." So it was; God made wild animals, cattle, and all reptiles, each according to its kind; and he saw that it was good. Then God said, "Let us make man in our image and likeness to rule the fish in the sea, the birds of heaven, the cattle, all wild animals on earth, and all reptiles that crawl upon the earth." So God created man in his own image; in the image of God he created him; male and female he created them. God blessed them and said to them, "Be fruitful and increase, fill the earth and subdue it, rule over the fish in the sea, the birds of heaven, and every living thing that moves upon the earth." God also said, "I give you all plants that bear seed everywhere on earth, and every tree bearing fruit which yields seed: they shall be yours for food. All green plants I give for food to the wild animals, to all the birds of heaven, and to all reptiles on earth, every living creature." So it was; and God saw all that he had made, and it was very good. Evening came, and morning came, a sixth day.

Thus heaven and earth were completed with all their mighty throng. On the sixth day God completed all the work he had been doing, and on the seventh day he ceased from all his work. God blessed the seventh day and made it holy, because on that day he ceased from all the work he had set himself to do.

This is the story of the making of heaven and earth when they were created.

4

ARISTOTLE

The Purpose of Nature

Now, we must first explain why nature is said to be one of the causes that are purposes, and then we must discuss necessity, and how it appears in natural objects. For necessity is a cause to which everyone refers things; they say that since the hot and the cold and all other such things are of a particular kind, particular things of necessity exist and come into being; even if they mention another cause, they merely touch upon it and then take leave of it: one will mention Love and Strife in this way, another, Mind.

There is the problem of knowing what there is to keep nature from acting without a purpose, and not because things are best as she does them; Zeus does not send the rain in order to make the corn grow, he sends it of necessity; for what is drawn up and evaporated must get cold, and what gets cold must come down again as water; and it is an accident that, when this has happened, the corn grows; similarly, if someone's corn is lost on the threshing floor, the rain did not fall with the purpose of destroying the corn, it was an accident that this happened. What is to keep this from being so with the parts in nature too? What is to keep it from being of necessity, for instance, that one's front teeth come up sharp and suitable for cutting things up, and that the molars are flat and useful for grinding the food? One would then say that these things did not happen purposely, but came about by accident. It is the same with all the other parts in which purpose seems to be present. On this view, all things that accidentally turned out to be what they would have become if they had had a purpose were preserved spontaneously, once they had come together in a suitable fashion; beings that did not turn out in this way perished, and continue to do so, as Empedocles says happened with his "man-faced oxen."

This argument, and others like it, are the ones that might make one at a

---

From Aristotle, *Physics,* Book 2, chap. 8 and 9.

loss to know whether there is a purpose in nature; but it is in fact impossible for things to be like that. For these and all natural objects either always or usually come into being in a given way, and that is not the case with anything that comes to be by chance or spontaneously. We do not think that it is by chance or by accident that it often rains in the winter, but we do think that it is if it rains in the dog days; nor do we think that it is by accident or by chance that it is hot in the dog days, although if it is hot in the winter we do think so. If, then, we think that things happen either by accident or for a purpose, and if it is not possible for them to happen by accident or spontaneously, then they must happen for a purpose. But all things of this kind happen by nature, as even those who maintain the view that we are criticizing would admit. Thus, there is purpose in things that come to be and exist by nature.

Further, in all cases where there is an end, the first and all the subsequent actions are carried out with that end as their purpose. Now, the course of nature corresponds to the course of action, and the course of any action corresponds to the course of nature—unless there is some obstacle in the way. But actions have a purpose; so nature must have one too. For instance, if a house were one of the things that come into being by nature, it would come into being in the same way that it now does through art; and if natural objects came into being not only by nature but also through art, they too would come into being in the same way that they do by nature. We may say, then, that one thing does have the next as its purpose. In general, art in some cases finishes what nature is unable to accomplish; in others, it imitates nature. If, then, things that happen in accordance with art have a purpose, plainly things that happen in accordance with nature will too. For the relation of the earlier and later stages to each other is the same in nature as it is in art.

This becomes particularly clear in the case of the other animals: they do not do things by art or after any inquiry or deliberation. This has led some people to wonder whether spiders and ants and things of that kind act through mind or by some other means. If one gradually goes on in this direction, one sees that in plants, too, things come into being that are conducive to their end: the leaves, for instance, come into being for the purpose of protecting the fruit. Thus, if it is both by nature and to fulfill a purpose that the swallow makes its nest and the spider spins its web, and if plants put forth their leaves for the sake of their fruit and send their roots down rather than up for the purpose of getting food, plainly a cause of this kind is present in things that come to be and exist by nature. And since nature is twofold—in one sense being matter, and in another shape, which is the end—and since everything else has the end as its purpose, it is in fact the shape or form that will be the cause, in the sense of its being the purpose.

Mistakes occur in things that are done according to art: the literate man will write incorrectly, the doctor will give the wrong dose; so it is clearly possible, too, for mistakes to happen in things that are in accordance with nature. Now, just as in the case of art, if things are done correctly, they serve a purpose, whereas if they go wrong, the attempt is made to serve a purpose, but it fails; so the situation must be with natural objects, and monsters must be failures to achieve a purpose. And in the original combinations, the oxlike creatures, since they were unable to come to a defined end, must have come into being through the corruption of some principle in them, just as it is now through the corruption of the seed that monsters are produced. Further, there must have been a seed first; the animals cannot have come into being straightaway; and the "primal generator of all" must have been such a seed.

Purpose is present in plants, too, but it has been less clearly articulated in them. Did what is supposed to have happened with animals also happen with them? Did there come into being, corresponding to the oxen with men's faces, vines with the appearance of olives? This is absurd; but some such thing would have to happen, if it happened too among animals.

Further, on this theory, things would have had to come into being from the seeds just as they chanced to; but the man who holds this kind of view does away with natural objects and with nature. For natural things are things that are continuously moved by some principle within themselves and attain some end; it is not the same thing that comes to be from each principle in each case, nor is it just what it chance to be; but it always tends toward the same thing if there is nothing to prevent it. The purpose for which a thing is done, and what is done for that purpose, may come to be by chance: we say, for instance, that the stranger came by chance and went off after ransoming the man when he acts as though he had come for this purpose but had in fact not come for it. This is accidental, for, as we said earlier, chance is an accidental cause; but when it happens always or usually, it is not accidental, and does not happen by chance. And in natural occurrences, things always are like this, unless there is some impediment.

It is strange to suppose that things do not happen for a purpose simply because one does not see the mover deliberate. Art does not deliberate; and if the art of shipbuilding were present in the wood, it would act in the same way by nature; so that if purpose is present in art, it is present in nature too. This becomes most clear when someone heals himself, for that is just what nature is like.

> It is clear, then, that nature is a cause, and is a cause in the sense of being a purpose. . . .
>
> Does necessity apply in nature absolutely, or only on the basis of certain assumptions?

For at the moment people suppose that the necessity occurs in the process of coming-to-be; it is as if one thought that a wall had come into being of necessity because the heavy parts naturally moved downwards and the light parts up to the surface, so that the stones and foundations were therefore at the bottom, the earth above them because of its lightness, and the wood right at the top because it is the lightest of them all. But, in fact, although the wall has not come into being without these, it has not come into being because of them, except insofar as they are matter; it has, rather, come into being for the purpose of concealing and preserving various things. Similarly with all other things in which purpose is present, they do not come into being without the things that possess the necessary nature, but they do not come into being because of them, except insofar as these things are matter; they, rather, come into being for a purpose. Why, someone asks, is the saw like *this*? So that it can do *this,* we say, and with *this* purpose. But this purpose cannot come to be unless the saw is of iron; and so there must be iron if the saw and its activity are going to exist. The necessary, then, is present only on the basis of some assumption, it is not there as end; for the necessity is present in the matter, whereas the purpose is present in the form or account.

Necessity in mathematics is in a way very similar to necessity in things that come into being by nature; because the straight is what it is, the triangle must contain angles equal to two right angles; but it does not follow from the fact that the latter is true that the straight is what it is; if, however, the latter proposition is not true, the straight will not be what it is said to be either. In the case of things that come into being for a purpose, it is the other way around: if the end is to exist either now or in the future, what leads up to it must do so too; but if what leads up to the end does not exist, the end and purpose will not exist either, just as there will be no premise if the conclusion does not hold. For it is the purpose which is the starting point, not, indeed, of the activity, but of the calculation leading to it; and in the case of mathematics, too, the premise is the starting point of the calculation, since there is no activity involved. Thus, if there is going to be a house, particular things must come into being or be there: matter must necessarily exist for the achievement of any purpose—bricks and stones must be there, for instance, for a house. But it is not because of these things that the end exists, except insofar as they are matter, nor will it do so in the future because of them. In general, if these things do not exist, neither the house nor the saw will exist: the house will not exist if there are no stones, the saw will not exist if there is no iron; for in the other case the premises will not be true unless the triangle contains two right angles.

Clearly, then, necessity in natural objects is what is described as matter together with its affections. Both causes must be named by the natural scientist, but more especially the purpose; for it is the cause of the matter, but the matter is not the cause of the end. The end is the purpose, and the starting point is the definition and account, as it is too in things that have to do with art: since, we say, the house is to be of a particular kind, these particular things must come into being and be present of necessity; since health is like this, particular things must come into being and be present of necessity; similarly, since man is a particular thing, other particular things must be there; and if these other things are to be there, still others must be, too.

5

St. Augustine

The City of God

Of all visible things, the universe is the greatest; of all invisible realities, the greatest is God. That the world exists we can see; we believe in the existence of God. But there is no one we can more safely trust than God Himself in regard to the fact that it was He who made the world. Where has He told us so? Nowhere more distinctly than in the Holy Scriptures where His Prophet said: "In the beginning God created the heavens and the earth." Well, but was the Prophet present when God made heaven and earth? No; but the Wisdom of God by whom all things were made was there. And this Wisdom, entering into holy souls, makes of them the friends and prophets of God and reveals to them, silently and interiorly, what God has done.

They are taught, also, by the angels of God who "always behold the face of the Father" and are commissioned to announce His will to others. Among these Prophets was the one who announced in writing: "In the beginning God created the heavens and the earth." And it was so fitting that faith in God should come through such a witness that he was inspired by the same Spirit of God, who had revealed these truths to him, to predict, far in advance, our own future faith.

But, why did it please the eternal God to create heaven and earth at that special time, seeing that He had not done so earlier? If the purpose of those who pose this question is to protest that the world is eternal, without beginning, and, therefore, not created by God, then they are far from the truth and are raving with the deadly disease of irreligion. For, quite apart from the voice of the Prophets, the very order, changes, and movements in the universe, the very beauty of form in all that is visible, proclaim, however silently, both that the world was created and also that its Creator could be none other than God whose greatness and beauty are both ineffable and invisible.

From St. Augustine, *City of God,* Book 15, chap. 4, Book 11.

There are those who say that the universe was, indeed, created by God, denying a "temporal" but admitting a "creational" beginning, as though, in some hardly comprehensible way, the world was made, but made from all eternity. Their purpose seems to be to save God from the charge of arbitrary rashness. They would not have us believe that a completely new idea of creating the world suddenly occurred to Him or that a change of mind took place in Him in whom there can be no change.

I do not see, however, how this position is consistent with their stand in other matters, especially in regard to the soul. For, if, as they must hold, the soul is co-eternal with God, they have no way to explain how a completely new misery can begin in an eternally existing soul.

For, if they say that its misery and happiness ceaselessly alternate, then they are obliged to conclude that this alternation will go on forever. Thus, an absurdity follows: though the soul is called blessed, it will not be so in fact, since it foresees its future misery and disgrace; and, even if it does not foresee its future disgrace or misery but thinks that it will be happy forever, its happiness will depend upon deception. And this is as foolish a statement as could possibly be made.

But, if they suppose that the soul has been alternately happy and unhappy through infinite ages but that, from now on, being set free, it will never return to its former misery, they are, in fact, convinced that the soul was never truly blessed but that at last it begins to enjoy a new and genuine happiness. Thus, they admit that something new, important, and remarkable happens within the soul which had never occurred to it before from all eternity. And, if they deny that God's eternal providence included the cause of this new experience of the soul, they likewise deny that He is the Author of its beatitude—which is an abominable piece of impiety. If, on the other hand, they claim that by a new decree God determined that the soul should be eternally blessed, how can they show that He is free from that mutability which even they repudiate?

Finally, if they say that the soul was created in time but will not perish in any future time, like numbers which begin with "one" but never end, and, therefore, that having experienced misery, it will be freed from it, never again to return to it, they will surely have no hesitation in admitting that this is compatible with the immutability of God's decision. This being so, they should also believe that the world could be made in time without God who made it having to change the eternal decision of His will.

Before attempting to reply to those who, while agreeing with us that God is the Creator of the world, question us about the time at which it was created, we must see what response they make when we ask them about the space in which it was created. For, just as they ask why it was made then and not earlier, we may ask why it was made here and not elsewhere. Because, if they excogitate infinite periods of time before the world, in which they cannot see how God could have had nothing to do, they ought to conceive of infinite reaches of space beyond the visible universe. And, if they maintain that the Omnipotent can never be inactive, will they not logically be forced to dream with Epicurus of innumerable universes? (There will be merely this difference, that, while he asserts that these worlds originate and disintegrate by the fortuitous movements of atoms, they will hold that they are created by the work of God.) This is the conclusion if they insist on the premise that there is an interminable immensity of space stretching in all directions in which God cannot remain passive and that those imaginary worlds, like this visible one, are indestructible.

The present discussion is limited to those who believe with us that God is spiritual and the Creator of all existences except Himself; first, because there is something improper in inviting materialists to discuss a religious question; and second, because even in pagan circles the Platonists have gained a prestige and authority beyond that of other philosophers—for the simple reason that, however far they are from the truth, they are much nearer to it than any of the others.

Now, the Platonists hold that the divine substance is neither confined nor limited nor distributed in space; they acknowledge very properly that He is spiritually and completely present everywhere. Will they then say that He is absent from the infinitely immense spaces out beyond and is occupied only in the relatively tiny space that contains this cosmos? I do not think that they will be foolish enough to go this far.

Let us agree, then, that they admit a single cosmos of immense material bulk, indeed, yet, finite and determined in its own place, and created by the work of God. Now, whatever reason they can give for God's cessation from work in the infinite spaces outside the world, let them offer the same solution to their problem of God ceasing from activity during the infinite stretches of time before the creation of the world.

Now, it does not follow that it was by chance rather than by a divine reason that God localized the world in this spot instead of in another, even though no human reason can comprehend the divine reason and although this particular place has no special merit that it should be chosen in preference to an infinite number of others. Nor, in the same way, does it follow that we should suppose that it was by accident that God created the world at that specific time rather than before, even though previous times had been uniformly passing by throughout an infinite past and there was no difference which would cause this time to be chosen in preference to another.

As for the city of this world, it is neither to last forever nor even to be a city, once the final doom of pain is upon it. Nevertheless, while history lasts, it has a finality of its own; it reaches such happiness by sharing a common good as is possible when there are no goods but the things of time to afford it happiness. This is not the kind of good that can give those who are content with it any freedom from fear. In fact, the city of man, for the most part, is a city of contention with opinions divided by foreign wars and domestic quarrels and by the demands for victories which either end in death or are merely monetary respites from further war. The reason is that whatever part of the city of the world raises the standard of war, it seeks to be lord of the world, when, in fact, it is enthralled in its own wickedness. Even when it conquers, its victory can be mortally poisoned by pride, and if, instead of taking pride in the success already achieved, it takes account of the nature and normal vicissitudes of life and is afraid of future failure, then the victory is merely momentary. The fact is that the power to reach domination is not the same as the power to remain in perpetual control.

Nevertheless, it is wrong to deny that the aims of human civilization are good, for this is the highest end that mankind of itself can achieve. For, however lowly the goods of earth, the aim, such as it is, is peace. The purpose even of war is peace. For, where victory is not followed by resistance there is a peace that was impossible so long as rivals were competing, hungrily and unhappily, for something material too little to suffice for both. This kind of peace is a product of the work of war, and its price is a so-called glorious victory; when victory goes to the side that had a juster cause it is surely a matter for human rejoicing, and the peace is one to be welcomed. . . .

The things of earth are not merely good; they are undoubtedly gifts from God. But, of course, if those who get such goods in the city of men are reckless about the better goods of the City of God, in which there is to be the ultimate victory of an eternal, supreme, and untroubled peace, if men so love the goods of earth as to believe that these are the only goods or if they love them more than the goods they know to be better, then the consequence is inevitable: misery and more misery.

6

SAM GILL

Creation in Light of Luiseño Religion

In the recorded oral traditions of the Luiseño, these accounts of creation seem to be preliminary to the more developed story of Wiyot, a male figure who is something of a culture hero.[1]

All things born at the time of origin were in the form of people. Among these people was Wiyot. In some versions of the story, it seems that the birth of Wiyot was the principal cosmogonic objective, yet in others his origin is not even told. As described in the story, Wiyot was "very wise and knew more than anyone living. He taught the people, watched over them, and made provision for their needs, so that he called them all his children. They were not born to him as children, but he stood to them in the relation of a father."[2] Yet it seems that Wiyot was born to die, for the principle event of his story is his death.

In Wiyot's time, it was the custom for people to bathe every morning. When Wiyot went to bathe he noticed a beautiful woman and he grew to admire her greatly. She had a beautiful face and long hair that completely covered her back. One day when watching her bathe, Wiyot noticed that her back was hollow and flat like that of a frog and his admiration for her turned to disgust. She was, in fact, a frog and was empowered by witchcraft. She knew Wiyot's thoughts and set out to kill him. When he became ill, all of the doctors were called, but none could save him. Importantly, it was not until Wiyot knew that he was to die that he began to reveal to the people the elements that were to characterize Luiseño culture. He told them

---

Reprinted with permission from *Mother Earth: An American Story* by Sam D. Gill (Chicago: University of Chicago Press, 1987), pp. 96–106.

the names of the months; he dispersed the peoples and set apart their languages; he revealed that he was to become the moon and that if they would run races and shout at the time when he returned to life as the new moon, they would live longer. As Wiyot knew he was about to die, he set forth the manner in which his body was to be treated. Wiyot was the first to die and his introduction of death not only set a pattern for Luiseño funerary customs, it set the precedent for the many Luiseño religious themes that focus on death.[3]

Puberty rites for girls, one of the major Luiseño ceremonial occasions, dealt extensively with images and themes of death. The initiates were buried up to their necks in heated sand for several days. This practice combines the death and rebirth imagery of entering and emerging from the grave with that of cooking the initiate, both common initiatory motifs.[4]

Luiseño boys entered their formal religious lives in an initiation rite that involved their drinking a datura mixture. *Toloache,* the Spanish word for datura, is the term commonly used for this initiation ceremony. Intoxicated by the datura, the youths were assembled around a fire and given a display of the magical powers of the adepts. These were performances in a shamanic style in which all manner of mortal wounds were seemingly suffered, often self-inflicted ones, with the wounds then being miraculously healed. While the effects of datura were felt only during one night, the initiates continued to fast for a period of days. Three days after drinking the datura brew, the youths were taken to a pit in which a net representing the Milky Way had been placed, along with three stones forming a crude human shape. The Milky Way is the spirit to whom human spirits go when human beings die. The initiates had to enter the pit and leap from stone to stone. A misstep or fall presaged an early death. The danger of this crossing was heightened because the initiates had been fasting. Crossing the Milky Way expressed the Luiseño wish that, upon death, their spirits would be free from the earth and go to be caught in the net which is the Milky Way. The leaping from stone to stone enacted the escape of the spirit from the grave and enacted the pattern established by Wiyot at his death.[5]

Apart from initiation ceremonies, the Luiseño ritual practice centers upon funerary rites and mourning ceremonies in which the dead are remembered.

The Luiseño emphasis upon rituals of death and the extensive use of death imagery in religion are relatively common among California tribes, as Alfred L. Kroeber has shown. . . .[6]

A suggestion of how Wiyot and the Luiseño emphasis upon death relate to the incestuous rape by which the elements of the world were created can be found in the oral traditions. After Wiyot's death the people met to consider its meaning for them. Some thought that should they die, they, like

Wiyot, would return to life. Eagle, who was very wise, had attempted to find a place where death did not exist but returned to tell the others that death was everywhere. All had to die. The subject then turned to how, in death, some of them might be useful to the others. Some thought that Deer would be good to eat. They considered killing him and having a gathering in which the meat would be eaten. Deer did not care for the idea and an argument ensued. It is of such importance that one example of the argument must be presented, although this theme is well developed in most versions.

> They told him [Deer] they would kill him with the sacred stones. He said, No, he had the same. Then they got a stone arrow-straightener and said they would kill him with that. He said, No, he had that too. They said they had the feathers for the head-dresses and would kill him with them. He said, No, he had some of them too. They showed him arrowheads and said they would kill him with them. He said, No, he had those also. They showed him a bow and said they would kill him with that. Deer said he also had that. They told him they had sinew and would kill him with that. He said, No, he had that too. They told him they would kill him with blood. Deer said, No, he had that. They told him they would kill him with the tracks of their footprints. He said, No, some of those were his too. They told him they would kill him with marrow. Deer said, No, he also had marrow. They told him they would kill him with their ears. He said they could not do that. He had ears too. They told him they would kill him with their eyes. He said, No, he had eyes too. They told him they would kill him with the skin of the deer's head and antlers worn on the head by the hunter to deceive the deer. He said, No, he had that too. They told him they would kill him with tobacco. He said, No, he had some of that too. They told him they would kill him with wood-ticks. He said, No, he had those also. They told him they would kill him with one of the big blueflies. He said, No, he had that too. Then at last he gave up when they told him they would kill him with the feathers that wing the arrows.[7]

In like manner they argued with each of the animals until the weakness of each, represented by the lack of some property, was found and each, in turn, gave up to serve the others through death. Thus was established a hierarchy of beings, although the parties involved in that hierarchy accept their plight and role somewhat unwillingly and only after a contest of rights and powers.

R.C. White addressed this aspect of Luiseño thought:

> The ecological relationships observable within the environment clearly do not exist upon a one-to-one basis. This is reflected in the cosmological stories concerning the hierarchical organization of nature. The eater is not necessarily directly responsible for having cosmologically overcome the eaten. For example, Deer is a principal food animal for the Indians, but humans are not directly responsible for the plight of Deer. . . . All the intricate ecological phenomena of nature thus becomes a matter for intensive observation upon

> the part of the Indians. The behavior of every "living" thing depends upon its individualistic personal "knowledge," as well as its hierarchical characteristics. The most acute observation of every detail becomes necessary if one is to have sufficient food in the face of the internecine warfare existing throughout the nature—nobody wants to be eaten; everybody strains his utmost to avoid personal power.[8]

Since this hierarchical structure is the basis of the Luiseño world view, giving order to the myriad life-forms and their interrelationships, the accomplishment of Wiyot's death can now be more fully appreciated. It is death which is the basis for the order of life, and while Luiseño, as their oral traditions as well as their cultural history show, do not desire death or enjoy its occurrence, they nonetheless recognize its great power for bringing order into the world.

With this understanding of the Luiseño worldview the cosmogonic acts may be considered again. An important and constant dimension of most accounts is the struggle between the brother and sister. They argued about who was the older and who was the stronger; and, in some versions, in a manner exactly like the argument between Deer and the other animals, their claim to power was demonstrated by a display of objects. The creation process itself attests to these ordering principles. In this light, incestuous rape is consistent with the process of ordering that establishes the Luiseño world. Internal evidence in the stories suggests that incest is not a culturally condoned action, yet, even as death is necessary for the world to have meaningful order—for the world to be even possible—so must such acts occur. The connection between the creative force of death and sexuality is most strongly made in a version of the story in which the female figure is first unwillingly subjected to her brother's sexual assault, the act in which the forms of the world are conceived, and then has her belly ripped open with a knife, as in a ritual sacrifice, the resulting wound permitting the forms of the world to emerge from her body.

Simply put, hierarchy, a system of dominance, is the ordering power of the created Luiseño world. Only with the dominance of brother over sister, male over female, sky (night) over earth, accomplished by such a vile act as incestuous rape, did the precreation unity, characterized as emptiness and darkness, give way to the formation of the world and all of its attributes, peoples, and powers.

Other Considerations

In order to more fully comprehend the nature of the female figures in the story traditions of the Luiseño and other cultures of the region and to understand why these have been understood as examples of earth-mother goddesses, there are other considerations that must be pursued.

First, it must be asked what the Luiseño call this female figure in their creation story and what her name means. In the story accounts she is often referred to as "earth" or as "earth who is female," and, variously, as Tai-mai-ya-wurt, Ta-no-wish, and Tomaiyowit (transformed from Harurai Chatutai). In none of the accounts is she referred to by the proper name "Mother Earth" or any of its several variants. Linguistic evidence helps reveal the meaning of her name. Sparkman's Luiseño grammar gives "*tamá-yawot* (mythologically) 'the earth, first female,' "[9] although in the entry for the stem indicating north, he includes: "from *tamá-yawot* the first woman, mother earth, who lay in the north."[10] DuBois was the first to refer to the figure by the proper name "Earth-mother" in her 1905 study, "Religious Ceremonies and Myths of the Mission Indians."[11] When she made the reference she was not considering the creation story, but an incidental relationship between the order of things created and ritual objects used in the *toloache* ceremony.

Another line that should be followed is the existence of world parents or earth mothers in the creation stories of other tribes in the southern California and southwestern region. Stith Thompson's *Tales of the North American Indians* (1929) indicates that we should expect to find evidence among the Diegueño (another Mission tribe), the Pima, Mohave, Yuma, and Zuni.[12] A brief review of the story traditions of these tribes is worthwhile.

The Diegueño and the Luiseño are often considered the most prominent of the Mission tribes. While they share some ceremonial practices and doubtless have long maintained close cultural contact, their conceptions of world creation are distinct. It must also be remembered that their languages and cultures stem from quite different stocks. A search through all the accounts of the Diegueño creation story reveals only one in which there is even a mention of the earth and sky as male and female creators. It is in an account collected by DuBois and published in 1901. The account begins:

> When Tu-chai-pai made the world, the earth is the world, the earth is the woman, the sky is the man. The sky came down upon the earth. The world in the beginning was pure lake covered with tules. Tu-chai-pai and Yo-ko-mat-is, the brother, sat together, stooping far over, bowed down under the weight of the sky.[13]

The account then continues with the story of the two brothers who emerge from the ocean to model humankind and the animals out of clay. This theme of two brothers as creators is found in all other Diegueño accounts. Waterman, in an early comparative study of the accounts of several southern California cultures, concluded that "these two sentences [the first sentences in DuBois's account] came into the myths in question either from a bias on the part of the author, or from a combination of Luiseño and Diegueño story-elements by the native narrator."[14]

Among the Mohave there is but a hint of the belief in the earth and sky as mother and father of creation. There are many well-developed Mohave accounts of the creation by the two brothers, as described above. Yet, there are several brief references to the world-parent theme. In 1886, John G. Bourke visited Fort Mohave. For his tour of several Mohave villages he was assigned a guide by the name of Merryman who had served as a scout and had traveled widely. Merryman spoke, read, and wrote English. During the tour, Merryman recounted for Bourke many Mohave beliefs and practices. After a comment about Mohave hunting practices, Bourke wrote the following, apparently quoting Merryman.

> This Earth is a woman; the Sky is a man. The Earth was sterile and barren and nothing grew upon it; but, by conjunction with the Sky—(here he repeated almost the very same myth that the Apaches and Pimas have to the effect that the Earth was asleep and a drop of rain fell upon her causing conception,)—two gods were born, in the west, thousands of miles away from here. They were Ku-ku-matz and his brother, To-chi-pa. I don't know much about them: I heard they jumped down a burning mountain, what you call a volcano. They are not dead, but we do not see them any more.[15]

Merryman made another reference to the earth and sky as parents of other children, but Bourke found the evidence contradictory to what he had already been told and, while noting this peculiarity, claimed he did not question Merryman for fear he would cease giving him information.

In a couple of other accounts, there are statements which indicate the earth is female or a mother, but the bulk of evidence of Mohave belief about the creation is in contradiction to these statements.[16]

Bourke noted that Merryman told a story about the impregnation of the earth by rain and he identified this as a story he knew to exist among the Apache and Pima. I have yet to find any published evidence of such a story told by the Pima, yet it could certainly have existed. It is a well-known story among the Apache and Navajo.

The reference to a Pima belief in earth and sky parents comes in the midst of the long and complicated saga of creation recorded by Frank Russell and published in 1908.

> In the beginning there was nothing where now are earth, sun, moon, stars, and all that we see. Ages long the darkness was gathering, until it formed a great mass in which developed the spirit of Earth Doctor, who, like the fluffy

> wisp of cotton that floats upon the wind, drifted to and fro without support or place to fix himself. Conscious to his power, he determined to try to build an abiding place, so he took from his breast a little dust and flattened it into a cake. Then he thought to himself, "Come forth, some kind of plant," and there appeared the creosote bush.[17]

Through thought and song, the power of Earth Doctor manifested itself in the world and it was peopled. But death did not exist and the world became overcrowded, and for want of food people began eating one another. Earth Doctor became distressed and decided to destroy all that he had created.

> Earth Doctor said, "I shall unite earth and sky; the earth shall be as a female and the sky as a male, and from their union shall be born one who will be a helper to me. Let the sun be joined with the moon, also even as man is wedded to woman, and their offspring shall be a helper to me." Then he caught the hook of his staff into the sky and pulled it down, crushing to death the people and all other living things. Thrusting his stick through the earth, Earth Doctor went through the hole and came out alone on the other side. He called upon the sun and moon to come forth from the wreck of world and sky, and they obeyed him. But there was no sky for them to travel through, no stars nor milky way, so he created all these anew. Then he called for the offspring of earth and sky, but there was no response. Then he created a race of men, as he had done before; these were the Rsasanatc. . . . After a time the earth gave birth to one who was afterwards known as Itany and later as Siuuhu, Elder Brother.[18]

Elder Brother then comes forth to challenge the work of Earth Doctor, threatening to destroy these things of his creation. From here a complex saga of creation and destruction unfolds. There is no other mention of the earth and sky as creators.

In the context of this story it seems that the conjoining of the earth and sky is an act primarily motivated by the need to destroy the initial world created by Earth Doctor because that world had run amok, and thus the act is somewhat the reverse of the separation of parents common to the world-parent type creation. While Earth Doctor states that he will have the earth and sky serve as parents in the manner of a man and a woman, when he calls forth their offspring there is no response. Only later does Elder Brother appear, and it seems that he is born from the earth.

There is in this aspect of the story something of an enigma which cannot be resolved, yet it seems beyond question that the union of earth and sky is not central to Pima creation, nor does a further examination of Pima religious culture reveal evidence that the sky and earth are significant figures.

Despite some of the difficulties of the existing recorded accounts, the variety of the stories of creation that exist among several tribes in southern California and Arizona are well known. While several of these include the female personification of the earth, she is in no place a major creator, nor is there any extensive development in ritual or story of a female personification of the earth. What then led to these stories being so commonly referred to as examples of world-parent creations? Why has the figure Mother Earth been so commonly seen as present, particularly in the Luiseño stories?

The Scholarly Contribution

As indicated, in 1905 DuBois was the first to use the term "Earth-mother" to refer to a Luiseño belief. She occasionally used the term after that in publications on the Luiseño. In his *Handbook of Indians of California* (1925) Kroeber includes a discussion of Luiseño creation. He is obviously dependent upon DuBois's latest account, but he does not use the term "Earth-mother."[19] Robert Heizer's recent summary of California mythology also presents the Luiseño story, and this is obviously dependent upon Kroeber. Heizer does not use any form of the Earth-mother name.[20] Ake Hultkrantz considers Luiseño creation stories in his *The Religions of the American Indians* (1979). He too is dependent upon Kroeber, and in his way of seeing the story he finds it appropriate to introduce the proper name "Mother Earth" for the Luiseño female figure. Hultkrantz writes, "In the southern California myth of the cosmic parents, . . . the spirits, human beings, and all of nature emanate from the union of the skyfather with Mother Earth."[21]

From this review of the way students of California, and in particular Luiseño, story traditions have referred to the female figure in the story, we see that only DuBois and Hultkrantz have actually referred to her by the name Earth-mother or Mother Earth, yet all have seen Luiseño concepts of creation as of the world-parent type. Perhaps most remarkable is the virtual absence of discussion of the Luiseño stories beyond identification as being of the world-parent type. It is the more remarkable in light of the common and fundamental elements of the story accounts. Every account of the story identifies the male and female figures as not only associated with sky and earth but as siblings. Every account presents their union as one of incest and as a shameful one. Every account presents their union as one of dominance and violence, that is, rape. Given these constant and central aspects of all Luiseño story accounts, it is more than surprising to find that not one of the scholarly interpreters of the story so much as mentions these salient details.

There is not a single mention, not a single expressed concern, either about the incestuous nature of their relationship, the forceful nature of the sexual contact, or the violence threatened by the brother and carried out by him on his sister. Only Boscana seems to have been at all concerned with any of these factors and, according to his notes, he was only gauging the morality of the people he served. Surely this indicates that the scholarly interest in these stories has been so predisposed as to have missed their most fundamental features. Observing the presence of male and female figures whose union is associated with the creation of features of the earth, they assumed, all too quickly, the adequacy of classifying the cosmogony as being of the world-parent type. I believe that there is evidence for this predisposition in what I call "the Polynesian connection."

In Kroeber's discussion of Luiseño creation stories in his *Handbook* (1925), he focuses primarily upon demonstrating their sophistication, thus contradicting the common view that the Luiseño culture is extremely primitive. He summarizes, with considerable liberty, the last version published by DuBois (which is the most unusual and complex of all the versions). He indicates that this account is basically the same as all other accounts, with certain expected minor variations. In his tribute to the sophistication of the story, Kroeber remarks, "the beginning of the Luiseño genesis reads far more, in spirit at least, like the opening of a Polynesian cosmogonic chant than like an American Indian tradition of the world origin."[22] This point was picked up and restarted by both Hultkrantz and Heizer. No one of the three indicates the specific Polynesian connection, which is quite likely the classic Polynesian text "The Children of Heaven and Earth."[23] Had this connection been developed by any of the authors who suggested it, they might have been encouraged to consider the more central issues in the Luiseño stories, for the Polynesian story begins with the statement that all beings had but one pair of ancestors, springing either from the heaven above or the earth below. It is a tale which in its full extent is focused upon the efforts of the created children to force the separation of the earth and sky so that light and life might be attained. It was a difficult and unwilling separation. The children argued and finally warred among themselves. They did much violence to their parents and, as a result of the creative separation, the price of light and life was darkness, war, death, and strife borne by siblings on a cosmic scale. Here too the order that constitutes creation is inseparable from strife, hierarchy, destruction, darkness, and despair,[24] but in the Luiseño stories the order is effected not by the separation of the world parents by the children they have created, but rather by an incestuous rape. . . .

Notes

1. Another figure in Luiseño oral traditions and ritual, similar in many ways to Wiyot, is Chungichnish. There is an extensive cycle of stories centered on this figure. Many scholars believe that the origins of this figure and the accompanying ritual practices are of relatively recent date. See Raymond C. White, "The Luiseño Theory of 'Knowledge,'" *American Anthropologist,* 59 (1957): pp. 1–19.

2. Constance G. DuBois, "Mythology of the Mission Indians," *Journal of American Folklore,* 19 (1906):145.

3. For the stories related to Wiyot, see John P. Harrington, "Yuma Account of Origins," *Journal of American Folklore,* 21 (1908): 324–48; Constance G. DuBois, "Religion of the Luiseño," *University of California Publications in American Archaeology and Ethnology,* 8 (1908): 69–186; DuBois, "Mythology of the Mission Indians" (1906), pp. 55–60.

4. See DuBois, "Religion of the Luiseño," pp. 93–97, for a description of the girls' initiation rites.

5. See ibid., pp. 77–87, for a description of the Toloache and Milky Way rituals.

6. Alfred L. Kroeber, *Handbook of Indians in California* (Washington, DC: Bureau of American Ethnology, 1925).

7. DuBois, "Religion of the Luiseño," p. 147.

8. White, "Luiseño Social Organization," pp. 142, 143.

9. Alfred L. Kroeber and George W. Grace, "The Sparkman Grammar of Luiseño," *University of California Publications in Linguistics,* 16 (Berkeley and Los Angeles: University of California Press, 1960), p. 80.

10. Ibid., p. 122.

11. DuBois, "Religious Ceremonies," p. 629.

12. Stith Thompson, *Tales of the North American Indians* (Bloomington: University of Indiana Press, 1929), p. 280, n. 37.

13. Constance G. DuBois, "The Mythology of the Diegueño," *Journal of American Folk-Lore,* 14 (1901): 181.

14. Thomas Waterman, "Analysis of the Mission Indian Creation Story," *American Anthropologist* n.s. 2 (1909): 46.

15. John G. Bourke, "Notes on the Cosmogony and Theogony of the Mojave Indians," *Journal of American Folk-Lore,* 2 (1889): 46.

16. Edward S. Curtis, *The North American Indian,* Frederick W. Hodge, ed. 20 vols. Norwood, Mass.: Plimpton Press, 1907–30. (Reprinted: Johnson Reprint, New York, 1970), vol. 2, pp. 56–57, and p. 86, attributes creation to the earth and sky, as mother and father, for the Mohave and the Maricopa tribes. Alfred L. Kroeber, "More Mohave Myths," *Anthropological Records,* 27 (1972): 5, notes the Mohave belief in the earth as woman and mother. The search of other records on these tribes has failed to produce any corroborative evidence and has suggested these ideas to be inconsistent with the arguing-brother creation theme which is well developed and dominant. Cyril Forde discusses mythic themes of the various southern California tribes, with some suggestions about their relatedness and history, in his "Ethnography of the Yuma Indians," *University of California Publications in American Archaeology and Ethnography* 28 (1931): 178. I do not find evidence to confirm the presence of the general theme of sky-earth cosmogony among the Luiseño and Mohave.

17. Frank Russell, "The Pima Indians," *Twenty-sixth Annual Report of the Bureau of American Ethnology,* 1904–1905, (Washington, D.C.: Government Printing Office, 1908), p. 206.

18. Ibid., pp. 208–9.

19. Kroeber, *Handbook of Indians of California,* p. 677.

20. Robert F. Heizer, "Mythology: Regional Patterns and History of Research," in *California: Handbook of North American Indians,* vol. 8, ed. William C. Sturtevant (Washington, D.C.: Smithsonian Institution, 1978), p. 656.

21. Ake Hultkrantz, *The Religious of the American Indians* (Berkeley: University of California Press, 1979), p. 31.

22. Kroeber, *Handbook of Indians of California,* p. 677.

23. Sir George Grey, *Polynesian Mythology and Ancient Traditional History* (Auckland: H. Brett, 1885), pp. 1–8.

24. The importance of the separation of the world parents as part of the cosmic creation process is discussed by Charles H. Long, *Alpha: The Myths of Creation* (New York: George Braziller, 1963), pp. 66–80.

7

Frank Waters

The Hopi Myth of Creation

Tokpela: The First World

The first world was Tokpeia [Endless Space].

But first, they say, there was only the Creator, Taiowa. All else was endless space. There was no beginning and no end, no time, no shape, no life. Just an immeasurable void that had its beginning and end, time, shape and life in the mind of Taiowa the Creator.

Then he, the infinite, conceived the finite. First he created Sótuknang to make it manifest, saying to him, "I have created you, the first power and instrument as a person, to carry out my plan for life in endless space. I am your Uncle. You are my Nephew. Go now and lay out these universes in proper order so they may work harmoniously with one another according to my plan."

Sótuknang did as he was commanded. From endless space he gathered that which was to be manifest as solid substance, molded it into forms, and arranged them into nine universal kingdoms: one for Taiowa the Creator, one for himself, and seven universes for the life to come. Finishing this, Sótuknang went to Taiowa and asked, "Is this according to your plan?"

"It is very good," and Taiowa. "Now I want you to do the same thing with the waters. Place them on the surfaces of these universes so they will be divided equally among all and each."

So Sótuknang gathered from endless space that which was to be manifest

---

as the waters and placed them on the universes so that each would be half solid and half water. Going now to Taiowa, he said, "I want you to see the work I have done and if it pleases you."

"It is very good," said Taiowa. "The next thing now is to put the forces of air into peaceful movement about all."

This Sótuknang did. From endless space he gathered that which was to be manifest as the airs, made them into great forces, and arrange them into gentle ordered movements around each universe.

Taiowa was pleased. "You have done a great work according to my plan, Nephew. You have created the universes and made them manifest in solids, waters, and winds, and put them in their proper places. But your work is not yet finished. Now you must create life and its movement to complete the four parts, Túwqachi, of my universal plan."

Spider Woman and the Twins

Sótuknang went to the universe wherein was that to be Tokpela, the First World, and out of it he created her who was to remain on that earth and be his helper. Her name was Kókyangwúti, Spider Woman.

When she awoke to life and received her name, she asked, "Why am I here?"

"Look about you," answered Sótuknang. "Here is this earth we have created. It has shape and substance, direction and time, a beginning and an end. But there is no life upon it. We see no joyful movement. We hear no joyful sound. What is life without sound and movement? So you have been given the power to help us create this life. You have been given the knowledge, wisdom, and love to bless all the beings you create. That is why you are here."

Following his instructions, Spider Woman took some earth, mixed with it some túchvala [liquid from mouth: saliva], and molded it into two beings. Then she covered them with a cape made of white substance which was the creative wisdom itself, and sang the Creation Song over them. When she uncovered them the two beings, twins, sat up and asked, "Who are we? Why are we here?"

To the one on the right Spider Woman said, "You are Pöqánghoya and you are to help keep this world in order when life is put upon it. Go now around all the world and put your hands upon the earth so that it will become fully solidified. This is your duty."

Spider Woman then said to the twin on the left, "You are Palöngawhoya and you are to help keep this world in order when life is put upon it. This is your duty now: go about all the world and send out sound so that it may be heard throughout all the land. When this is heard you will also be known as 'Echo,' for all sound echoes the Creator."

Pöqánghoya, traveling throughout the earth, solidified the higher reaches into great mountains. The lower reaches he made firm but still pliable enough to be used by those beings to be placed upon it and who would call it their mother.

Palöngawhoya, traveling throughout the earth, sounded out his call as he was bidden. All the vibratory centers along the earth's axis from pole to pole resounded his call; the whole earth trembled; the universe quivered in tune. Thus he made the whole world an instrument of sound, and sound an instrument for carrying messages, resounding praise to the Creator of all.

"This is your voice, Uncle," Sótuknang said to Taiowa. "Everything is tuned to your sound."

"It is very good," said Taiowa.

When they had accomplished their duties, Pöqánghoya was sent to the north pole of the world axis and Palöngawhoya to the south pole, where they were jointly commanded to keep the world properly rotating. Pöqánghoya was also given the power to keep the air in gentle ordered movement, and instructed to send out his call for good or for warning through the vibratory centers of the earth.

"These will be your duties in time to come," said Spider Woman.

She then created from the earth trees, bushes, plants, flowers, all kinds of seed-bearers and nut-bearers to clothe the earth, giving to each a life and name. In the same manner she created all kinds of birds and animals—molding them out of earth, covering them with her white-substance cape, and singing over them. Some she placed to her right, some to her left, others before and behind her, indicating how they should spread to all four corners of the earth to live.

Sótuknang was happy, seeing how beautiful it was—the land, the plants, the birds and animals, and the power working through them all. Joyfully he said to Taiowa, "Come see what our world looks like now!"

"It is very good," said Taiowa. "It is ready now for human life, the final touch to complete my plan."

Creation of Mankind

So Spider Woman gathered earth, this time of four colors, yellow, red, white, and black; mixed with túchvala, the liquid of her mouth; molded them; and covered them with her white-substance cape which was the creative wisdom itself. As before, she sang over them the Creation Song, and when she uncovered them these forms were human beings in the image of

Sótuknang. Then she created four other beings after her own form. They were *wúti*, female partners, for the first four male beings.

When Spider Woman uncovered them the forms came to life. This was at the time of the dark purple light, Qoyangnuptu, the first phase of the dawn of Creation, which first reveals the mystery of man's creation.

They soon awakened and began to move, but there was still a dampness on their foreheads and a soft spot on their heads. This was at the time of the yellow light, the second phase of the dawn of Creation, when the breath of life entered man.

In a short time the sun appeared above the horizon, drying the dampness on their foreheads and hardening the soft spot on their heads. This was the time of the red light, Tálawva, the third phase of the dawn of Creation, when man, fully formed and firmed, proudly faced his Creator. . . .

"That is the Sun," said Spider Woman. "You are meeting your Father the Creator for the first time. You must always remember and observe these three phases of your Creation. The time of the three lights, the dark purple, the yellow, and the red reveal in turn the mystery, the breath of life, and warmth of love. These comprise the Creator's plan of life for you as sung over you in the Song of Creation:

Song of Creation

The dark purple light rises in the north,
A yellow light rises in the east.
Then we of the flowers of the earth come forth
To receive a long life of joy.
We call ourselves the Butterfly Maidens.

Both male and female make their prayers to the east.
Make the respectful sign to the Sun our Creator.
The sounds of bells ring through the air,
Making a joyful sound throughout the land,
Their joyful echo resounding everywhere.

Humbly I ask my Father,
The perfect one, Taiowa, our Father.
The perfect one creating the beautiful life
Shown to us by the yellow light,
To give us perfect light at the time of the red light.

The perfect one laid out the perfect plan
And gave to us a long span of life,

Creating song to implant joy in life.
On this path of happiness, we the Butterfly Maidens
Carry out his wishes by greeting our Father Sun.

The song resounds back from our Creator with joy,
And we of the earth repeat it to our Creator.
At the appearing of the yellow light,
Repeats and repeats again the joyful echo,
Sounds and resounds for times to come.

The First People of the First World did not answer her; they could not speak. Something had to be done. Since Spider Woman received her power from Sótuknang, she had to call him and ask him what to do. So she called Palöngawhoya and said, "Call your Uncle. We need him at once."

Palöngawhoya, the echo twin, sent out his call along the world axis to the vibratory centers of the earth, which resounded his message throughout the universe. "Sótuknang, our Uncle, come at once! We need you!"

All at once, with the sound as of a mighty wind, Sótuknang appeared in front of them. "I am here. Why do you need me so urgently?"

Spider Woman explained. "As you commanded me, I have created these First People. They are fully and firmly formed; they are properly colored; they have life; they have movement. But they cannot talk. That is the proper thing they lack. So I want you to give them speech. Also the wisdom and the power to reproduce, so that they may enjoy their life and give thanks to the Creator."

So Sótuknang gave them speech, a different language to each color, with respect for each other's difference. He gave them the wisdom and the power to reproduce and multiply.

Then he said to them, "With all these I have given you this world to live on and to be happy. There is only one thing I ask of you. To respect the Creator at all times. Wisdom, harmony, and respect for the love of the Creator who made you. May it grow and never be forgotten among you as long as you live."

So the First People sent their directions, were happy, and began to multiply.

Tokpa: The Second World

So the First People kept multiplying and spreading over the face of the land and were happy. Although they were of different colors and spoke different languages, they felt as one and understood one another without talking. It was the same with the birds and animals. They all suckled at the breast of their Mother Earth, who gave them her milk of grass, seeds, fruit, and corn, and they all felt as one, people and animals.

But gradually there were those who forgot the commands of Sótuknang and the Spider Woman to respect their Creator. More and more they used the vibratory centers of their bodies solely for earthly purposes, forgetting that their primary purpose was to carry out the plan of the Creator.

There then came among them Lavaíhoya, the Talker. He came in the form of a bird called Mochni [bird like a mockingbird], and the more he kept talking the more he convinced them of the differences between them: the difference between people and animals, and the differences between the people themselves by reason of the colors of their skins, their speech, and belief in the plan of the Creator.

It was then that animals drew away from people. The guardian spirit of animals laid his hands on their hind legs just below the tail, making them become wild and scatter from the people in fear. You can see this slightly oily spot today on deer and antelope—on the sides of their back legs as they throw up their tails to run away.

In the same way, people began to divide and draw away from one another—those of different races and languages, then those who remembered the plan of Creation and those who did not. . . .

There came among them a handsome one, Káto'ya, in the form of a snake with a big head. He led the people still farther away from one another and their pristine wisdom. They became suspicious of one another and accused one another wrongfully until they became fierce and warlike and began to fight one another.

All the time Mochni kept talking and Káto'ya became more beguiling. There was no rest, no peace.

But among all the people of different races and languages there were a few in every group who still lived by the laws of Creation. To them came Sótuknang. He came with the sound as of a mighty wind and suddenly appeared before them. He said, "I have observed this state of affairs. It is not good. It is so bad I talked to my Uncle, Taiowa, about it. We have decided this world must be destroyed and another one created so you people can start over again. You are the ones we have chosen."

They listened carefully to their instructions.

Said Sótuknang, "You will go to a certain place. Your *kópavi* [vibratory center on top of the head] will lead you. This inner wisdom will give you the sight to see a certain cloud, which you will follow by day, and a certain star, which you will follow by night. Take nothing with you. Your journey will not end until the cloud stops and the star stops."

So all over the world these chosen people suddenly disappeared from their homes and people and began following the cloud by day and the star by night. Many other people asked them where they were going and, when they were told, laughed at them. "We don't see any cloud or any star either!" they said. This was because they had lost the inner vision of the *kópavi* on the crown of their head; the door was closed to them. Still there were a very few who went along anyway because they believed the people who did see the cloud and the star. This was all right.

After many days and nights the first people arrived at the certain place. Soon others came and asked, "What are you doing here?" And they said, "We were told by Sótuknang to come here." The other people said, "We too were led here by the vapor and the star!" They were all happy together because they were of the same mind and understanding even though they were of different races and languages.

When the last ones arrived Sótuknang appeared. "Well, you are all here, you people I have chosen to save from the destruction of this world. Now come with me."

He led them to big mound where the Ant People lived, stamped on the roof, and commanded the Ant People to open up their home. When an opening was made on top the anthill, Sótuknang said to the people, "Now you will enter this Ant kiva, where you will be safe when I destroy the world. While you are here I want you to learn a lesson from these Ant People. They are industrious. They gather food in the summer for the winter. They keep cool when it is hot and warm when it is cool. They live peacefully with one another. They obey the plan of Creation."

So the people went down to live with the Ant People. When they were all safe and settled, Taiowa commanded Sótuknang to destroy the world. Sótuknang destroyed it by fire because the Fire Clan had been its leaders. He rained fire upon it. He opened up the volcanoes. Fire came from above and below and all around until the earth, the waters, the air, all was one element, fire, and there was nothing left except the people safe inside the womb of the earth.

This was the end of Tokpela, the First World.

Emergence to the Second World

While this was going on the people lived happily underground with the Ant People. Their homes were just like the people's homes on the earth-surface being destroyed. There were rooms to live in and rooms where they stored their food. There was light to see by, too. The tiny bits of crystal in the sand of the anthill had absorbed the light of the sun, and by using the inner vision of the center behind their eyes they could see by its reflection very well.

Only one thing troubled them. The food began to run short. It had not taken Sótuknang long to destroy the world, nor would it take him long to create another one. But it was taking a long time for the First World to cool off before the Second World could be created. That was why the food was running short.

"Do not give us so much of the food you have worked so hard to gather and store," the people said.

"Yes, you are our guests," the Ant People told them. "What we have is yours also." So the Ant People continued to deprive themselves of food in order to supply their guests. Every day they tied their belts tighter and tighter. That is why ants today are so small around the waist.

Finally that which had been the First World cooled off. Sótuknang purified it. Then he began to create the Second World. He changed its form completely, putting land where the water was and water where the land had been, so the people upon their Emergence would have nothing to remind them of the previous wicked world.

When all was ready he came to the roof of the Ant kiva, stamped on it, and gave his call. Immediately the Chief of the Ant People went up to the opening and rolled back the *núta.* "*Yung-ai!* Come in! You are welcome!" He called.

Sótuknang spoke first to the Ant People. "I am thanking you for doing your part in helping to save these people. It will always be remembered, this you have done. The time will come when another world will be destroyed; and when wicked people know their last day on earth had come, they will sit by an anthill and cry for the ants to save them. Now, having fulfilled your duty, you may go forth to this Second World I have created and take your place as ants."

Then Sótuknang said to the people, "Make your Emergence now to this Second World I have created. It is not quite so beautiful as the First World, but it is beautiful just the same. You will like it. So multiply and be happy. But remember your Creator and the laws he gave you. When I hear you singing joyful praises to him I will know you are my children, and you will be close to me in your hearts.

So the people emerged to the Second World. Its name was Tokpa (Dark Midnight). Its direction was south, its color blue, its mineral *qöchásiva,* silver. Chiefs upon it were *salavi,* the spruce; *kwáhu,* the eagle; and *kolíchiyaw,* the skunk.

It was a big land, and the people multiplied rapidly, spreading over it to all directions, even to the other side of the world. This did not matter, for they were so close together in spirit they could see and talk to each other from the center on top of the head. Because this door was still open, they felt close to Sótuknang and they sang joyful praises to the Creator, Taiowa.

They did not have the privilege of living with the animals, though, for the animals were wild and kept apart. Being separated from the animals, the people tended to their own affairs. They built homes, then villages and trails between them. They made things with their hands and stored food like the Ant People. Then they began to trade and barter with one another.

This was when the trouble started. Everything they needed was on this Second World, but they began to want more. More and more they traded for things they didn't need, and the more goods they got, the more they wanted. This was very serious. For they did not realize they were drawing away, step by step, from the good life given them. They just forgot to sing joyful praises to the Creator and soon began to sing praises for the goods they bartered and stored. Before long it happened as it had to happen. The people began to quarrel and fight, and then wars between villages began.

Still there were a few people in every village who sang the song of their Creation. But the wicked people laughed at them until they could sing it only in their hearts. Even so, Sótuknang heard it through their centers and the centers of the earth. Suddenly one day he appeared before them.

"Spider Woman tells me your thread is running out on this world," he said. "That is too bad. The Spider Clan was your leader, and you were making good progress until this state of affairs began. Now my Uncle, Taiowa, and I have decided we must do something about it. We are going to destroy this Second World just as soon as we put you people who still have the song in your hearts in a safe place."

So again, as on the First World, Sótuknang called on the Ant People to open up their underground world for the chosen people. When they were safely underground, Sótuknang commanded the twins, Pöqánghoya and Palöngawhoya, to leave their post at the north and south ends of the world's axis, where they were stationed to keep the earth properly rotating.

The twins had hardly abandoned their stations when the world, with no one to control it, teetered off balance, spun around crazily, then rolled over twice. Mountains plunged into seas with a great splash, seas and lakes sloshed over the land; and as the world spun through cold and lifeless space it froze into solid ice.

This was the end of Tokpa, the Second World.

Emergence to the Third World

For many years all the elements that had comprised the Second World were frozen into a motionless and lifeless lump of ice. But the people were happy and warm with the Ant People in their underground world. They watched their food carefully, although the ants' waists became still smaller. They wove sashes and blanket together and told stories.

Eventually Sótuknang ordered Pöqánghoya and Palöngawhoya back to their stations at the poles of the world axis. With a great shudder and a splintering of ice the planet began rotating again. When it was revolving smoothly about its own axis and stately moving in its universal orbit, the ice began to melt and the world began to warm to life. Sótuknang set about creating the Third World: arranging earths and seas, planting mountains and plains with their proper coverings, and creating all forms of life.

When the earth was ready for occupancy, he came to the Ant kiva with the proper approach as before and said, "Open the door. It is time for you to come out."

Once again when the *núta* was rolled back he gave the people their instructions. "I have saved you so you can be planted again on this new Third World. But you must always remember the two things I am saying to you now. First, respect men and one another. And second, sing in harmony from the tops of the hills. When I do not hear you singing praises to your Creator I will know you have gone back to evil again."

So the people climbed up the ladder from the Ant kiva, making their Emergence to the Third World.

Kuskurza: The Third World

Its name was Kuskurza, its direction east, its color red. Chiefs upon it were the mineral *palásiva* (copper); the plant *píva,* tobacco; the bird *angwusi,* crow; and the animal *chöövio,* antelope.

Upon it once more the people spread out, multiplied, and continued their progress on the Road of Life. In the First World they had lived simply with the animals. In the Second World they had developed handicrafts, homes, and villages. Now in the Third World they multiplied in such numbers and advanced so rapidly that they created big cities, countries, a whole civilization. This made it difficult for them to conform to the plan of Creation and to sing praises to Taiowa and Sótuknang. More and more of them became wholly occupied with their own earthly plans.

Some of them, of course, retained the wisdom granted them upon their Emergence. With this wisdom they understood that the farther they proceeded on the Road of Life and the more they developed, the harder it was. That was why their world was destroyed every so often to give them a fresh start. They were especially concerned because so many people were using their reproductive power in wicked ways. There was one woman who was becoming known throughout the world for her wickedness in corrupting so many people. She even boasted that so many men were giving her turquoise necklaces for her favors she could wind them around a ladder that reached to the end of the world's axis. So the people with wisdom sang louder and longer their praises to the Creator from the tops of their hills.

The other people hardly heard them. Under the leadership of the Bow Clan they began to use their creative power in another evil and destructive way. Perhaps this was caused by that wicked woman. But some of them made a *pátuwvota* [shield made of hide] and with their creative power made it fly through the air. On this many of the people flew to a big city, attacked it, and returned so fast no one knew where they came from. Soon the people of many cities and countries were making *pátuwvotas* and flying on them to attack one another. So corruption and war came to the Third World as it had to the others.

This time Sótuknang came to Spider Woman and said, "There is no use waiting until the thread runs out this time. Something has to be done lest the people with the song in their hearts are corrupted and killed off too. It will be difficult, with all this destruction going on, for them to gather at the far end of the world I have designated. But I will help them. Then you will save them when I destroy this world with water."

"How shall I save them?" asked Spider Woman.

"When you get there look about you," commanded Sótuknang. "You will see these tall plants with hollow stems. Cut them down and put the people inside. Then I will tell you what to do next."

Spider Woman did as he instructed her. She cut down the hollow reeds; and as the people came to her, she put them inside with a little water and *hurúsuki* (white cornmeal dough) for food, and sealed them up. When all the people were thus taken care of, Sótuknang appeared.

"Now you get in to take care of them, and I will seal you up," he said. "Then I will destroy the world."

So he loosed the waters upon the earth. Waves higher than mountains rolled in upon the land. Continents broke asunder and sank beneath the seas. And still the rains fell, the waves rolled in.

The people sealed up in their hollow reeds heard the mighty rushing of the waters. They felt themselves tossed high in the air and dropping back in the water. Then all was quiet, and they knew they were floating. For a long, long time—so long a time that it seemed it would never end—they kept floating.

Finally their movement ceased. The Spider Woman unsealed their hollow reeds, took them by the tops of their heads, and pulled them out. "Bring out all the food that is left over," she commanded.

The people brought out their *hurúsuki*; it was still the same size, although they had been eating it all this time. Looking about them, they saw they were on a little piece of land that had been the top of one of their highest mountains. All else, as far as they could see, was water. This was all that remained of the Third World.

"There must be some dry land somewhere we can go to," they said. "Where is the new Fourth World that Sótuknang has created for us?" They sent many kinds of birds, one after another, to fly over the waters and find it. But they all came back tired out without having seen any sign of land. Next they planted a reed that grew high into the sky. Up it they climbed and stared over the surface of the waters. But they saw no sign of land.

So Spider Woman directed the people to make round, flat boats of the hollow reeds they had come in and to crawl inside. Again they entrusted themselves to the water and the inner wisdom to guide them. So the people kept traveling toward the rising sun in their reed boats. After awhile they said, "There is that low rumbling noise we heard. We must be coming to land again."

So it was. A big land, it seemed, with grass and trees and flowers beautiful to their weary eyes. On it they rested a long time. Some of the people wanted to stay, but Spider Woman said, "No. It is not the place. You must continue on."

Leaving their boats, they traveled by foot eastward across the island to the water's edge. Here they found growing some more of the hollow plants like reeds or bamboo, which they cut down. Directed by Spider Woman, they laid some of these in a row with another row on top of them in the opposite direction and tied them all together with vines and leaves. This made a raft big enough for one family or more. When enough rafts were made for all, Spider Woman directed them to make paddles.

"You will be going uphill from now on and you will have to make your own way. So Sótuknang told you: The farther you go, the harder it gets."

After long and weary traveling, still east and a little north, the people began to hear the low rumbling noise and saw land. One family and clan after another landed with joy. The land was long, wide, and beautiful. The earth was rich and flat, covered with trees and plants, seed-bearers and nut-bearers, providing lots of food. The people were happy and kept staying there year after year.

"No. This is not the Fourth World," Spider Woman kept telling them. "It is too easy and pleasant for you to live on, and you would soon fall into evil ways again. You must go on. Have we not told you the way becomes harder and longer?"

Reluctantly the people traveled eastward by foot across the island to the far shore. Again they made rafts and paddles. When they were ready to set forth Spider Woman said, "Now I have done all I am commanded to do for you. You must go on alone and find your own place of emergence. Just keep your doors open, and your spirits will guide you."

At last they saw land. It rose high above the waters, stretching from north to south as far as they could see. A great land, a mighty land, their inner wisdom told them. "The Fourth World!" they cried to each other.

As they got closer, its shores rose higher and higher into a steep wall of mountains. There seemed no place to land. "Let us go north. There we will find our Place of Emergence," said some. So they went north, but the mountains rose higher and steeper.

"No! Let us go south! There we will find our Place of Emergence!" cried others. So they turned south and traveled many days more. But here too the mountain wall reared higher.

Not knowing what to do, the people stopped paddling, opened the doors on top their heads, and let themselves be guided. Almost immediately the water smoothed out, and they felt their rafts caught up in a gentle current. Before long they landed and joyfully jumped out upon a sandy shore. "The Fourth World!" they cried. "We have reached our Place of Emergence at last!"

Soon all the others arrived and when they were gathered together Sótuknang appeared before them. "Well, I see you are all here. That is good. This is the place I have prepared for you. Look now at the way you have come."

Looking to the west and the south, the people could see sticking out of the water the islands upon which they had rested.

"They are the footprints of your journey," continued Sótuknang, "the tops of the high mountains of the Third World, which I destroyed. Now watch."

As the people watched them the closest one sank under the water, then the next, until all were gone, and they could see only water.

"See," said Sótuknang, "I have washed away even the footprints of your Emergence; the stepping-stones which I left for you. Down on the bottom of the seas lie all the proud cities, the flying *pátuwvotas,* and the worldly treasures corrupted with evil, and those people who found no time to sing praises to the Creator from the tops of their hills. But the day will come, if you preserve the memory and the meaning of your Emergence, when these stepping-stones will emerge again to prove the truth you speak."

This at last was the end of the Third World, Kuskurza [an ancient name for which there is no modern meaning].

Tuwaqachi: The Fourth World

"I have something more to say before I leave you," Sótuknang told the people as they stood at their Place of Emergence on the shore of the present Fourth World. This is what he said:

"The name of this Fourth World is Túwaqachi, World Complete. You will find out why. It is not all beautiful and easy like the previous ones. It has height and depth, heat and cold, beauty and barrenness; it has everything for you to choose from. What you choose will determine if this time you can carry out the plan of Creation on it or whether it must in time be destroyed too. Now you will separate and go different ways to claim all the earth for the Creator. Each group of you will follow your own star until it stops. There you will settle. Now I must go. But you will have help from the proper deities, from your good spirits. Just keep your own doors open and always remember what I have told you. This is what I say. . . ."

Part II
Law and Property

8

Rory O'Brien

Law, Property, and the Environment: An Introduction

Two of the most important areas concerning the environment are property and justice. Defining property as something that is privately held immediately impacts the environment. If land can be held under law by an individual, the implication is that the individual is able to do what she wants with the land. As long as property owners are concerned about the state of the environment, there is no threat to the well-being of the land. But owners are often more interested in the gains they can make through the use or exploitation of property (or the natural resources that are part of a piece of property) than they are concerned about a healthy environment.

The way a society understands justice informs the laws that will either protect the environment or protect the interests of those who own property. If the rule of law is used to protect property ownership, the environment itself is not regarded as a primary good that has precedence over the rights of individuals. By thinking about notions of justice, we can start to have some idea about how to create laws that serve the best interests of all members of society. This includes notions of the collective good in addition to the rights of individuals. The underlying concepts of justice reflect how people view their relationship with nature. Having an idea about what we think is just, especially in terms of property rights, helps us to understand how we will treat the environment.

In this chapter we will explore some of the ways in which property ownership has traditionally been defined. From Jean-Jacques Rousseau, John Locke, and Karl Marx we'll get some idea about how property rights and ownership have developed over time. Locke's ideas are especially instructive here as they lay the foundation for much of American political thought. Additionally, we will take a look at the theories of the German philosopher Immanuel Kant and of John Rawls, a contemporary American philosopher, in order to gain a better understanding of the role justice plays in terms of the environment. Finally, both Herbert Marcuse and Matthew Alan Cahn's separate discussions of the nature of modern industrial society will help prepare us to move into the next section.

A State of Nature and Beyond

The English philosopher John Locke (1632–1704) is considered the progenitor of the political perspective commonly called Liberalism. Liberal thought is predicated on certain assumptions about nature, humankind, and social structures. From this perspective, human beings are born into this world as a *tabula rasa,* or a clean slate ready to be filled with sensory data and other information gathered through the process of learning. For liberals, human talent is unequally distributed, as are wealth, status, and power in society. So the fundamental goal of a society is to create an equality of opportunity for all, which allows individuals with natural talents to assume the wealth and power they are capable of attaining. Government's role in all of this is to equalize society so that equality of opportunity truly exists, and then to step back. Locke's philosophy is based on the ideas of natural law and natural rights that allow individuals to reach the fullness of their potential.

As was common among philosophers from the sixteenth to the eighteenth centuries, Locke embeds his ideas about society in a device called *the state of nature.* What this means is that philosophers often need a starting point, or a foundation, for the concepts they want to develop. In order to fully explicate a notion about the way society should be organized, for instance, it is sometimes convenient to be able to discuss the shortcomings, or advantages, of the same society at an earlier stage. The state of nature usually refers to a period of time in the distant past when society was in a lesser state of development. The opposite of the state of nature is what we call civil society. After describing some aspect of the social order during this earlier time, a philosopher can highlight ideas about contemporary society.

In his *Two Treatises of Government,* Locke makes reference to a time before the notion of ownership was fully developed so that he can explain his theory of property. Simply put, Locke believed that human beings found themselves alive and with possession of their own minds and bodies. Additionally, the world in which humans find themselves is full of naturally occurring resources. By using the natural talents and abilities with which they are endowed, humans then mix their labor with resources they find all around them. Through the process of mixing human energy with natural resources, humans gain the right to own what they have produced. For

Locke, labor is whatever we do to change or transform resources. So the ability to fell trees, build fences, and enclose property is a way humans can use their talents to modify nature, thus claiming its fruits for their own. Locke argues, however, that humankind is not to spoil that which has been given freely by God.

Property ownership is a right that humans possess on the basis of the law of nature. It is Locke's view that the strongest desire that humans have is for self-preservation. As this is a part of our very nature as persons, following this law is tantamount to following God's will. Self-preservation is linked to property ownership in that by preserving ourselves we mix our labor with resources, again producing the result of property. With possession theoretically tied so closely to self-preservation and the law of nature, it is no wonder that the philosophical descendants of Lockean liberalism have considered private property to be nearly sacred.

The French philosopher Jean-Jacques Rousseau (1712–1778) offers another view of human society starting with the state of nature. In a selection from his *Discourse on Inequality,* Rousseau gives us a romantic view of the development of human society. In Rousseau's version of the state of nature, humankind enjoyed a golden age of social cooperation and mutually satisfying interdependence before the development of private property and the division of labor. At each step as society progressed, however, inequalities in property ownership, which went along with limitations on freedom, brought on the transformation of humanity into civilized beings. Rousseau, as a critic of French society of his day, was not particularly sympathetic with civilization and considered the stability of social order more a nuisance than a blessing.

As we trace humankind's development through Rousseau's eyes, we see the beauty of simple human interaction and crude society destroyed by ever more sophisticated modes of social relationships. As humans developed greater skills, their minds became more enlightened. This, in turn, led to even more advances in skill and ability. Soon people were living not in caves or under trees but in huts and then in homes. It is truly property ownership itself that implies the use of money and the exchange of commodities, which, for Rousseau, signals the downfall of mankind. With the advent of ownership, people were forced to defend something for the first time against others.

Rousseau's overriding concern was with freedom. As humans became more dependent on property, turning eventually to a settled agricultural life, they forfeited the freedom they had previously known. Along with the development of property came the laws necessary to protect ownership. Finally, people began to judge one another on the basis of the possessions they owned, leading to status in society being determined by wealth. As society develops from its earliest forms, humankind becomes more and more alienated from nature itself. Civil society, which for Rousseau is an outcome of the definition of private property, is responsible for wars and destruction. What this eighteenth-century thinker could not have foreseen was the destruction of the environment wrought by civil society as it progressed even further.

Nature as a Commodity

Contrary to how we think of him in the light of twentieth-century history, Karl Marx was perhaps most powerful as a critic of capitalism. In a variety of ways Marx's work helps to clarify how societies operating under capitalism transform resources, goods, and even individuals through the process of production. In *Capital,* Marx outlines the way that resources are turned into commodities. According to Marx, what we think of as the wealth of a capitalist society is actually an accumulation of commodities. A commodity is "an external object, a thing which through its qualities satisfies human needs of whatever kind."

Marx wants to carefully define how commodities are counted in terms of both their use-value and their exchange-value. The use-value of a particular thing is dependent upon its usefulness, and has nothing to do with the amount of work it takes to extract or appropriate its value. Exchange-value, on the other hand, has to do with what a commodity can be traded for, and changes constantly, depending upon numerous factors such as the time and place of trading, as well as for what it is being traded. None of this would seem to matter much except, as Marx points out, things need not have either use- or exchange-value to be useful to people. For instance, the natural environment may be most useful when left undisturbed. And even if resources are turned to the advantage of humans (which would give them a use-value), they do not have to become commodities. The point here is that the appropriation of objects especially for their exchange-value transforms them into commodities. Indeed capitalist economics, which depends upon the appropriation of privately held goods, forces the commodification of the environment.

Universality and Temporal Problems of Justice

If civil society has been built upon private property ownership that does little to ensure the protection of the environment, and if the usefulness of even natural objects becomes commodified in modern economies, then where does that leave us in terms of nature? Philosophers often address questions about justice through an area called ethics or moral philosophy. One of the most influential thinkers in the Western tradition was Immanuel Kant, who is perhaps best known for his contribution of the categorical imperative. Kant is interested in exploring ways of understanding what humans should and should not do, and he explains in *Foundations of the Metaphysics of Morals* that an imperative is a sort of command that tells us what to do.

In other words, imperatives are rules that involve notions of what we ought to do. Some imperatives are hypothetical in nature and state something to the effect of: *If you want outcome x, you ought to do y.* A hypothetical circumstance involves creating a situation in which to test an idea or assumption, or to prove a theory. In terms of our discussion of the environment, we might construct a hypothetical imperative along these lines: *If we want clear air, we ought to allow fewer emissions.* In other words, if we want the particular outcome of cleaner air (based on some set of agreed-upon criteria), we ought to limit emissions. This is what Kant would call a practical reason for doing something. The hypothetical argument we make by stating "if" we are interested in a certain outcome appeals to our sense of reason.

The categorical imperative differs from hypothetical imperatives in that it is not an appeal to reason but instead asserts an action that is necessary in and of itself, without making reference to assumptions about the outcome of the action. For Kant, the categorical imperative ultimately takes only one form: "Act only according to that maxim (or rule) by which you can at the same time will that it should become a universal law." Our imperative about air quality would now have to become: *Emissions will not be allowed to go above healthful levels.* The distinction is that, based on the hypothetical assumption, we would act in accordance with the imperative *if* we were interested in cleaner air, and under the greater strength of the categorical imperative, we would act in accordance with what we perceive to be a universal rule that we ought not pollute the air. Kant's view is that, in order for our actions to be morally acceptable, we should base our ideas of what to do on what we feel to be right.

Much of the power of Kant's assertion seems lost in modern society. We tend to think that what societies and individuals do should be based on contingencies rather than absolutes. Most often the contingencies on the basis of which we operate are related to expediency; we seek solutions to our problems that are convenient, simple, or developed in the light of utilitarian calculations such as cost-effectiveness. None of these reasons for doing things meets Kant's rigorous criteria for moral actions. There are always relative considerations, that make it difficult to do what is right. From the Kantian perspective, as long as we base solutions to our environmental problems on relative considerations, we do nothing more than create more practical reasons.

Contemporary political theorists and philosophers still struggle with Kant's views on justice. In his *A Theory of Justice,* John Rawls lays out what he finds to be the necessary foundations for a just society. Rawls is sometimes referred to as being a neo-Kantian, in the sense that, like Kant, he places the highest priority on what is right rather than on what is expedient. As was the case with both Locke and Rousseau, Rawls is also a contract theorist; his view of society is based upon the notion that governments rule by consent. Rawls's society is based on principles of justice that ensure persons equal rights to liberty and equal opportunities to economic and social advantages, and he uses his own version of the state of nature in order to explain how the foundations of his society would be built.

Rawls focuses on what he refers to as a "just savings principle" in order to address the problem of justice between generations. He is referring here to how much debt or surplus contemporary members of a society leave to future generations. But it is easy enough for us to imagine replacing monetary savings in Rawls's schema with saving nature itself for those yet unborn. The argument remains pretty much the same. It is questionable whether the current members of society would restrain spending in the present for the benefit of future generations if purely utilitarian considerations are used as a basis for judgment. Calculations of this sort can be inaccurate, or even manipulated so as to bring about a certain conclusion. If the same question is considered in the light of what is right to do (in this case, saving for the future), then the debate is about how to save rather than whether or not savings should be set aside.

In the same respect, we can think about the protection of environmental purity as a good in itself. In order to pass that good on to successive generations, we must work in the present to protect nature. This involves thinking about what we do in the present in a very different way than we usually do. Modern societies generally are more concerned with the profitability of short-term solutions to problems rather than long-range planning that would secure environmental protection. The industrialization of the modern world has led to ever greater differences between what is profitable and what is right in terms of the environment.

Living in the Industrialized World

Herbert Marcuse, as an exponent of what is referred to as "Critical Theory," provides an interesting perspective on how modern societies commodify all objects. Critical theorists have developed critiques of capitalist social orders in the twentieth century. In Marcuse's view, what advanced industrialized civilization has done is to replace people's desires for freedom and liberty with desires for things. The idea of commodification that we saw first in Marx is developed further by Marcuse in *One Dimensional Man*.

A major concern of Marcuse is that modern society strips life of meaning by focusing the attention of individuals on objects. People are no longer interested in discovering the meaning in their lives when they are more concerned with things than anything else. Marcuse's work functions as a bridge between the moral theories of Kant and Rawls and the more current literature on the environment. Couched in terms that are familiar to students of Marx and Marxist thought, Marcuse discusses the ways in which commodification removes personal value by emphasizing material possessions. In terms of our relationship with the environment, it is increasingly difficult for individuals to feel a connection with or even an interest in the preservation of nature when they are most concerned with owning new cars or entertaining gadgets. Furthermore, when all objects are commodified by industrial civilization, the intrinsic value of the natural environment is obscured by our desire to extract the greatest exchange value from all resources.

In contrast to Marcuse's denial of advanced society and its achievements, Matthew Alan Cahn allows us to view the tensions inherent in the relationship between environmental protection and industrial capitalism while making prescriptions for the creation of future public policy. Invoking the language and philosophy of contract theorists such as Locke and Rawls, Cahn offers a critique of liberalism in the light of the low priority that capitalism generally assigns to the environment. Liberal societies, which are predicated on the notion of individual self-interest, are faced with tremendous problems when trying to deal with issues requiring communal solutions.

Again we return to Kantian ideas about morals. As liberalism is based on a set of assumptions that places the greatest emphasis on individuals, moral schemes under capitalism are often constructed so as to work to the advantage of those individuals, rather than to the benefit of all members of society. But developing a moral or ethical system rooted in these ideas will most likely allow for expediency to overwhelm the right. The tension we see in advanced industrial societies between the continual development of efficient economies and the preservation of the environment is a result of the emphasis on profit over nature. By making natural resources into commodities, and by relying solely on the Lockean view of property ownership as a fundamental of natural law (without making reference to Locke's injunction about destroying nature), modern industrial society has allowed itself to institute a system of justice that leaves little room for the protection of nature.

9

JEAN-JACQUES ROUSSEAU

The Nature of Private Property

The first man who, having enclosed a piece of land, took it into his head to say, "This is mine," and found people simple enough to believe him, was the true founder of civil society. The human race would have been spared endless crimes, wars, murders, and horrors if someone had pulled up the stakes or filled in the ditch and cried out to his fellow men, "Do not listen to this impostor! You are lost if you forget that the fruits of the earth belong to everyone, and the earth to no one!" But it is highly probable that by then things had already reached a point where they could no longer continue as they had been, for this idea of property, depending on many prior ideas which could only have arisen successively, was not formed all at once in the human mind. Men had to make great progress, acquire many kinds of knowledge and skill, and transmit and augment them from one age to another, before they reached that final stage in the state of nature. Let us therefore go farther back and try to consider that slow succession of events and discoveries from a single point of view, in their most natural order.

Man's first feeling was that of his own existence; his first concern was self-preservation. The earth produced everything he needed, and instinct prompted him to make use of it. Hunger and other appetites made him successively experience different ways of existing. There was one which invited him to perpetuate his species, and that blind urge, devoid of any sentiment of the heart, led to a purely animal act. Once their need had been satisfied, the two sexes ceased paying any attention to each other; even the child no longer meant anything to its mother as soon as it could do without her.

Such was the condition of earliest man. It was the life of an animal limited at first to pure sensations. Far from even thinking of forcing any-

From Jean-Jacques Rousseau, "Discourse on Inequality," in *The Essential Rousseau*, Lowell Bair, trans. (New York: New American Library, 1974).

thing from nature, he scarcely took advantage of the gifts she offered him. But he soon encountered difficulties and had to learn to overcome them. The height of trees that prevented him from gathering their fruit, the competition of other animals seeking the same food, the ferocity of those intent on killing him—everything obliged him to develop his physical abilities. He had to become vigorous in combat, agile, and swift-footed. He soon found natural weapons: stones and clubs. He learned to surmount the obstacles of nature, to fight other animals when necessary, to compete even with other men for his sustenance, and to make up for what he had to yield to those stronger than himself.

As the human race multiplied, its cares increased. Differences in terrains, climates, and seasons must have forced men to alter their ways of living. Barren years, long, harsh winters, and hot summers that seared everything made new skills necessary. On the seashore and the banks of rivers, they invented the hook and line, and became fishermen and fish-eaters. In cold regions they covered themselves with the skins of the animals they had killed. Lightning, a volcano, or some lucky accident made them acquainted with fire, a new resource against the rigors of winter. They learned to conserve it, then to reproduce it, and finally to use it for cooking meat, which they had previously eaten raw.

As man repeatedly interacted with various living beings and observed their interactions with one another, he must naturally have been led to perceive certain relations. These relations, which we express by the words "large," "small," "strong," "weak," "fast," "slow," "cowardly," "brave," and so on, were compared when necessary, almost unthinkingly, and finally produced in him a kind of reflection, or rather an automatic prudence which indicated to him the precautions that were most important for his security.

The new understanding that resulted from this development increased his superiority to other animals by making him aware of it. He became skilled in setting traps for them and outwitted them in countless ways. Although some surpassed him in speed or strength, in time he became the master of those that could be useful to him, and the scourge of those that could harm him. Thus his first contemplation of himself gave him his first surge of pride. Still scarcely able to grasp the concept of a hierarchical order, he saw that his species ranked above all others, and this was the remote beginning of the idea of rank among individuals.

Although his fellow men were not to him what ours are to us, and although he had little more to do with them than with other animals, they were not forgotten in his observations. The conformities that he eventually perceived among them, and between himself and his female, made him judge those that he did not perceive. Seeing that others all acted as he would have done in similar circumstances, he concluded that their ways of thinking and feeling were the same as his own. When this important truth had been firmly established in his mind, and intuition that was as reliable as dialectical reasoning and more rapid, it prompted him to behave toward them in accordance with the rules best suited to furthering his own advantage and security.

Taught by experience that love of well-being is the sole motive of human actions, he was able to distinguish the rare occasions when mutual interest ought to make him rely on the assistance of his fellow men, and the still rarer occasions when competition ought to make him wary of them. In the first case, he joined them in a herd, or at most in some sort of free association that obligated no one and lasted only as long as the temporary need that had formed it. In the second case, everyone sought his own advantage, either by open force, if he believed himself capable of it, or by adroitness and cunning, if he felt that he was too weak to do otherwise.

That is how men may have gradually acquired a crude idea of mutual commitments and the advantage of fulfilling them, but only insofar as their present and obvious interest required it, because they knew nothing of foresight, and far from concerning themselves with the distant future, they did not even think of the next day. If a group of them set out to take a deer, they were fully aware that they would all have to remain faithfully at their posts in order to succeed; but if a hare happened to pass near one of them, there can be no doubt that he pursued it without a qualm, and that once he had caught his prey, he cared very little whether or not he had made his companions miss theirs.

It is easy to understand that such undertakings did not require a language much more refined than that of crows and monkeys, which troop together in almost the same way. For a long time the universal language must have been composed of inarticulate cries, many gestures, and a few imitative noises. When these were augmented in each country by a few conventional articulate sounds, whose establishment, as I have already said, is not very easy to explain, there were individual languages, crude and imperfect, similar to those still spoken by various savage peoples today.

Urged on by the passing of time, the great number of things I have to say, and the almost imperceptible rate of the progress that took place at the beginning, I am swiftly passing over multitudes of centuries; for the more slowly events succeeded one another, the more rapidly they can be described.

These first advances finally enabled men to make others more quickly. The more their minds were enlightened, the more their skills were improved. They ceased sleeping under trees or in caves and found various tools of hard, sharp stone which they used for cutting wood, digging, and making huts of branches, which they later learned to cover with clay and mud. This was the period of a first revolutionary change that established and distinguished families, and introduced a kind of property, already a source of much quarreling and fighting. However, since the strongest were no doubt the first to make dwellings that they felt capable of defending, we may assume that the weak found it quicker and safer to imitate them, rather than trying to dislodge them; and as for those who already had huts, none of them must have had any great inclination to take possession of his neighbor's, less because it did not belong to him than because he did not need it, and because he could not have seized it without the danger of a fierce fight with the family that occupied it.

The first developments of the heart were the result of a new situation in which husbands and wives, fathers and children, were united in a common dwelling. The habit of living together gave rise to the sweetest feeling known to man; conjugal love and paternal love. Each family became a small society, all the better united because mutual attachment and freedom were its only ties. This was the time when the first differences appeared in the two sexes' ways of living, which had previously been the same. The women grew more sedentary and became accustomed to keeping the hut and the children while the men went off in search of food for all. With their somewhat softer life, both sexes began to lose some of their ferocity and vigor; but while individuals became less capable of fighting wild beasts separately, it was easier for them to assemble to resist them in common.

In this new state, with a simple and solitary life, very few needs, and implements that they had invented to provide for those needs, men had abundant leisure and used it to procure various kinds of conveniences that had been unknown to their forefathers. This was the first yoke that they had unwittingly imposed on themselves, and the first source of evils that they prepared for their descendants. For besides continuing to soften their bodies and minds, through habit these conveniences lost all their charm and degenerated into real needs, so that the pain of being deprived of them was much greater than the pleasure of having them, and men were unhappy to lose them without being happy to possess them.

We can see a little better at this point how the use of speech gradually arose, or became improved, within each family; and we can also conjecture how various particular causes may have extended language and accelerated its progress by making it more necessary. Great floods or earthquakes caused inhabited areas to be surrounded by water or precipices; upheavals of the earth broke off parts of the mainland and made them islands. It is clear that a common language must first have been formed among men thus brought together and forced to live with one another, rather than among those who wandered freely in the forests of the mainland. It is therefore quite possible that after their first attempts at seafaring, islanders brought the use of speech to other men; and it is at least highly probable that society and languages came into existence on islands and were well developed there before they became known on the mainland.

Everything now began to take on a new aspect. After having previously roamed the forests, men became more settled, slowly began coming together in different bands, and finally formed in each region a separate nation, with shared customs and a distinctive character, unified not by regulations and laws, but by a single way of life, the same kinds of food, and the common influence of climate. With time, permanent proximity could not fail to bring about certain connections among different families. Young people of both sexes lived in neighboring huts; the fleeting relations demanded by nature soon led them, by way of regular contact with each other, to form equally pleasant and more lasting relations. They became accustomed to considering different men or women and making comparison; they gradually acquired ideas of merit and beauty that produced feelings of preference. Seeing each other often gave them a need to continue seeing each other. A sweet, tender feeling permeated their souls, and was turned into an impetuous fury by the slightest opposition. Jealousy was thus born with love; discord triumphed, and the gentlest of passions received sacrifices of human blood.

As ideas and feelings succeeded one another, as the mind and the heart grew more active, the human race continued to become more sociable. Connections were extended, ties became closer. People acquired the habit of gathering in front of their huts or around a large tree; singing and dancing, true children of love and leisure, became the amusement, or rather the occupation, of idle men and women who had formed themselves into groups. Each began looking at the others and wanting them to look at him; public esteem came to be valued, and it went to those who were the best singers or dancers, the most beautiful or handsome, the strongest, the most dexterous, or the most eloquent. This was the first step toward inequality, and also toward vice. From these first preferences arose vanity and contempt, on the one hand, and shame and envy, on the other; and the fermentation caused by these new leavens finally produced compounds that were deadly to happiness and innocence.

As soon as men had begun evaluating each other and the idea of esteem had been formed in their minds, everyone claimed a right to it as it was no longer possible to withhold it from anyone with impunity. Hence came the first duties of civility, even among savages; and hence any deliberate wrong that was done to someone became an outrage, for besides being harmed by it, he also saw it as evidence of contempt for him, which was often more intolerable than the harm itself. Each man punished contempt that had been shown for him in a manner proportionate to the esteem in which he held himself; it was thus that vengeance became terrible, and men bloodthirsty and cruel. This is precisely the stage that has been reached by most of the savage peoples known to us. Because some writers have not made adequate distinctions among their ideas, and have not discerned how far these peoples already are from the first state of nature, they have hastily concluded that man is naturally cruel and needs political rule to keep his cruelty under control. The fact is that nothing is gentler than man in his original state; placed by nature at an equal distance from the stupidity of brutes and the pernicious understanding of man in the civil state, and limited by both instinct and reason to warding off dangers that threaten him, he is restrained by natural compassion from harming others needlessly, even if he has been harmed by them. For, according to the axiom of the wise Locke, "Where there is no property there is no injustice."

But it must be noted that early society, and the relations already established among men, required qualities different from those given to them by their original constitution. When morality had begun to be introduced into human acts and, before the existence of laws, each man was the sole judge and avenger of offenses committed against him, the goodness that had suited the state of nature was not the kind that was called for by the newborn society. Punishments had to become more severe as opportunities for offenses became more frequent, and fear of vengeance had to perform the restraining function of law. Thus, although men had become more irascible and natural compassion had already deteriorated to some extent, this period of development of human faculties, midway between the indolence of the original state and the irrepressible activity of our egotism, must have been mankind's happiest and most stable epoch. The more we reflect on it, the more clearly we see that this state was the least subject to upheavals and the best for man, and that he must have left it as the result to some unfortunate accident which, for the common good, should never have happened. The example of savages, most of whom have been found in this state, seems to confirm the view that the human race was meant to remain in it forever, that it is the true youth of the world, and that while all later advances have appeared to be so many steps toward the perfection of the individuals, they have actually been leading toward the decay of the species.

As long as men were content with their rustic huts, as long as they limited themselves to making clothes of animal skins sewn together with thorns or fish bones, to adorning themselves with feathers and shells, painting their bodies in various colors, improving or embellishing their bows and arrows, using sharp-edged stones as tools for making fishing boats and crude musical instruments; in short, as long as they limited themselves to artifacts that could be made by one man, and to arts that did not need the concurrence of several hands, they were as free, healthy, good, and happy as their nature permitted them to be, and they continued to enjoy the pleasures of independent intercourse with one another. But as soon as one man needed another's help, as soon as one man realized that it was useful to have enough provisions for two, equality disappeared, property came into being, work became necessary, and vast forests were changed into smiling fields which man had to water with his sweat, and in which slavery and poverty soon germinated and grew with the crops.

Metallurgy and agriculture were the two arts whose invention produced this great revolution. To the poet it is gold and silver, but to the philosopher it is iron and grain that made men civilized and brought on the downfall of the human race. They were both unknown to the savages of America, who for that reason are still savages. Other peoples seem to have remained barbarians as long as they practiced one of those arts without the other. And perhaps one of the best reasons why Europe has been, if not longer, at least more constantly and better civilized than any other part of the world, is that it is both the most abundant in iron and the most fertile in grain.

It is very difficult to conjecture how men first came to know and use iron, for it is impossible to believe that, of themselves, they thought of mining ore and preparing it for smelting, before knowing what the result would be. On the other hand, it is all the more implausible to attribute the discovery to an accidental fire, because mines are formed only in arid regions that are bare of trees and plants; it almost seems as if nature had taken precautions to withhold that fateful secret from us. There remains only the extraordinary possibility that a volcano ejecting molten metal may have been observed by men who conceived the idea of imitating that operation of nature. We must further assume that they were industrious enough to undertake such a laborious task, and had the great foresight that they would have needed in order to realize the advantages they could gain from it, which almost necessarily presupposes minds more highly developed than theirs must have been.

As for agriculture, its principle was known long before its practice was established; it is scarcely possible that men, constantly occupied in obtaining food from trees and plants, should not have soon gained some understanding of the ways in which nature assures the propagation of plant life. But they probably did not begin to turn their industry in that direction until very late, either because trees, which along with hunting and fishing supplied their food, had no need of their care; or because they did not know how to use grain, or had no implements with which to cultivate it; or, finally, because they had no means of preventing others from appropriating the fruits of their labor. We may assume that when they became more industrious, they began by cultivating a few vegetables or roots around their huts, using sharp stones and pointed sticks, long before they knew how to prepare grain and had the implements necessary for cultivation on a large scale. Moreover, to sow a field for such cultivation, one must resolve to lose something in the present in order to gain much more in the future, and this attitude is alien to the mind of savage man, who, as I have said, finds it very difficult even to think in the morning of what he will need at night.

The invention of other arts was therefore necessary to make the human race apply itself to the art of agriculture. When men were needed for smelting and forging iron, others had to feed them. The more the number of artisans increased, the fewer hands there were to obtain food for the community, with no decrease in the number of mouths to feed; and since the artisans required food in exchange for their iron, the others finally found means of using iron to increase the amount of food available. Thus plowing and agriculture arose, on the one hand, and the art of working metals and multiplying their uses, on the other.

The division of land necessarily followed from its cultivation, and once property had been recognized it gave rise to the first rules of justice, for if each man is to be assured of what is rightfully his, all must be able to have something. Furthermore, when men began to look forward into the future and realize that they had something to lose, they all had reason to fear reprisals for any wrongs they might do to others. This origin is all the more natural because it is impossible to imagine property arising from anything but labor, since the only way in which a man can take possession of something he has not made is to put his own work into it. It is work alone that gives a farmer title to the produce of the land he has tilled, and consequently to the land itself, at least until he has harvested his crop. If this possession is continued uninterruptedly from year to year, it is easily transformed into ownership. When the ancients, says Grotius, called Ceres "the lawgiver" and gave the name of Thesmaphoria to a festival celebrated in her honor, they implied that the division of land had produced a new kind of right: the right of property, different from that which derives from natural law.

Things in this state might have remained equal if abilities had been equal and if, for example, the use of iron and the consumption of food had always remained in the same proportion. But this proportion, which nothing worked to preserve, was soon broken. The strongest did more work; the most skillful turned their efforts to better advantage; the most ingenious found ways to shorten their labor; the farmer needed more iron, or the blacksmith more grain; and doing equal amounts of work, some prospered while others were barely able to stay alive. It is thus that natural inequality gradually becomes accentuated by inequalities of exchange, and differences among men, developed by differences in circumstances, become more noticeable and more permanent in their efforts, and begin to influence the fate of individuals in the same proportion.

Things having reached this point, it is easy to imagine the rest. I shall not take time to describe the successive inventions of the other arts, the progress of language, the testing and employment of talents, the inequality of fortunes, the use or abuse of wealth, and all the details connected with them, which the reader can easily supply for himself. I shall limit myself to taking a glance at the human race in that new state of affairs.

Let us assume, then, that all human faculties had developed, memory and imagination were functioning, egotism had come into play, reason had become active, and the mind had almost reached the greatest perfection of which it was capable. Let us assume that all natural qualities were in action, and that each man's rank and condition had been established, on the basis not only of his property and his power to help or harm others, but also of his wit, beauty, strength, skill, merit, and talent. Since these were the only qualities that could win respect, it soon became necessary for him either to have them or seem to have them; for his own advantage, he had to show himself as different from what he actually was. Being and appearing became two quite different things, and from that distinction came ostentation, deceptive guile, and all the vices that follow in their wake. On the other hand, whereas man had previously been free and independent, his multitude of new needs now placed him in subjection to all of nature, so to speak, and especially to his fellow men. He became their slave, in a sense, even when he became their master: If he was rich, he needed their services; if he was poor, he needed their help; and no condition anywhere between those two extremes enabled him to do without them. He therefore had to be constantly seeking to make them take an interest in his fate and see their advantage, real or apparent, in working to further his. This made him crafty and devious with some, harsh and imperious with others, and forced him to deceive all those whom he needed, when he could not make them fear him and did not feel that it was to his interest to be useful to them. Finally, consuming ambition, a drive to raise the relative level of their fortunes, less from real need than from a desire to place themselves above others, aroused in all men a vile inclination to harm one another, a secret jealousy that was all the more dangerous because it often wore the mask of benevolence in order to strike its blow more safely; in short, there was competition and rivalry on the one hand, opposition of interests on the other, and always the hidden desire to profit at the expense of others. All these evils were the first effect of property, and the inseparable accompaniments of incipient inequality.

Before the invention of signs to represent wealth, it could scarcely have consisted of anything but land and livestock, the only real property that men can have. When inheritances had grown in number and size to the point where they covered all the land and bordered on one another, a man could increase his property only at the expense of others. Those who were excluded from ownership, who because of weakness or indolence had acquired nothing, became poor without having lost anything, because while everything around them was changing, they themselves had not changed. They were forced to receive or steal their sustenance from the rich, and this gave rise, according to differences of character, to domination and servitude, or violence and theft. As soon as the rich had discovered the pleasure of dominating, they disdained all others: using their present slaves to acquire new ones, they thought only of subjugating their neighbors, like those ravenous wolves which, once they have tasted human flesh, reject all other food and seek only to devour men.

Thus, when both the poorest and the most powerful men had come to regard their poverty or their power as a kind of right to take the belongings of others which was equivalent, in their view, to the right of property, the destruction of equality was followed by terrible disorders; and it was thus that the usurpations of the rich, the banditry of the poor, and the unbridled passions of both, stifling natural compassion and the still weak voices of justice, made men grasping, ambitious, and malicious. Between the right of the strongest and the right of first occupancy, there arose constant conflicts which inevitably led to fighting and murder. Nascent society gave way to the most horrible state of war; the human race, degraded and devastated, unable to retrace its steps or give up the unfortunate acquisitions it had made, and working only for its shame by misusing the faculties that honor it, brought itself to the brink of ruin. "Terrified by this new evil, rich and miserable, he wants to flee from wealth, and now hates what he once desired."

It is impossible that men should not eventually have begun to reflect on this wretched situation and on the calamities that overwhelmed them. The rich, especially, must soon have become aware of how disadvantageous it was for them to be in a state of incessant warfare whose cost was borne by them alone, and in which the risk of death was common to all, while the risk of losing property was individual. Moreover, no matter how they might try to place their usurpations in a favorable light, they knew that they rested on a precarious and spurious title, and that since they had acquired them only by force, they would have no right to complain if they were taken away from them by force. Even those who had become rich only through their own industry could scarcely base their ownership on a better title. It was useless for them to say, "I built this wall myself; I earned this land by my own work," because others could reply to them. "Who marked off boundaries for you, and by what right do you expect to be paid at our expense for work that we never forced you to do? Do you not see that many of your brothers are dying or suffering for lack of what you have too much of? Only the express and unanimous consent of the whole human race could have entitled you to take more from the common resources than what you require for your own needs." Lacking valid arguments to justify himself and sufficient forces to defend himself; easily able to crush an individual, but crushed himself by troops of bandits; alone against everyone, and unable, because of mutual jealousy, to unite with his equals against enemies who were united by the common hope of pillage, the rich man, pressed by necessity, finally devised the most shrewdly conceived plan that ever entered the human mind: to employ in his favor the very strength of those who attacked him, to turn his adversaries into his defenders, to instill different principles into them, and to give them different institutions that would be as favorable to him as natural right was unfavorable.

With this in mind, after having depicted to his neighbors the horrors of a situation which armed them all against each other and made their possessions as burdensome as their needs, and in which no one could find security in either wealth or poverty, he easily invented specious arguments to make them accept his plan. "Let us unite," he said to them, "to protect the weak from oppression, restrain the ambitious, and assure everyone of possessing what belongs to him; let us institute rules of justice and peace that will be binding on everyone and give preference to no one, and will to some extent make up for the whims of fortune by subjecting both the weak and the strong to mutual obligations. In short, rather than turning our forces against each other, let us assemble them in a supreme power that will govern us in accordance with wise laws, protect and defend all members of the association, repulse our common enemies, and keep us always in harmony."

Much less than an equivalent of this speech was needed to convince men who were so unsophisticated and easy to lead astray, and who, moreover, had too many disputes to settle among themselves to do without arbitrators, and too much greed and ambition to do without masters for very long. They all hastened to enchain themselves, believing that they were assuring their freedom; for although they had enough intelligence to realize the advantages of a political establishment, they did not have enough experience to foresee its dangers. Those most capable of anticipating abuses were precisely those who expected to profit from them; and even the wisest saw that they had to resign themselves to sacrificing part of their freedom to save the rest, as a wounded man allows his arm to be cut off to save the rest of his body.

Such was, or probably was, the origin of society and laws, which gave new fetters to the weak and new strength to the rich, permanently destroyed natural freedom, established the law of property and inequality forever, turned adroit usurpation into an irrevocable right, and for the advantage of a few ambitious men, subjected all others to unending work, servitude, and poverty. It is easy to see how the establishment of one society made others necessary, for if men were to hold their own against united forces, they had no choice but to unite theirs also. Societies rapidly multiplied and expanded until they covered the whole surface of the earth; it was no longer possible for a man to find any place in the world where he could escape servitude and withdraw his head from beneath the sword that everyone always saw suspended above him, often precariously. When civil laws had thus become the common rule of all citizens, the law of nature subsisted only among the different societies, where, under the name of the law of nations, it was tempered by a few tacit agreements to make commerce possible and serve as a substitute for natural compassion, which, between one society and another, and no longer exists in that form except in few great cosmopolitan souls who cross the imaginary barriers that separate peoples, and following the example of the Sovereign Being who created them, include the whole human race in their benevolence.

Remaining thus in the state of nature among themselves, societies soon began to feel the effects of the disadvantages that had forced individuals to leave that state, and it became even more harmful among those great bodies than it had been among the individuals who composed them. Hence came the national wars, battles, murders, and reprisals which offend reason and make nature shudder, and all those horrible prejudices which cause the shedding of human blood to be regarded as an honor and a virtue. Even the most decent citizens learned to consider killing their fellow men as one of their duties. Finally men began slaughtering one another by the thousands, without knowing why, and more murders were committed in one day of combat, and more atrocities in the capture of a single town, than had been committed in the state of nature during many centuries, all over the world. Such were the first perceptible results of the division of the human race into different societies.

10

John Locke

Of Property

Whether we consider natural *Reason,* which tells us, that Men, being once born, have a right to their Preservation, and consequently to Meat and Drink, and such other things, as Nature affords for their Subsistence: Or revelation, which gives us an account of those Grants God made of the World to *Adam,* and to *Noah,* and his Sons, 'tis very clear, that God, as King *David* says, Psal. CXV. xvi. *has given the Earth to the Children of Men,* given it to Mankind in common. But this being supposed, it seems to some a very great difficulty, how any one should ever come to have a *Property* in any thing: I will not content my self to answer, That if it be difficult to make out *Property,* upon a supposition, that God gave the World to *Adam* and his Posterity in common; it is impossible that any Man, but one universal Monarch, should have any *Property,* upon a supposition, that God gave the World to *Adam,* and his Heirs in Succession, exclusive of all the rest of his Posterity. But I shall endeavor to show, how Men might come to have a *property* in several parts of that which God gave to Mankind in common, and that without any express Compact of all the Commoners.

God, who hath given the World to Men in common, hath also given them reason to make use of it to the best advantage of Life, and convenience. The Earth, and all that is therein, is given to Men for the Support and Comfort of their being. And though all the Fruits it naturally produces, and Beasts it feeds, belong to Mankind in common, as they are produced by the spontaneous hand of Nature; and no body has originally a private Dominion, exclusive of the rest of Mankind, in any of them, as they are thus in their natural state; Yet being given for the use of Men, there must of necessity be a means to appropriate them some way or other before they can be of any

From John Locke, *Two Treatises of Government.*

use, or at all beneficial to any particular Man. The Fruit, or Venison, which nourishes the wild *Indian,* who knows no Inclosure, and is still a Tenant in common, must be his, and so his, i.e. a part of him, that another can no longer have any right to it, before it can do him any good for the support of his life.

Though the Earth, and all inferior Creatures by common to all Men, yet every man has a *Property* in his own *Person.* This nobody has any Right to but himself. The Labour of his Body, and the Work of his Hands, we may say, are properly his. Whatsoever then he removes out of the State that Nature hath provided, and left it in, he hath mixed his Labour with, and joyned to it something that is his own, and thereby makes it his Property. It being by him removed from the common state nature placed it in, hath by this Labour something annexed to it, that excluded the common right of other Men. For this Labour being the unquestionable Property of the Labourer, no Man but he can have a right to what that is once joyned to, at least where there is enough, and as good left in common for other.

He that is nourished by the Acorns he pickt up under an Oak, or the Apples he gathered from the Trees in the Wood, has certainly appropriated them to himself. No Body can deny but the nourishment is his. I ask then, When did they begin to be his? When he digested? Or when he ate? Or when he boiled? Or when he brought them home? Or when he pickt them up? And 'tis plain, if the first gathering made them not his, nothing else could. That labour put a distinction between them and common. That added something to them more than Nature, the common Mother of all, had done; and so they became his private right. And will any one say he had no right to those Acorns or Apples he thus appropriated, because he had not the consent of all Mankind to make them his? Was it a Robbery thus to assume to himself what belonged to all in Common? If such a consent as that was necessary, Man had starved, notwithstanding the Plenty God had given him. We see in Commons, which remain so by Compact, that 'tis the taking any part of what is common, and removing it out of the state Nature leaves it in, which begins the Property; without which the Common is of no use. And the taking of this or that part, does not depend on the express consent of all the Commoners. Thus the Grass my Horse has bit; the Turfs my Servant has cut; and the Ore I have digg'd in any place where I have a right to them in common with others, become my Property, without the assignation or consent of any body. The labour that was mine, removing them out of that common state they were in, hath fixed my Property in them.

By making an explicit consent of every Commoner, necessary to any ones appropriating to himself any part of what is given in common, Children or Servants could not cut the Meat which their Father or Master had provided for them in common, without assigning to every one his peculiar part. Though the Water running in the fountain be every ones, yet who can doubt, but that in the Pitcher is his only who drew it out? His Labour hath taken it out of the hands of Nature, where it was common, and belong'd equally to all her Children, and hath thereby appropriated it to himself.

Thus this Law of reason makes the Deer, that Indians who hath killed it; 'tis allowed to be his goods who hath bestowed his labour upon it, though before, it was the common right of every one. And amongst those who are counted the Civiliz'd part of Mankind, who have made and multiplied positive Laws to determine Property, this original Law of Nature for the beginning of Property, in what was before common, still takes place; and by vertue thereof, what Fish any one catches in the ocean, that great and still remaining Common of Mankind; or what Ambergriese any one takes up here, is by the Labour that removes it out of that common state Nature left it in, made his Property who takes that pains about it. And even amongst us the Hare that any one is Hunting, is thought his who pursues her during the Chase. For being a Beast that is still looked upon as common, and no Man's private Possession; whoever has imploy'd so much labour about any of that kind, as to find and pursue her, has thereby removed her from the state of Nature, wherein she was common, and hath begun Property.

It will perhaps be objected to this, That if gathering the Acorns, or other Fruits of the Earth, *&c.* makes a right to them, then any one may *ingross* as much as he will. To which I Answer, Not so. The same Law of Nature, that does by this means give us Property, does also bound that Property too. *God has given us all things richly,* 1 Tim. vi. 17. is the Voice of Reason confirmed by Inspiration. But how far has he given it us? To enjoy. As much as any one can make use of to any advantage of life before it spoils; so much he may by his labour fix a Property in. Whatever is beyond this, is more than his share, and belongs to others. Nothing was made by God for Man to spoil or destroy. And this considering the plenty of natural Provisions there was a long time in the World, and the few spenders, and to how small a part of that provision in industry of one Man could extend it self, and ingross it to the prejudice of others; especially keeping within the *bounds,* set by reason of what might serve for his *use;* there could be then little room for Quarrels or Contentions about Property so establish'd.

But the *chief matter of Property* being now not the Fruits of the Earth, and the Beasts that subsist on it, but the Earth it self; as that which takes in and carries with it all the rest: I think it is plain, that Property in that too is acquired as the former. *As much land* as a Man Tills, Plants, Improves, Cultivates, and can use the Product of, so much is his *Property*. He by his Labour does as it were, inclose it from the Common. Nor will it invalidate his right to say, Every body else has an equal Title to it; and therefore he cannot appropriate, he cannot inclose, without the Consent of all his Fellow-Commoners, all Mankind. God, when he gave the World in common to all Mankind, commanded Man also to labour, and the penury of his Condition required it of him. God and his reason commanded him to subdue the Earth, i.e. improve it for the benefit of Life, and therein lay out something upon it that was his own, his labour. He that in Obedience to this Command of God, subdued, tilled and sowed any part of it, thereby annexed to it something that was his *Property,* which another had no Title to, nor could without injury take from him.

Nor was this appropriation of any parcel of Land, by improving it, any prejudice to any other Man, since there was still enough and as good left; and more than the yet unprovided could use. So that in effect, there was never the less left for others because of his inclosure for himself. For he that leaves as much as another can make use of, does as good as take nothing at all. No Body could think himself injur'd by the drinking of another Man, though he took a good Draught, who had a whole River of the same Water left him to quench his thirst. And the Case of Land and Water, where there is enough of both, is perfectly the same.

God gave the World to Men in Common; but since he gave it them for their benefit, and the greatest Conveniences of Life they were capable to draw from it, it cannot be supposed he meant it should always remain common and uncultivated. He gave it to the use of the Industrious and Rational, (and *Labour* was to be his *Title* to it;) not to the Fancy or Covetousness of the Quarrelsom and Contentious. He that had as good left for his Improvement, as was already taken up, needed not complain, ought not to meddle with what was already improved by another's Labour: If he did, 'tis plain he desired the benefit of another's Pains, which he had no right to, and not the Ground which God had given him in common with others to labour on, and whereof there was as good left, as he already possessed, and more than he knew what to do with, or his Industry could reach to.

'Tis true in *Land* that is *common* in *England,* or any other Country, where there is Plenty of People under Government, who have Money and Commerce, no one can inclose or appropriate any part, without the consent of all his Fellow-Commoners: Because this is left common by Compact, i.e. by the Law of the Land, which is not to be violated. And though it be

Common, in respect of some Men, it is not so to all Mankind; but is the joint property of this Countrey, or this Parish. Besides, the remainder, after such inclosure, would not be as good to the rest of the Commoners as the whole was, when they could all make use of the whole; whereas in the beginning and first peopling of the great Common of the World, it was quite otherwise. The Law Man was under, was rather for *appropriating*. God Commanded, and his Wants forced him to labour. That was his *Property* which could not be taken from him where-ever he had fixed it. And hence subduing or cultivating the Earth, and having Dominion, we see are joyned together. The one gave Title to the other. So that God, by commanding to subdue, gave Authority so far to *appropriate*. And the Condition of Humane Life, which requires Labour and Materials to work on, necessarily introduces *private Passions*.

The measure of Property, Nature has well set, by the Extent of Mens' *Labour, and the Convenience of Life:* No Mans Labour could subdue, or appropriate all: nor could his Enjoyment consume more than a small part; so that it was impossible for any Man, this way, to intrench upon the right of another, or acquire, to himself, a Property, to the Prejudice of his Neighbour, who would still have room, for a good, and as large a Possession (after the other had taken out his) as before it was appropriated. This *measure* did confine every Man's *Possession,* to a very moderate Proportion, and such as he might appropriate to himself, without Injury to any Body in the first Ages of the World, when Men were more in danger to be lost, by wandering from their Company, in the then vast Wilderness of the Earth, than to be straitned for want of room to plant in. And the same *measure* may be allowed still, without prejudice to any Body, as fell as the World seems. For supposing a Man, or Family, in the state they were, at first peopling of the World by the Children of *Adam,* of *Noah;* let him plant in some in-land, vacant places of *America,* we shall find that the *Possessions* he could make himself upon the *measures* we have given, would not be very large, nor, even to this day, prejudice the rest of Mankind, or give them reason to complain, or think themselves injured by this Man's Incroachment, though the Rage of Men have now spread themselves to all the corners of the World, and do infinitely exceed the small number [which] was at the beginning. Nay, the extent of Ground is of so little value, *without labour,* that I have heard it affirmed, that in Spain it self, a Man may be permitted to plough, sow, and reap, without being disturbed, upon Land he has no other Title to, but only his making use of it. But, on the contrary, the Inhabitants think themselves beholden to him, who, by his Industry on neglected, and consequently waste Land, has increased the stock of Corn, which they wanted. But be this as it will, which I lay no stress on; This I dare boldly affirm, That the same *Rule of Property,* (viz.) That every Man should have as much as he could make use of, would hold still in the World, without straitning any body, since there is Land enough in the World to suffice double the Inhabitants had not the *Invention of Money,* and the tacit Agreement of Men to put a value on it, introduced (by Consent) larger Possessions, and a Right to them; which, how it has done, I shall, by and by, shew more at large.

This is certain, That in the beginning, before the desire of having more than Men needed, had altered the intrinsick value of things, which depends only on their usefulness to the Life of Man; or Men had agreed, that a little piece of yellow Metal, which would keep without wasting or decay, should be worth a great piece of Flesh, or a whole heap of Corn; though Men had a Right to appropriate, by their Labour, each one to himself, as much of the things of Nature, as he could use: Yet this could not be much, nor to the Prejudice of others, where the same plenty was still left, to those who would use the same Industry. To which let me add, that he who appropriates land to himself by his labour, does not lessen but increase the common stock of mankind. For the provisions serving to the support of humane life, produced by one acre of inclosed and cultivated land, are (to speak much within compasse) ten times more, than those, which are yielded by an acre of Land, of an equal richnesse, lyeing waste in common. And therefore he, that incloses Land and has a greater plenty of the conveniences of life from ten acres, than he could have from an hundred left to Nature, may truly be said, to give ninety acres to Mankind. For his labour now supplys him with provisions out of ten acres, which were but the product of an hundred lying in common. I have here rated the improved land very low in making its product but as ten to one, when it is much nearer an hundred to one. For I say whether in the wild woods and uncultivated wast of America left to Nature, without any improvement, tillage or husbandry, a thousand acres will yield the needy and wretched inhabitants as many conveniencies of life as ten acres of equally fertile land in Devonshire where they are well cultivated?

Before the Appropriation of Land, he who gathered as much of the wild Fruit, killed, caught, or tamed, as many of the Beasts as he could; he that so employed his Pains about any of the spontaneous Products of Nature, as any way to alter them, from the state which Nature put them in, by placing any of his Labour on them, did thereby acquire a Property in them: But if they perished, in his Possession, without their due use; if the Fruits rotted, or the Venison putrefied, before he could spend it, he offended against the common Law of Nature, and was liable to be punished; he invaded his Neighbours' share, for he had *no right, farther than his Use* called for any of them, and they might serve to afford him Conveniences of Life.

The same *measures* governed the *Possession of Land* too: Whatsoever he tilled and reaped, laid up and made use of, before it spoiled, that was his peculiar Right; whatsoever he enclosed, and could need, and make use of, the Cattle and Product was also his. But if either the Grass of his Inclose rotted on the Ground, or the Fruit of his planting perished without gathering, and laying up, this part of the Earth, notwithstanding his Inclosure, was still to be looked on a Waste, and might be the Possession of any other. Thus, as the beginning, Cain might take as much Ground as he could till, and make it his own Land, and yet leave enough to *Abel*'s Sheep to feed on; a few Acres would serve for both their Possessions. But as Families increased, and Industry inlarged their Stocks, their Possessions inlarged with the need of them; but yet it was commonly *without any fixed property in the ground they made use of,* till they incorporated, settled themselves together, and built cities, and then, by consent, they came in time, to set out the *bounds of their distinct Territories,* and agree on limits between them and their Neighbours, and by Laws within themselves, settled the *Properties* of those of the same Society. For we see, that in that part of the World which was first inhabited, and therefore like to be best peopled, even as low down as *Abraham*'s time, they wandered with their Flocks, and their Herds, which was their substance, freely up and down; and this *Abraham* did, in a Country where he was a Stranger. Whence it is plain, that at least, a great part of the *Land lay in common;* that the Inhabitants valued it not, nor claimed Property in any more than they made use of. But when there was not room enough in the same place, for their Herds to feed together, they, by consent, as *Abraham* and Lot did, Gen. Xii. 5. Separated and inlarged their pasture, where it best liked them. And for the same Reason *Esau* went from his Father, and his Brother, and planted in *Mount Seir,* Gen. xxxvi. 6.

And thus, without supposing any private Dominion, and property in *Adam,* over all the World, exclusive of all other Men, which can no way be proved, nor any ones Property be made out from it; but supposing the World given as it was to the Children of Men in common, we see how labour could make Men distinct titles to several parcels of it, for their private uses; wherein there could be no doubt of Right, no room for quarrel.

Nor is it so strange, as perhaps before consideration it may appear, that the Property of labour should be able to over-ballance the Community of Land. For 'tis Labour indeed that puts the difference of value on every thing; and let any one consider, what the difference is between an acre of Land planted with Tobacco, or Sugar, sown with Wheat or Barley; and an Acre of the same Land lying in common, without any Husbandry upon it, and he will find, that the improvement of labour makes the far greater part of the value. I think it will be but a very modest computation to say, that of the products of the Earth useful to the Life of Man 9/10 are the effects of labour: nay, if we will rightly estimate things as they come to our use, and cast up the several expenses about them, what in them is purely owing to Nature, and what to labour, we shall find, that in most of them 99/100 are wholly to be put on the account of labour.

There cannot be a clearer demonstration of any thing, than several Nations of the *American* are of this, who are rich in Land, and poor in all the Comforts of Life; whom Nature having furnished as liberally as any other people, with the materials of Plenty, i.e. a fruitful Soil, apt to produce in abundance, what might serve for food, rayment, and delight; yet for want of improving it by labour, have not one hundredth part of the Conveniencies we enjoy: And a King of a large fruitful Territory there feeds, lodges, and is clad worse than a day Labourer in *England.*

To make this a little clearer, let us but trace some of the ordinary provisions of Life, through their several progresses, before they come to our use, and see how much they receive of their value from Humane Industry. Bread, Wine and Cloth, are things of daily use, and great plenty, yet notwithstanding. Acorns, Water and Leaves, or Skins, must be our Bread, Drink and Clothing, did not *labour* furnish us with these more useful Commodities. For whatever *Bread* is more worth than Acorns, Wine than Water, and Cloth or Silk than Leaves, Skins, or Moss, that is wholly *owing to labour* and industry. The one of these being the Food and Rayment which unassisted Nature furnishes us with; the other provisions which our industry and pains prepare of us, which how much they exceed the other in value, when any one hath computed, he will then see, how much *labour makes the far greatest part of the value* of things, we enjoy in this world: And the ground which produces the materials, is scarce to be reckon'd in, as any, or at most, but a very small, part of it; So little that even amongst us, Land that is left wholly to Nature, that hath no improvement of Pasturage, Tillage, or Planting, is called, as indeed it is, *wast;* and we shall find the benefit of it amount to little more than nothing. This shews, how much numbers of men are to be prefered to largeness of dominions, and that the increase of lands and the right imploying of them is the great art of government. And that Prince who shall be so wise and godlike as by established laws of liberty to secure protection and incouragement to the honest industry of Mankind against the oppression of power and narrownesse of Party will quickly be too hard for his neighbours. But this bye the bye. To return to the argument in hand. . . .

From all which it is evident, that though the things of Nature are given in common, yet Man (by being Master of himself, and Proprietor of his own Person, and the actions or Labour of it) had still in himself *the great Foun-*

dation of Property; and that which made up the great part of what he applied to the Support or Comfort of his being, when Invention and Arts had improved the conveniencies of Life, was perfectly his own, and did not belong in common to others.

Thus *Labour,* in the Beginning, *gave a Right of Property,* where-ever any one was pleased to imploy it, upon what was common, which remained, a long while, the far greater part, and is yet more than Mankind makes use of. Men, at first, for the most part, contented themselves with what un-assisted Nature Offered to their Necessities: and though afterwards, in some parts of the World, (where the Increase of People and Stock, with the Use of Money) had made Land scarce, and so of some Value, the several *Communities* settled the Bounds of their distinct Territories, and by Laws within themselves, regulated the Properties of the private Men of their Society, and so, by Compact and Agreement, *settled the Property* which Labour and Industry began; and the Leagues that have been made between several States and Kingdoms, either expressly or tacitly disowning all Claim and Right to the Land in the others Possession, have, by common Consent, given up their Pretences to their natural common Right, which originally they had to those Countries, and so have, by *positive agreement, settled a Property* amongst themselves, in distinct Parts and parcels of the Earth: yet there are still *greatest Tracts of Ground* to be found, which (the Inhabitants thereof not having joyned with the rest of Mankind, in the consent of the Use of their common Money) *lie wasts,* and are more than the People, who dwell on it, do, or can make use of, and so still lie in common. Tho' this can scarce happen amongst that part of Mankind, that have consented to the use of Money.

The greatest part of *things really useful* to the Life of Man, and such as the necessity of subsisting made the first Commoners of the World look after, as it doth the *Americans* now, are generally things of short duration; such as, if they are not consumed by use, will decay and perish of themselves: Gold, Silver, and Diamonds, are things, that Fancy or Agreement hath put the Value on, more then real Use, and the necessary Support of Life. Now of those good things which Nature hath provided in common, every one had a Right (as hath been said) to as much as he could use, and had a Property in all that he could affect with his Labour: all that his Industry could extend to, to alter from the State Nature had put it in, was his. He that *gathered* a Hundred Bushels of Acorns or Apples, had thereby a *Property* in them; they were his goods as soon as gathered. He was only to look that he used them before they spoiled; else he took more than his share, and robb'd others. And indeed it was a foolish thing, as well as dishonest, to hoard up more than he could make use of. If he gave away a part to any body else, so that it perished not uselessly in his Possession, these he also made use of. And if he also bartered away Plumbs that would have rotted in a week, for Nuts that would last good for his eating a whole Year, he did no injury; the portion of Goods that belonged to others, so long as nothing perished uselessly in his hands. Again, if he would give us Nuts for a piece of Metal, pleased with its colour; or exchanged his Sheep for Shells, or Wool for a sparkling Pebble or a Diamond, and keep those by him all his Life, he invaded not the Right of others, he might heap up as much of these durable things as he pleased; the *exceeding of the bounds of his* just Property not lying in the largeness of his Possession, but the perishing of any thing uselessly in it.

And thus *came in the use of Money,* some lasting thing that Men might keep without spoiling, and that by mutual consent Men would take in exchange for the truly useful, but perishable Supports of Life.

And as different degrees of Industry were apt to give Men Possessions in different Proportions, so this Invention of Money gave them the opportunity to continue to enlarge them. For supposing an Island, separated from all possible Commerce with the rest of the World, wherein there were but a hundred Families, but there were Sheep, Horses, Cows, with other useful Animals, wholsome Fruits, and Land enough for Corn for a hundred thousand times as many, but nothing in the Island, either because of its Commonness, or Perishableness, fit to supply the place of Money: What reason could any one have there to enlarge his Possessions beyond the use of his Family, and a plentiful supply to its Consumption, either in what their own Industry produced, or they could barter for like perishable, useful Commodities, with others? Where there is not something both lasting and scarce, and so valuable to be hoarded up, there Men will not be apt to enlarge their *Possessions of Land,* were it never so rich, never so free for them to take. For I ask, What would a Man value TenThousand, or an Hundred Thousand acres of excellent land, ready cultivated, and well stocked too with Cattle, in the middle of the in-land parts of *America,* where had no hopes of commerce with other Parts of the world, to draw *Money* to him by the Sale of the Product? It would not be worth the inclosing, and we should see him give up again to the wild Common of Nature, whatever was more than would supply the conveniencies of Life to be had there for him and his Family.

Thus in the beginning all the World was *America,* and more so than that is now; for no such thing as Money was any where known. Find out something that hath the *Use and Value of Money* amongst his Neighbours, you shall see the same Man will begin presently to *enlarge his Possessions.* Life of Man in proportion to Food, Rayment, and Carriage, has its *value* only from the consent of Men, whereof Labour yet makes, in great part, *the measure,* it is plain, that Men have agreed to disproportionate an unequal Possession of the Earth, they having by a tacit and voluntary consent found out a way, how a man may fairly possess more land than he himself can use the product of, by receiving in exchange for the overplus, Gold and Silver, which may be hoarded up without injury to any one, these metalls not spoileing or decaying the hands of the possessor. This partage of things, in an inequality of private possessions, men have made practicable out of the bounds of Societie, and without compact, only by putting a value on gold and silver and tacitly agreeing in the use of Money. For in Governments the Laws regulate the right of property, and the possession of land is determined by positive constitutions.

And thus, I think, it is easie to conceive without any difficulty, *how labour could at first begin a title of Property* in the common things of nature, and how the spending it upon our uses bounded it. So that there could then be no reason of quarrelling about Title, nor any doubt about the largeness of Possession it gave. Right and conveniency went together; for as a Man had a Right to all he could imploy his Labour upon, so he had no temptation to labour for more than he could make use of. This left no room for Controversie about the Title, nor for Incroachment on the Right of others; what Portion a Man carved to himself, was easily seen; and it was useless as well as dishonest to carve himself too much, or take more than he needed.

11

KARL MARX

The Commodity

The wealth of societies in which the capitalist mode of production prevails appears as an "immense collection of commodities"; the individual commodity appears as its elementary form. Our investigation therefore begins with an analysis of the commodity.

The commodity is, first of all, an external object, a thing which through its qualities satisfies human needs of whatever kind. The nature of these needs, whether they arise, for example, from the stomach, or the imagination, makes no difference. Nor does it matter here how the thing satisfies man's need, whether directly as a means of subsistence, i.e., an object of consumption, or indirectly as a means of production.

Every useful thing, for example, iron, paper, etc., may be looked at from the two points of view of quality and quantity. Every useful thing is a whole composed of many properties; it can therefore be useful in various ways. The discovery of these ways and hence of the manifold uses of things is the work of history. So also is the invention of socially recognized standards of measurement for the quantities of these useful objects. The diversity of the measures for commodities arises in part from the diverse nature of the objects to be measured, and in part from convention.

The usefulness of a thing makes it a use-value. But this usefulness does not dangle in mid-air. It is conditioned by the physical properties of the commodity, and has no existence apart from the latter. It is therefore the physical body of the commodity itself, for instance iron, corn, a diamond, which is the use-value or useful thing. This property of a commodity is independent of the amount of labour required to appropriate its useful qualities. When examining use-values, we always assume we are dealing with definite quantities, such as dozens of watches, yards of linen, or tons of

From Karl Marx, *Capital,* Vol. 1.

iron. The use-values of commodities provide the material for special branch of knowledge, namely the commercial knowledge of commodities. Use-values are only realized in use or in consumption. They constitute the material content of wealth, whatever its social form may be. In the form of society to be considered here they are also the material bearers of . . . exchange-value.

Exchange-value appears first of all as the quantitative relation, the proportion, in which use-values of one kind exchange for use-values of another kind. This relation changes constantly with time and place. Hence exchange-value that is inseparably an intrinsic value, i.e., an exchange-value that is inseparably connected with the commodity, inherent in it, seems a contradiction in terms. Let us consider the matter more closely. A given commodity, a quarter of wheat for example, is exchanged for x boot-polish, y silk or z gold, etc. In short, it is exchanged for other commodities in the most diverse proportions. Therefore the wheat has many exchange values instead of one. But x boot-polish, y silk or z gold, etc., each represent the exchange-value of one quarter of wheat. Therefore x boot-polish, y silk, z gold, etc., must, as exchange-values, be mutually replaceable or of identical magnitude. It follows from this that, firstly, the valid exchange-values of a particular commodity express something equal, and secondly, exchange-value cannot be anything other than the mode of expression, the "form of appearance," of a content distinguishable from it.

Let us now take two commodities, for example corn and iron. Whatever their exchange relation may be, it can always be represented by an equation in which a given quantity of corn is equated to some quantity of iron, for instance 1 quarter of corn = x cwt of iron. What does this equation signify? It signifies that a common element of identical magnitude exists in two different things, in 1 quarter of corn and similarly in x cwt of iron. Both are therefore equal to a third thing, which in itself is neither the one nor the other. Each of them, so far as it is exchange-value, must therefore be reducible to this third thing.

A simple geometrical example will illustrate this. In order to determine and compare the areas of all rectilinear figures we split them up into triangles. Then the triangle itself is reduced to an expression totally different from its visible shape: half the product of the base and the altitude. In the same way the exchange values of commodities must be reduced to a common element, of which they represent a greater or a lesser quantity.

This common element cannot be a geometrical, physical, chemical or other natural property of commodities. Such properties come into consideration only to the extent that they make the commodities useful, i.e., turn them into use-values. But clearly, the exchange relation of commodities is characterized precisely by its abstraction from use-values. Within the exchange relation, one use-value is worth just as much as another, provided only that it is present in the appropriate quantity. Or, as old Barbon says: "One sort of wares are as good as another, if the value be equal. There is no difference or distinction in things of equal value. . . . One hundred pounds worth of lead or iron, is of as great a value as one hundred pounds worth of silver and gold."

If then we disregard the use-value of commodities, only one property remains, that of being products of labour. But even the product of labour has already been transformed in our hands. If we make abstraction from its use-value, we abstract also from the material constituents and forms which make it a use-value. It is no longer a table, a house, a piece of yarn or any other useful thing. All its sensuous characteristics are extinguished. Nor is it any longer the product of the labour of the joiner, the mason or the spinner, or of any other particular kind of productive labour. With the disappearance of the useful character of the products of labour, the useful character of the kinds of labour embodied in them also disappears; this in turn entails the disappearance of the different concrete forms of labour. They can no longer be distinguished, but are all together reduced to the same kind of labour, human labour in the abstract.

Let us now look at the residue of the products of labour. There is nothing left of them in each case but the same phantom-like objectivity; they are merely congealed quantities of homogeneous human labour, i.e., of human labour-power expended without regard to the form of its expenditure. All these things now tell us is that human labour-power has been expended to produce them, human labour is accumulated in them. As crystals of this social substance, which is common to them all, they are values—commodity values.

We have seen that when commodities are in the relation of exchange, their exchange-value manifests itself as something totally independent of their use-value. But if we abstract from their use-value, there remains their value, as it has just been defined. The common factor in the exchange relation, or in the exchange-value of commodity, is therefore its value. The progress of the investigation will lead us back to exchange-value as the necessary mode of expression, or form of appearance, of value. For the present, however, we must consider the nature of value independently of its form of appearance.

A use-value, or useful article, therefore, has value only because abstract human labour is objectified or materialized in it. How, then, is the magnitude of this value to be measured? By means of the quality of the "value-forming substance," the labour, contained in the article. This quality is measured by its duration, and the labour-time is itself measured on the particular scale of hours, days, etc.

It might seem that if the value of a commodity is determined by the quality of labour expended to produce it, it would be the more valuable the more unskillful and lazy the worker who produced it, because he would need more time to complete the article. However, the labour that forms the substance of value is equal human labour, the expenditure of identical human labour-power. The total labour-power of society, which is manifested in the values of the world of commodities, counts here as one homogeneous mass of human labour-power, although composed of innumerable individual units of labour-power. Each of these units is the same as any other, to the extent that it has the character of a socially average unit of labour-power and acts as such, i.e., only needs, in order to produce a commodity, the labour time which is necessary on an average, or in other words is socially necessary. Socially necessary labour-time is the labour-time required to produce any use-value under the conditions of production normal for a given society and the average degree of skill and intensity of labour prevalent in that society. The introduction of power-looms into England, for example, probably reduced by one half the labour required to convert a given quality of yarn into woven fabric. In order to do this, the England hand-loom weaver in fact needed the same amount of labour-time as before; but the product of his individual hour of labour now only represented half an hour of social labour, and consequently fell to one half its former value.

What exclusively determines the magnitude of the value of any article is therefore the amount of labour socially necessary, or the labour-time socially necessary for its production. The individual commodity counts here only as an average sample of its kind. Commodities which contain equal qualities of labour, or which can be produced in the same time, have therefore the same value. The value of a commodity is related to the value of any other commodity as the labour-time necessary for the production of the other. "As exchange-value, all commodities are merely definite quantities of congealed labour-time."

The value of a commodity would therefore remain constant, if the labour-time required for its production also remained constant. But the latter changes with every variation in the productivity of labour. This is determined by a wide range of circumstances; it is determined amongst other things by the workers' average degree of skill, the level of development of science and its technological application, the social organization of the process of production, the extent and effectiveness of the means of production, and the conditions found in the natural environment. For example, the same quality of labour is present in eight bushels of corn in favorable seasons and only four bushels in unfavourable seasons. The same quality of labour provides more metal in rich monies than in poor. Diamonds are of very rare occurrence on the earth's surface, and hence their discovery costs, on an average, a great deal of labour-time. Consequently much labour is represented in a small volume. Jacob questions whether gold has ever been paid for at its full value. This applies still more to diamonds. According to Eschwege, the total produce of the Brazilian diamond mines for the eighty years ending in 1823 still did not amount to the price of 1½ years' average product of the sugar and coffee plantation of the same country, although the diamonds represented much more labour, therefore more value. With richer mines, the same quality of labour would be embodied in more diamonds, and their value would fall. If man succeeded, without much labour, in transforming carbon into diamonds, their value might fall below that of bricks. In general, the greater the productivity of labour, the less the labour-time required to produce an article, the less the mass of labour crystallized in that article, and the less its value. Inversely, the less the productivity of labour, the greater the labour-time necessary to produce an article, and the greater its value. The value of a commodity, therefore, varies directly as the quality, and inversely as the productivity, of the labour which finds its realization within the commodity. (Now we know the substance of value. It is labour. We know the measure of its magnitude. It is labour-time. The form, which stamps value as exchange-value, remains to be analyzed. But before this we need to develop the characteristics we have already found somewhat more fully.)

A thing can be a use-value without being a value. This is the case whenever its utility to man is not mediated through labour. Air, virgin soil, natural meadows, unplanted forests, etc. fall into this category. A thing can be useful, and a product of human labour, without being a commodity. He who satisfies his own need with the product of his own labour admittedly creates use-values, but not commodities. In order to produce the latter, he must not only produce use-values, but use-values for others, social use-values. (And not merely for others. The medieval peasant produced a corn-rent for the feudal lord and a corn-tithe for the priest; but neither corn-rent nor the corn-tithe became commodities simply by being produced for others. In order to become a commodity, the product must be transferred to the other person, for whom it serves as a use-value, through the medium of exchange.) Finally, nothing can be a value without being an object of utility. If the thing is useless, so is the labour contained in it; the labour does not count as labour, and therefore creates no value.

The Historical Tendency of Capitalist Accumulation

What does the primitive accumulation of capital, i.e., its historical genesis, resolve itself into? In so far as it is not the direct transformation of slaves and serfs into wage-labourers, and therefore a mere change of form, it only means the expropriation of the immediate procedures, i.e., the dissolution of private property based on the labour of its owner. Private property, as the antithesis to social, collective property, exists only where the means of labour and the external conditions of labour belong to private individuals. But according to whether these private individuals are workers or non-workers, private property has a different character. The innumerable different shades of private property which appear at first sight are only reflections of the intermediate situations which lie between the two extremes.

The private property of the worker in his means of production as the foundation of small-scale industry is a necessary condition for the development of social production and of the free individuality of the worker himself. Of course, this mode of production also exists under slavery, serfdom and other situations of dependence. But it flourishes, unleashes the whole of its energy, attains its adequate classical form, only where the worker is the free proprietor of the conditions of his labour, and sets them in motion himself: where the peasant owns the land he cultivates, or the artisan owns the tool with which he is an accomplished performer.

This mode of production presupposes the fragmentation of holdings, and the dispersal of the other means of production. As it excludes the concentration of these means of production, so it also excludes co-operation, division of labour within each separate process of production, the social control and regulation of the forces of nature, and the free development of the productive forces of society. It is compatible only with a system of production and a society moving within narrow limits which are of natural origin. To perpetuate it would be, as Pecqueur rightly says, "to decree universal mediocrity." At a certain stage of development, it brings into the world the material means of its own destruction. From that moment, new forces and new passions spring up in the bosom of society, forces and passions which feel themselves to be fettered by that society. It has to be annihilated; it is annihilated. Its annihilation, the transformation of the individualized and scattered means of production into socially concentrated means of production, the transformation, therefore, of the dwarf-like property of the many into the giant property of the few, and the expropriation of the great mass of the people from the soil, from the means of subsistence and from the instruments of labour, this terrible and arduously accomplished expropriation of the mass of the people forms the pre-history of capital. It comprises a whole series of forcible methods, and we have only passed in review those that have been epoch-making as methods of the primitive accumulation of capital. The expropriation of the direct producers was accomplished by means of the most merciless barbarism, and under the stimulus of the most infamous, the most sordid, the most petty and the most odious of passions. Private property which is personally earned, i.e., which is based, as it were, on the fusing together of the isolated, independent working individual with the conditions of his labour, is supplanted by capitalist private property, which rests on the exploitation of alien, but formally free labour.

As soon as this metamorphosis has sufficiently decomposed the old society throughout its depth and breadth, as soon as the workers have been turned into proletarians, and their means of labour into capital, as soon as the capitalist mode of production stands on its own feet, the further socialization of labour and the further transformation of the soil and other means of production into socially exploited and therefore communal means of production takes on a new form. What is now to be expropriated is not the self-employed worker, but the capitalist who exploits a large number of workers.

This expropriation is accomplished through the action of the immanent laws of capitalist production itself, through the centralization of capitals. One capitalist always strikes down many others. Hand in hand with this centralization, or this expropriation of many capitalists by a few, other developments take place on an ever-increasing scale, such as the growth of the co-operative form of the labour process, the conscious technical application of science, the planned exploitation of the soil, the transformation of the means of labour into forms in which they can only be used in common, the economizing of all means of production of combined, socialized labour, the entanglement of all peoples in the net of the world market, and, with this, the growth of the international character of the capitalist regime. Along with the constant decrease in the number of capitalist magnates, who usurp and monopolize all the advantages of this process of transformation, the mass of misery, oppression, slavery, degradation and exploitation grows; but with this there also grows the revolt of the working class, a class constantly increasing in numbers, and trained, united and organized by the very mechanism of the capitalist process of production. The monopoly of capital becomes a fetter upon the mode of production which has flourished alongside and under it. The centralization of the means of production and the socialization of labour reach a point at which they become incompatible with their capitalist integument. This integument is burst asunder. The knell of capitalist private property sounds. The expropriators are expropriated.

The capitalist mode of appropriation, which springs from the capitalist mode of production, produces capitalist private property. This is the first negation of individual private property, as founded on the labour of its proprietor. But capitalist production begets, with the inexorability of a natural process, its own negation. This is the negation of the negation. It does not re-establish private property, but it does indeed establish individual property on the basis of the achievements of the capitalist era: namely co-operation and the possession in common of the land and the means of production produced by labour itself.

The transformation of scattered private property resting on the personal labour of the individuals themselves into capitalist private property is naturally an incomparably more protracted, violent and difficult process than the transformation of capitalist private property, which in fact already rests on the carrying on of production by society, into social property. In the former case, it was a matter of the expropriation of the mass of the people by a few usurpers; but in this case, we have the expropriation of a few usurpers by the mass of the people.

Property and Capital

Although the formation of capital and the capitalist mode of production are essentially founded not merely on the abolition of feudal production but also on the *expropriation* of the peasantry, craftsmen and in general of the mode of production based on the *private ownership by the immediate producer of his conditions of production;* although, once capitalist production has been introduced, it continues to develop at the same rate as that private property and the mode of production based on it is destroyed, so that those immediate producers are expropriated in the name of the *concentration of capital* (centralization); although the subsequent systematic repetition of the process of *expropriation* in the "clearing of estates" is in part the act of violence that *inaugurates* the capitalist mode of production—although all this is the case, both *the theory of capitalist production* (political economy, philosophy of law, etc.) and the capitalist himself in *his own mind* is pleased to confuse his mode of property and appropriation, which is based on the expropriation of the immediate producer in its origins, and on the acquisition of the labour of others in its further progress, with its opposite: with a mode of production that presupposes that the *immediate producer privately owns his own conditions of production*—a premise which would actually render capitalist production in agriculture and manufacture, etc. impracticable. In consequence he regards every attack on this latter *form of appropriation* as an attack on the former and indeed as an attack on *property as such.* Not unnaturally, the capitalist always finds it extremely difficult to represent the expropriation of the working masses as the precondition of property based on labour. (Incidentally, in private property of every type the *slavery* of the members of the family at least is always implicit since they are made use of and exploited by the head of the family.) Hence, the general juridical notion from Locke to Ricardo is always that of *petty-bourgeois ownership,* while the relations of production they describe belong to the *capitalist mode of production.* What make this possible is the relationship of *buyer* and *seller* which *formally* remains the same in both cases. In all these writers the following dualism is apparent:

(1) *Economically* they are opposed to *private property based on labour;* they present the advantages of the *expropriation of the masses* and the *capitalist mode of production;*

(2) *Ideologically* and *juridically* the ideology of private property founded on labour is transferred without more ado to property founded on the *expropriation of the immediate producers.*

Thus, for example, the talk of eliminating present burdens by means of government debts which put them on the shoulders of future generations. When B lends A goods either in reality or in appearance, A can give him a promissory note on the *products of the future,* just as there are poets and composers of the future. But A and B together never consume an atom of the produce of the future. Every age must pay its own way. A worker, on the other hand, is able to spend in advance this year the labour of the next three.

"In pretending to stave off the expenses of the present hour to a future day, in pretending that you can burthen posterity to supply the wants of the existing generation," the absurd claim is made "that you can consume what does not yet exist, that you can feed on provisions before their seeds have been sown in the earth. . . . All the wisdom of our statesmen will have ended in a great transfer of property from one class of persons to another, in creating an enormous fund for the rewards of job speculation" (Piercy Ravenstone, M.A., *Thoughts on the Funding System and Its Effects,* London, 1824, pp. 8, 9).

12

IMMANUEL KANT

The Categorical Imperative

The conception of an objective principle, so far as it constrains a will, is a command (of reason), and the formula of this command is called an *imperative.*

All imperatives are expressed by an "ought" and thereby indicate the relation of an objective law of reason to a will which is not in its subjective constitution necessarily determined by this law. This relation is that of constraint. Imperatives say that it would be good to do or to refrain from doing something, but they say it to a will which does not always do something simply because it is presented as a good thing to do. Practical good is what determines the will by means of the conception of reason and hence not by subjective causes but, rather, objectively, i.e., on grounds which are valid for every rational being as such. It is distinguished from the pleasant as that which has an influence on the will only by means of a sensation from merely subjective causes, which hold only for the senses of this or that person and not as a principle of reason which holds for everyone.[1]

A perfectly good will, therefore, would be equally subject to objective laws (of the good), but it could not be conceived as constrained by them to act in accord with them, because, according to its own subjective constitution, it can be determined to act only through the conception of the good. Thus no imperatives hold for the divine will or, more generally, for a holy will. The "ought" is here out of place, for the volition of itself is necessarily in unison with the law. Therefore imperatives are only formulas expressing the relation of objective laws of volition in general to the subjective imperfection of the will of this or that rational being, e.g., the human will.

All imperatives command either hypothetically or categorically. The for-

Beck, Lewis White, trans. *Foundations of the Metaphysics of Morals,* copyright © 1959, pp. 30–39. Reprinted by permission of Prentice Hall, Upper Saddle River, New Jersey.

mer present the practical necessity of a possible action as a means to achieving something else which one desires (or which one may possibly desire). The categorical imperative would be one which presented an action as of itself objectively necessary, without regard to any other end.

Since every practical law presents a possible action as good and thus as necessary for a subject practically determinable by reason, all imperatives are formulas of the determination of action which is necessary by the principle of a will which is in any way good. If the action is good only as a means to something else, the imperative is hypothetical; but if it is thought of as good in itself, and hence as necessary in a will which of itself conforms to reason as the principle of this will, the imperative is categorical.

The imperative thus says what action possible to me would be good, and it presents the practical rule in relation to a will which does not forthwith perform an action simply because it is good, in part because the subject does not always know that the action is good and in part (when he does know it) because his maxims can still be opposed to the objective principles of practical reason.

The hypothetical imperative, therefore, says only that the action is good to some purpose, possible or actual. In the former case it is a problematical,[2] in the latter an assertorical, practical principle. The categorical imperative, which declares the action to be of itself objectively necessary without making any reference to a purpose, i.e., without having any other end, holds as an apodictical (practical) principle.

We can think of that which is possible through the mere powers of some rational being as a possible purpose of any will. As a consequence, the principles of action, in so far as they are thought of as necessary to attain a possible purpose which can be achieved by them, are in reality infinitely numerous. All sciences have some practical part which consists of problems of some end which is possible for us to understand and of an imperative as to how it can be reached. These can therefore generally be called imperatives of skill. Whether the end is reasonable and good is not in question at all, for the question is only of what must be done in order to attain it. The precepts to be followed by a physician in order to cure his patient and by a poisoner in order to bring about certain death are of equal value in so far as each does that which will perfectly accomplish his purpose. Since in early youth we do not know what ends may occur to us in the course of life, parents seek to let their children learn a great many things and provide for skill in the use of means to all sorts of arbitrary ends among which they cannot determine whether any one of them may late become an actual purpose of their pupil, though it is possible that he may some day have it as his actual purpose. And this anxiety is so great that they commonly neglect to form and correct their judgment on the worth of things which they may make their ends.

There is one end, however, which we may presuppose as actual in all rational beings so far as imperatives apply to them, i.e., so far as they are dependent beings; there is one purpose not only which they can have but which we can presuppose that they all do have by a necessity of nature. This purpose is happiness. The hypothetical imperative which represents the practical necessity of action as means to the promotion of happiness is an assertorical imperative. We may not expound it as merely necessary to an uncertain and a merely possible purpose, but as necessary to a purpose which we can a priori and with assurance assume for everyone because it belongs to his essence. Skill in the choice of means to one's own highest welfare can be called prudence[3] in the narrowest sense. Thus the imperative which refers to the choice of means to one's own happiness, i.e., the precept of prudence, is still only hypothetical; the action is not absolutely commanded but commanded only as a means to another end.

Finally, there is one imperative which directly commands a certain conduct without making its condition some purpose to be reached by it. This imperative is categorical. It concerns not the material of the action and its intended result but the form and the principle from which it results. What is essentially good in it consists in the intention, the result being what it may. This imperative may be called the imperative of morality.

Volition according to these three principles is plainly distinguished by dissimilarity in the constraint to which they subject the will. In order to clarify this dissimilarity, I believe that they are most suitably named if one says that they are either rules of skill, counsels of prudence, or commands (laws) of morality, respectively. For law alone implies the concept of an unconditional and objective and hence universally valid necessity, and commands are laws which must be obeyed, even against inclination. Counsels do indeed involve necessity, but a necessity that can hold only under a subjectively contingent condition, i.e., whether this or that man counts this or that as part of his happiness; but the categorical imperative, on the other hand, is restricted by no condition. As absolutely, though practically, necessary it can be called a command in the strict sense. We could also call the first imperative technical (belonging to art), the second pragmatic[4] (belonging to welfare), and third moral (belonging to free conduct as such, i.e., to morals).

The question now arises: how are all these imperatives possible? This question does not require an answer as to how the action which the imperative commands can be performed but merely as to how the constraint of the will, which the imperative expresses in the problem, can be conceived. How an imperative of skill is possible requires no particular discussion. Whoever wills the end, so far as reason has decisive influence on his action, wills also the indispensably necessary means to it that lie in his power. This proposition, in what concerns the will, is analytical; for, in willing an object as my effect, my causality as an acting cause, i.e., the use of the means, is already thought, and the imperative drives the concept of necessary actions to this end from the concept of willing this end. Synthetical propositions undoubtedly are necessary in determining the means to a proposed end, but they do not concern the ground, the act of the will, but only the way to make the object real. Mathematics teaches, by synthetical propositions only, that in order to bisect a line according to an infallible principle I must make two intersecting arcs from each of its extremities; but if I know the proposed result can be obtained only by such an action, then it is an analytical proposition that, if I fully will the effect, I must also will the action necessary to produce it. For it is one and the same thing to conceive of something as an effect which is in a certain way possible through me and to conceive of myself as acting in this way.

If it were only easy to give a definite concept of happiness, the imperatives of prudence would completely correspond to those of skill and would be likewise analytical. For it could be said in this case as well as in the former that whoever wills the end wills also (necessarily according to reason) the only means to it which are in his power. But it is a misfortune that the concept of happiness is so indefinite that, although each person wishes to attain it, he can never definitely and self-consistently state what it is he really wishes and wills. The reason for this is that all elements which belong to the concept of happiness are empirical, i.e., they must be taken from experience, while for the idea of happiness and absolute whole, a maximum, of well-being is needed in my present and in every future condition. Now it is impossible even for a most clear-sighted and most capable but finite being to form here a definite concept of that which he really wills. If he wills riches, how much anxiety, envy, and intrigue might he not thereby draw upon his shoulders! If he wills much knowledge and vision, perhaps it might become only an eye that much sharper to show him as more dreadful the evils which are now hidden from him and which are yet unavoidable, or to burden his desires—which already sufficiently engage him—with even more needs! If he wills a long misery? If he wills at least health, how often has not the discomfort of the body restrained him from excesses into which perfect health would have led him? In short, he is not capable, on any principle and with complete certainty, of ascertaining what would make him truly happy; omniscience would be needed for this. He cannot, therefore, act according to definite principles so as to be happy, but only according to empirical counsels, e.g., those of diet, economy, courtesy, restraint, etc., which are shown by experience best to promote welfare on the average. Hence the imperatives of prudence cannot, in the strict sense, command, i.e., present actions objectively as practically necessary; thus they are to be taken as counsels rather than as commands of reason, and the task of determining infallibly and universally what action will promote the happiness of a rational being is completely unsolvable. There can be no imperative which would, in the strict sense, command us to do what makes for happiness, because happiness is an ideal not of reason but of imagination,[5] depending only on empirical grounds which one would expect in vain to determine an action through which the totality of consequences—which is in fact infinite—could be achieved. Assuming that the means to happiness could be infallibly stated, this imperative of prudence would be an analytical proposition, for it differs from the imperative of skill only in that its end is given while in the latter case it is merely possible. Since both, however, only command the means to that which one presupposes, the imperative which commands the willing of the means to him who wills the end is in both cases analytical. There is, consequently, no difficulty in seeing the possibility of such an imperative.

To see how the imperative of morality is possible is, then, without doubt the only question needing an answer. It is not hypothetical, and thus the objectively conceived necessity cannot be supported by any presupposition, as was the case with the hypothetical imperatives. But it must not be overlooked that it cannot be shown by any example (i.e., it cannot be empirically shown) whether or not there is such an imperative; it is rather to be suspected that all imperatives which appear to be categorical may yet be hypothetical, but in a hidden way. For instance, when it is said, "Thou shalt not make a false promise," we assume that the necessity of this avoidance is not a mere counsel for the sake of escaping some other evil, so that it would read, "Thou shalt not make a false promise so that, if it comes to light, thou ruinest thy credit"; we assume rather that an action of this kind must be regarded as of itself bad and that the imperative of the prohibition is categorical. But we cannot show with certainty by any example that the will is here determined by the law alone without any other incentives, even though this appears to be the case. For it is always possible that secret fear of disgrace, and perhaps also obscure apprehension of other dangers, may have had an influence on the will. Who can prove by experience the nonexistence of a cause when experience shows us only that we do not perceive the cause? But in such a case the so-called moral imperative, which as such appears to be categorical and unconditional, would be actually only a pragmatic precept which makes us attentive to our own advantage and teaches us to consider it.

Thus we shall have to investigate purely a priori the possibility of a categorical imperative, for we do not have the advantage that experience would give us the reality of this imperative, so that the [demonstration of its] possibility would be necessary only for its explanation and not for its establishment. In the meantime, this much may at least be seen: the categorical imperative alone can be taken as a practical law, while all the others may be called principles of the will but not laws. This is because what is necessary merely for the attainment of an arbitrary purpose can be regarded as itself contingent, and we get rid of the precept once we give up the purpose, whereas the unconditional command leaves the will no freedom to choose the opposite. Thus it alone implies the necessity which we require of a law.

Secondly, the case of the categorical imperative or law of morality, the cause of difficulty in discerning its possibility is very weighty. This imperative is an a priori synthetical practical proposition,[6] and, since to discern the possibility of propositions of this sort is so difficult in theoretical knowledge, it may well be gathered that it will be no less difficult in the practical.

In attacking this problem, we will first inquire whether the mere concept of a categorical imperative does not also furnish the formula containing the proposition which alone can be a categorical imperative. For even when we know the formula of the imperative, to learn how such an absolute law is possible will require difficult and special labors which we shall postpone to the last section.

If I think of a hypothetical imperative as such, I do not know what it will contain until the condition is stated [under which it is an imperative]. But if I think of categorical imperative, I know immediately what it contains. For since the imperative contains besides the law only the necessity that the maxim[7] should accord with this law, while the law contains no condition to which it is restricted, there is nothing remaining in it except the universality of law as such to which the maxim of the action should conform; and in effect this conformity alone is represented as necessary by the imperative.

There is, therefore, only one categorical imperative. It is: Act only according to that maxim by which you can at the same time will that it should become a universal law.

Now if all imperatives of duty can be derived from this one imperative as a principle, we can at least show what we understand by the concept of duty and what it means, even though it remain undecided whether that which is called duty is an empty concept or not.

The universality of law according to which effects are produced constitutes what is properly called nature in the most general sense (as to form), i.e., the existence of things so far as it is determined by universal laws. [By analogy], then, the universal imperative of duty can be expressed as follows: Act as though the maxim of your action were by your will to become a universal law of nature.

Notes

1. The dependence of the faculty of desire on sensations is called inclination, and inclination always indicates a need. The dependence of a contingently determinable will on principles of reason, however, is called interest. An interest is present only in a dependent will which is not of itself always in accord with reason; in the divine will we cannot conceive of an interest. But even the human will can take an interest in something without thereby acting from interest. The former means the practical interest in the action; the latter, the pathological interest in the object of the action. The former indicates only the dependence of the will on principles of reason in themselves, while the latter indicates dependence on the principles of reason for the purpose of inclination, since reason gives only the practical rule by which the needs of inclination are to be aided. In the former case the action interests me, and in the latter the object of the action (so far as it is pleasant for me) interests me. In the first section we have seen that, in the case of an action performed from duty, no regard must be given to the interest in the object, but merely in the action itself and its principle in . . . reason (i.e., the law).

2. [The *First Introduction to the Critique of Judgment* says: "This is the place to correct an error into which I fell in the *Foundations of the Metaphysics of Morals.* After I had stated that the imperatives of prudence commanded only conditionally, and indeed only under the condition of merely possible, i.e., problematic, ends, I called that kind of practical precept "problematic imperatives." But there is certainly a contradiction in this expression. I should have called them "technical imperatives," i.e., imperatives of art. The pragmatic imperatives, or rules of prudence which command under the condition of an actual and even subjectively necessary end, belong also among the technical imperatives. (For what is prudence but the skill to use free men and even the natural dispositions and inclinations of oneself for one's own designs?) Only the fact that the end to which we submit ourselves and others, namely, our own happiness, does not belong to the merely arbitrary ends [which we may or may not have] justifies a special name for these imperatives because the problem does not require merely a mode of reaching the end as is the case with technical imperatives, but also requires a definition of what constitutes this end itself (happiness). The end must be presupposed as known in the case of technical imperatives" (Akademie ed., XX, 200 n.).]

3. The word "prudence" may be taken in two senses, and it may bear the name of prudence with reference to things of the world and private prudence. The former sense means the skill of a man in having an influence on others so as to use them for his own purposes. The latter is the ability to unite all these purposes to his lasting advantage. The worth of the first is finally reduced to the latter, and of one who is prudent in the former sense but not in the latter we might better say that he is clever and cunning yet, on the whole, imprudent.

4. It seems to me that the proper meaning of the word "pragmatic" could be most accurately defined in this way. For sanctions which properly flow not from the law of states as necessary statutes but from provision for the general welfare are called pragmatic. A history is pragmatically composed when it teaches prudence, i.e., instructs the world how it could provide for its interest better than, or at least as well as, has been done in the past.

5. [The distinction between happiness and pleasure, which Kant says the followers of Epicurus confused, is explained in a fragment dating back to perhaps 1775: "Happiness is not something sensed but something thought. Nor is it a thought which can be taken from experience but a thought which only makes its experience possible. Not as if one had to know happiness in all its elements, but [one must know] the a priori condition by which alone one can be capable of happiness" (*Lose Blätter* [Reicke ed.], trans. Schilpp, in *Knat's Precritical Ethics,* p. 129).]

6. I connect a priori, and hence necessarily, the action with the will without supposing as a condition that there is any inclination [to the action] (though I do so only objectively, i.e., under the idea of a reason which would have complete power over all subjective motives). This is, therefore, a practical proposition which does not analytically derive the willing of an action from some other volition already presupposed (for we do not have such a perfect will); it rather connects it directly with the concept of the will of a rational being as something which is not contained within it.

7. A maxim is the subjective principle of acting and must be distinguished from the objective principle, i.e., the principle law. The former contains the practical rule which reason determines according to the conditions of the subject (often its ignorance or inclinations) and is thus the principle according to which the subject acts. The law, on the other hand, is the objective principle valid for every rational being, and the principle by which it ought to act, i.e., an imperative.

13

JOHN RAWLS

The Problem of Justice Between Generations

We must now consider the question of justice between generations. There is no need to stress the difficulties that this problem raises. It subjects any ethical theory to severe if not impossible tests. Nevertheless, the account of justice as fairness would be incomplete without some discussion of this important matter. The problem arises in the present context because the question is still open whether the social system as a whole, the competitive economy surrounded by the appropriate family of background institutions, can be made to satisfy the two principles of justice. The answer is bound to depend, to some degree anyway, on the level at which the social minimum is to be set. But this in turn connects up with how far the present generation is bound to respect the claims of its successors.

So far I have said nothing about how generous the social minimum should be. Common sense might be content to say that the right level depends upon the average wealth of the country and that, other things equal, the minimum should be higher when the average increases. Or one might say that the proper level is determined by customary expectations. But these suggestions are unsatisfactory. The first is not precise enough since it does not say how the minimum depends on average wealth and it overlooks other relevant aspects such as distribution; while the second provides no criterion for telling when customary expectations are themselves reasonable. Once the difference principle is accepted, however, it follows that the minimum is to be set at that point which, taking wages into account, maximizes the expectations of the least advantaged group. By adjusting the amount of

---

transfers (for example, the size of supplementary income payments), it is possible to increase or decrease the prospects of the more disadvantaged, their index of primary goods (as measured by wages plus transfers), so as to achieve the desired result.

Now offhand it might seem that the difference principle requires a very high minimum. One naturally imagines that the greater wealth of those better off is to be scaled down until eventually everyone has nearly the same income. But this is a misconception, although it might hold in special circumstances. The appropriate expectation in applying the difference principle is that of the long-term prospects of the least favored extending over future generations. Each generation must not only preserve the gains of culture and civilization, and maintain intact those just institutions that have been established, but it must also put aside in each period of time a suitable amount of real capital accumulation. This saving may take various forms from net investment in machinery and other means of production to investment in learning and education. Assuming for the moment that a just savings principle is available which tells us how great investment should be, the level of the social minimum is determined. Suppose for simplicity that the minimum is adjusted by transfers paid for by proportional expenditure (or income) taxes. In this case raising the minimum entails increasing the proportion by which consumption (or income) is taxed. Presumably as this fraction becomes larger there comes a point beyond which one of two things happens. Either the appropriate savings cannot be made or the greater taxes interfere so much with economic efficiency that the prospects of the least advantaged in the present generation are no longer improved but begin to decline. In either event the correct minimum has been reached. The difference principle is satisfied and no further increase is called for.

These comments about how to specify the social minimum have led us to the problem of justice between generations. Finding a just savings principle is one aspect of this question.[1] Now I believe that it is not possible, at present anyway, to define precise limits on what the rate of savings should be. How the burden of capital accumulation and of raising the standard of civilization and culture is to be shared between generations seems to admit of no definite answer. It does not follow, however, that certain bounds which impose significant ethical constraints cannot be formulated. As I have said, a moral theory characterizes a point of view from which policies are to be assessed; and it may often be clear that a suggested answer is mistaken even if an alternative doctrine is not ready to hand. Thus it seems evident, for example, that the classical principle of utility leads in the wrong direction for questions of justice between generations. For if one takes the size of the population as variable, and postulates a high marginal productivity of capital and a very distant time horizon, maximizing total utility may lead to an excessive rate of accumulation (at least in the near future). Since from a moral point of view there are no grounds for discounting future well-being on the basis of pure time preference, the conclusion is all the more likely that the greater advantages of future generations will be sufficiently large to compensate for present sacrifices. This may prove true if only because with more capital and better technology it will be possible to support a sufficiently large population. Thus the utilitarian doctrine may direct us to demand heavy sacrifices of the poorer generations for the sake of greater advantages for later ones that are far better off. But this calculus of advantages, which balances the losses of some against benefits to others, appears even less justified in the case of generations than among contemporaries. Even if we cannot define a precise just savings principle, we should be able to avoid this sort of extreme.

Now the contract doctrine looks at the problem from the standpoint of the original position. The parties do not know to which generation they belong or, what comes to the same thing, the stage of civilization of their society. They have no way of telling whether it is poor or relatively wealthy, largely agricultural or already industrialized, and so on. The veil of ignorance is complete in these respects. Thus the persons in the original position are to ask themselves how much they would be willing to save at each stage of advance on the assumption that all other generations are to save at the same rates. That is, they are to consider their willingness to save at any given phase of civilization with the understanding that the rates they propose are to regulate the whole span of accumulation. In effect, then, they must choose a just savings principle that assigns an appropriate rate of accumulation to each level of advance. Presumably this rate changes depending upon the state of society. When people are poor and saving is difficult, a lower rate of saving should be required; whereas in a wealthier society greater savings may reasonably be expected since the real burden is less. Eventually once just institutions are firmly established, the net accumulation required falls to zero. At this point a society meets its duty of justice by maintaining just institutions and preserving their material base. Of course, the just savings principle applies to what a society is to save as a matter of justice. If its citizens wish to save for various grand projects, that is another matter.

The question of time preference and matters of priority I shall leave aside until the next sections. For the present I wish to point out the main features of the contractarian approach. First of all, while it is evident that a just savings principle cannot literally be adopted democratically, the conception of the original position achieves the same result. Since no one knows to which generation he belongs, the question is viewed from the standpoint of each and a fair accommodation is expressed by the principle adopted. All generations are virtually represented in the original position, since the same principle would always be chosen. An ideally democratic decision will result, one that is fairly adjusted to the claims of each generation and therefore satisfying the precept that what touches all concerns all. Moreover, it is immediately obvious that every generation, except possibly the first, gains when a reasonable rate of saving is maintained. The process of accumulation, once it is begun and carried through, is to the good of all subsequent generations. Each passes on to the next a fair equivalent in real capital as defined by a just savings principle. (It should be kept in mind here that capital is not only factories and machines, and so on, but also the knowledge and culture, as well as the techniques and skills, that make possible just institutions and the fair value of liberty.) This equivalent is in return for what is received from previous generations that enables the later ones to enjoy a better life in a more just society. Only those in the first generation do not benefit, let us say, for while they begin the whole process, they do not share in the fruits of their provision. Nevertheless, since it is assumed that a generation cares for its immediate descendants, as fathers say care for their sons, a just savings principle, or more accurately, certain limits on such principles, would be acknowledged.

It is also characteristic of the contract doctrine to define a just state of society at which the entire course of accumulation aims. This feature derives from the fact that an ideal conception of a just basic structure is embedded in the principles chosen in the original position. In this respect, justice as fairness contrasts with utilitarian views. The just savings principle can be regarded as an understanding between generations to carry their fair share of the burden of realizing and preserving a just society. The end of the savings process is set up in advance, although only the general outlines can be discerned. Particular circumstances as they arise will in time determine the more detailed aspects. But in any event we are not bound to go on maximizing indefinitely. Indeed, it is for this reason that the savings principle is agreed to after the principles of justice for institutions, even though this principle constrains the difference principle. These principles tell us what to strive for. The savings principle represents an interpretation, arrived at in the original position, of the previously accepted natural duty to uphold and to further just institutions. In this case the ethical problem is that of agreeing on a path over time which treats all generations justly during the whole course of a society's history. What seems fair to persons in the original position defines justice in this instance as in others.

The significance of the last stage of society should not, however, be misinterpreted. While all generations are to do their part in reaching the just state of things beyond which no further net saving is required, this state is not to be thought of as that alone which gives meaning and purpose to the whole process. To the contrary, all generations have their appropriate aims. They are not subordinate to one another any more than individuals are. The life of a people is conceived as a scheme of cooperation spread out in historical time. It is to be governed by the same conception of justice that regulates the cooperation of contemporaries. No generation has stronger claims than any other. In attempting to estimate the fair rate of saving, the persons in the original position ask what is reasonable for members of adjacent generations to expect of one another at each level of advance. They try to piece together a just savings schedule by balancing how much at each stage they would be willing to save for their immediate descendants against what they would feel entitled to claim of their immediate predecessors. Thus imagining themselves to be fathers, say, they are to ascertain how much they should set aside for their sons by noting what they would believe themselves entitled to claim of their fathers. When they arrive at an estimate that seems fair from both sides, with due allowance made for the improvement in their circumstances, then the fair rate (or range of rates) for that stage is specified. Now once this is done for all stages, we have defined the just saving principle. When this principle is followed, adjacent generations cannot complain of one another; and in fact no generation can find fault with any other no matter how far removed in time.

The last stage at which saving is called for is not one of great abundance. This consideration deserves perhaps some emphasis. Further wealth might not be superfluous for some purposes; and indeed average income may not, in absolute terms, be very high. Justice does not require that early generations save so that later ones are simply more wealthy. Saving is demanded as a condition of bringing about the full realization of just institutions and the fair value of liberty. If additional accumulation is to be undertaken, it is for other reasons. It is a mistake to believe that a just and good society must wait upon a high material standard of life. What men want is meaningful work in free association with others, these associations regulating their relations to one another within a framework of just basic institutions. To achieve this state of things great wealth is not necessary. In fact, beyond some point it is more likely to be a positive hindrance, a meaningless distraction at best if not a temptation to indulgence and emptiness.

We should now observe that there is a peculiar feature of the reciprocity principle in the case of just savings. Normally this principle applies when there is an exchange of advantages and each party gives something as a fair return to the other. But in the course of history no generation gives to the preceding generations, the benefits of whose saving it has received. In following the savings principle, each generation makes a contribution to later generations and receives from its predecessors. The first generations may benefit hardly at all, whereas the last generations, those living when no further saving is enjoined, gain the most and give the least. Now this may appear unjust. Herzen remarks that human development is a kind of chronological unfairness, since those who live later profit from the labor of their predecessors without paying the same price. And Kant thought it disconcerting that earlier generations should carry their burdens only for the sake of the later ones and that only the last should have the good fortune to dwell in the completed building.[2] These feelings while entirely natural are misplaced. For although the relation between generations is a special one, it gives rise to no insuperable difficulty.

It is a natural fact that generations are spread out in time and actual exchanges between them take place only in one direction. We can do something for posterity but it can do nothing for us. This situation is unalterable, and so the question of justice does not arise. What is just or unjust is how institutions deal with natural limitations and the way they are set up to take advantage of historical possibilities. Obviously if all generations are to gain (except perhaps the first), they must choose a just savings principle which if followed brings it about that each receives from its predecessors and does its fair share for those which come later. The only reciprocal exchanges between generations are virtual ones, that is, compensating adjustments that can be made in the original position in drawing up the just savings principle. But these adjustments I imagine each generation to make for itself, leaving it to the veil of ignorance and the other constraints to lead any one generation to look out for all.

It is now clear why the difference principle does not apply to the savings problem. There is no way for later generations to improve the situation of the least fortunate first generation. The principle is inapplicable and it would seem to imply, if anything, that there be no saving at all. Thus, the problem of saving must be treated in another fashion. If we imagine that the original position contains representatives from all actual generations, the veil of ignorance would make it unnecessary to change the motivation assumption. But as we noted earlier, it is best to take the present time of entry interpretation. Those in the original position know, then, that they are contemporaries, so unless they care at least for their immediate successors, there is no reason for them to agree to undertake any saving whatever. To be sure, they do not know to which generation they belong, but this does not matter. Either earlier generations have saved or they have not; there is nothing the parties can do to affect it. It seems best to preserve the present time of entry interpretation and therefore to adjust the motivation condition. The parties are regarded as representing family lines, say, with ties of sentiment between successive generations. This modification seems natural enough, and has been used already in the argument for equal liberty. Although the savings problem presents a special situation, the characterization of justice remains the same. The criteria for justice between generations are those that would be chosen in the original position.

We now have to combine the just savings principle with the two principles of justice. This is done by supposing that this principle is defined from the standpoint of the least advantaged in each generation. It is the representative men from this group as it extends over time who by virtual adjustments are to specify the rate of accumulation. They undertake in effect to constrain the application of the difference principle. In any generation their expectations are to be maximized subject to the condition of putting aside the savings that would be acknowledged. Thus the complete statement of the difference principle includes the savings principle as a constraint. Whereas the first principle of justice and the principle of fair opportunity limit the application of the difference principle within generations, the savings principle limits its scope between them.

Of course, the saving of the less favored need not be done by their taking an active part in the investment process. Rather it normally consists of their approving of the economic and other arrangements necessary for the appropriate accumulation. Saving is achieved by accepting as a political judgement those policies designed to improve the standard of life of later generations to the least advantaged, thereby abstaining from the immediate gains which are available. By supporting these arrangements the required saving can be made, and no representative man in any generation of the most disadvantaged can complain of another for not doing his part. It should also be observed that for much of the time, especially during the earlier stages, the general conception of justice is likely to apply rather than the two principles in serial order. But the same idea holds and I shall not trouble to state it.

So much, then, for a brief sketch of some of the main features of the just savings principle. We can now see that persons in different generations have duties and obligations to one another just as contemporaries do. The present generation cannot do as it pleases but is bound by the principles that would be chosen in the original position to define justice between persons at different moments of time. In addition, men have a natural duty to uphold and to further just institutions and for this the improvement of civilization up to a certain level is required. The derivation of these duties and obligations may seem at first a somewhat farfetched application of the contract doctrine. Nevertheless these requirements would be acknowledged in the original position, and so the conception of justice as fairness covers these matters without any change in its basic idea.

Notes

1. This problem is often discussed by economists in the context of the theory of economic growth. For an exposition see A.K. Sen, "On Optimizing the Rate of Saving," *Economic Journal,* vol. 7 (1961); James Tobin, *National Economic Policy* (New Haven, Yale University Press, 1966), ch. IX; and R.M. Solow, *Growth Theory* (New York, Oxford University Press, 1970), ch. V. In an extensive literature, see F.P. Ramsey, "A Mathematical Theory of Saving," *Economic Journal,* vol. 38 (1928), reprinted in Arrow and Scitovsky, *Readings in Welfare Economics:* T.C. Koopmans, "On the Concept of Optimal Economic Growth" (1965) in Scientific Papers of T.C. Koopmans (Berlin, Springer Verlag, 1970). Sukamoy Chakravarty, *Capital and Development Planning* (Cambridge, M.I.T. Press, 1969), is a theoretical survey which touches upon the normative questions. If for theoretical purposes one thinks of the ideal society as one whose economy is in a steady state of growth (possibly zero), and which is at the same time just, then the savings problem is to choose a principle for sharing the burdens of getting to that growth path (or to such a path if there is more than one), and of maintaining the justice of the necessary arrangements once this is achieved. In the text, however, I do not pursue this suggestion; my discussion is at a more primitive level.

2. The remark of Alexander Herzen is from Isaiah Berlin's introduction to Franco Venturi, *Roots of Revolution* (New York, Alfred Knopf, 1960), p. xx. For Kant, see "Idea for a Universal History with a Cosmopolitan Purpose," in *Political Writings,* ed. Hans Reiss and trans. H.B. Nisbet (Cambridge, The University Press, 1970), p. 44.

14

HERBERT MARCUSE

The New Forms of Control

Freedom of enterprise was from the beginning not altogether a blessing. As the liberty to work or to starve, it spelled toil, insecurity, and fear for the vast majority of the population. If the individual were no longer compelled to prove himself on the market, as a free economic subject, the disappearance of this kind of freedom would be one of the greatest achievements of civilization. The technological processes of mechanization and standardization might release individual energy into a yet uncharted realm of freedom beyond necessity. The very structure of human existence would be altered; the individual would be liberated from the work world's imposing upon him alien needs and alien possibilities. The individual would be free to exert autonomy over a life that would be his own. If the productive apparatus could be organized and directed toward the satisfaction of the vital needs, its control might well be centralized; such control would not prevent individual autonomy, but render it possible.

This is a goal within the capabilities of advanced industrial civilization, the "end" of technological rationality. In actual fact, however, the contrary trend operates: the apparatus imposes its economic and political requirements for defense and expansion on labor time and free time, on the material and intellectual culture. By virtue of the way it has organized its technological base, contemporary industrial society tends to be totalitarian. For "totalitarian" is not only a terroristic political coordination of society, but also a nonterroristic economic-technical coordination which operates through the manipulation of needs by vested interests. It thus precludes the emergence of an effective opposition against the whole. Not only a specific form of government or party rule makes for totalitarianism, but also a specific system of production and distribution which may well be compatible with a "pluralism" of parties, newspapers, "countervailing powers," etc.

Today political power asserts itself through its power over the machine process and over the technical organization of the apparatus. The government of advanced and advancing industrial societies can maintain and secure itself only when it succeeds in mobilizing, organizing, and exploiting the technical, scientific, and mechanical productivity available to industrial civilization. And this productivity mobilizes society as a whole, above and beyond any particular individual or group interests. The brute fact that the machine's physical (only physical?) power surpasses that of the individual, and of any particular group of individuals, makes the machine the most effective political instrument in any society whose basic organization is that of the machine process. But the political trend may be reversed; essentially the power of the machine is only the stored-up and projected power of man. To the extent to which the work world is conceived of as a machine and mechanized accordingly, it becomes the *potential* basis of a new freedom for man.

Contemporary industrial civilization demonstrates that it has reached the stage at which "the free society" can no longer be adequately defined in the traditional terms of economic, political, and intellectual liberties, not because these liberties have become insignificant, but because they are too significant to be confined within the traditional forms. New modes of realization are needed, corresponding to the new capabilities of society.

Such new modes can be indicated only in negative terms because they would amount to the negation of the prevailing modes. Thus economic freedom would mean freedom from the economy—from being controlled by economic forces and relationships; freedom from the daily struggle for existence, from earning a living. Political freedom would mean liberation of the individuals from politics over which they have no effective control. Similarly, intellectual freedom would mean the restoration of individual thought now absorbed by mass communication and indoctrination, abolition of "public opinion" together with its makers. The unrealistic sound of these propositions is indicative, not of their utopian character, but of the strength of the forces which prevent their realization. The most effective and enduring form of warfare against liberation is the implanting of material and intellectual needs that perpetuate obsolete forms of the struggle for existence.

The intensity, the satisfaction, and even the character of human needs, beyond the biological level, have always been preconditioned. Whether or not the possibility of doing or leaving, enjoying or destroying, possessing or rejecting something is seized as a *need* depends on whether or not it can be seen as desirable and necessary for the prevailing societal institutions and interests. In this sense, human needs are historical needs and, to the extent to which the society demands the repressive development of the individual, his needs themselves and their claim for satisfaction are subject to overriding critical standards.

We may distinguish both true and false needs. "False" are those which are superimposed upon the individual by particular social interests in his repression: the needs which perpetuate toil, aggressiveness, misery, and injustice. Their satisfaction might be most gratifying to the individual, but this happiness is not a condition which has to be maintained and protected if it serves to arrest the development of the ability (his own and others) to recognize the disease of the whole and grasp the chances of curing the disease. The result then is euphoria in unhappiness. Most of the prevailing needs to relax, to have fun, to behave and consume in accordance with the advertisements, to love and hate what others love and hate, belong to this category of false needs.

Such needs have a societal content and function which are determined by external powers over which the individual has no control; the development and satisfaction of these needs is heteronomous. No matter how much such needs may have become the individual's own, reproduced and fortified by the conditions of his existence; no matter how much he identifies himself with them and finds himself in their satisfaction, they continue to be what they were from the beginning—products of a society whose dominant interest demands repression.

The prevalence of repressive needs is an accomplished fact, accepted in ignorance and defeat, but a fact that must be undone in the interest of the happy individual as well as all those whose misery is the price of his satisfaction. The only needs that have an unqualified claim for satisfaction are the vital ones—nourishment, clothing, lodging at the attainable level of culture. The satisfaction of these needs is the prerequisite for the realization of all needs, of the unsublimated as well as the sublimated ones.

For any consciousness and conscience, for any experience which does not accept the prevailing societal interest as the supreme law of thought and behavior, the established universe of needs and satisfactions is a fact to be questioned—questioned in terms of truth and falsehood. These terms are historical throughout, and their objectivity is historical. The judgment of needs and their satisfaction, under the given conditions, involves standards of *priority*—standards which refer to the optimal development of the individual, of all individuals, under the optimal utilization of the material and intellectual resources available to man. The resources are calculable. "Truth" and "falsehood" of needs designate objective conditions to the extent to which the universal satisfaction of vital needs and, beyond it, the progressive alleviation of toil and poverty, are universally valid standards. But as historical standards, they do not only vary according to area and stage of development, they also can be defined only as (greater or lesser) *contradiction* to the prevailing ones. What tribunal can possibly claim the authority of decision?

In the last analysis, the question of what are true and false needs must be answered by the individuals themselves, but only in the last analysis; that is, if and when they are free to give their own answer. As long as they are kept incapable of being autonomous, as long as they are indoctrinated and manipulated (down to their very instincts), their answer to this question cannot be taken as their own. By the same token, however, no tribunal can justly arrogate to itself the right to decide which needs should be developed and satisfied. Any such tribunal is reprehensible, although our revulsion does not do away with the question: how can the people who have been the object of effective and productive domination by themselves create the conditions of freedom?

. . . Indeed, in the most highly developed areas of contemporary society, the transplantation of social into individual needs is so effective that the difference between them seems to be purely theoretical. Can one really distinguish between the mass media as instruments of information and entertainment, and as agents of manipulation and indoctrination? Between the automobile as nuisance and as convenience? Between the horrors and the comforts of functional architecture? Between the work for national defense and the work for corporate gain? Between the private pleasure and the commercial and political utility involved in increasing the birth rate?

We are again confronted with one of the most vexing aspects of advanced industrial civilization: the rational character of its irrationality. Its productivity and efficiency, its capacity to increase and spread comforts, to turn waste into need, and destruction into construction, the extent to which this civilization transforms the object world into an extension of man's mind and body makes the very notion of alienation questionable. The people recognize themselves in their commodities; they find their soul in their automobile, hi-fi set, split-level home, kitchen equipment. The very mechanism which ties the individual to his society has changed, and social control is anchored in the new needs which it has produced.

The prevailing forms of social control are technological in a new sense. To be sure, the technical structure and efficacy of the productive and destructive apparatus has been a major instrumentality for subjecting the population to the established social division of labor throughout the modern period. Moreover, such integration has always been accompanied by more obvious forms of compulsion: loss of livelihood, the administration of justice, the police, the armed forces. It still is. But in the contemporary period, the technological controls appear to be the very embodiment of Reason for the benefit of all social groups and interests—to such an extent that all contradiction seems irrational and all counteraction impossible.

No wonder then that, in the most advanced areas of this civilization, the social controls have been introjected to the point where even individual protest is affected at its roots. The intellectual and emotional refusal "to go along" appears neurotic and impotent. This is the socio-psychological aspect of the political event that marks the contemporary period: the passing of the historical forces which, at the preceding stage of industrial society, seemed to represent the possibility of new forms of existence.

But the term "introjection" perhaps no longer describes the way in which the individual by himself reproduces and perpetuates the external controls exercised by his society. Introjection suggests a variety of relatively spontaneous processes by which a Self (Ego) transposes the "outer" into the "inner." Thus introjection implies the existence of an inner dimension distinguished from and even antagonistic to the external exigencies—an individual consciousness and an individual unconscious *apart from* public opinion and behavior. The idea of "inner freedom" here has its reality: it designates the private space in which man may become and remain "himself."

Today this private space has been invaded and whittled down by technological reality. Mass production and mass distribution claim the *entire* individual, and industrial psychology had long since ceased to be confined to the factory. The manifold processes of introjection seem to be ossified in almost mechanical reactions. The result is, not adjustment but *mimesis:* an immediate identification of the individual with his society and, through it, with the society as a whole.

This immediate, automatic identification (which may have been characteristic of primitive forms of association) reappears in high industrial civilization; its new "immediacy," however, is the product of a sophisticated, scientific management and organization. In this process, the "inner" dimension of the mind in which opposition to the status quo can take root is whittled down. The loss of this dimension, in which the power of negative thinking—the critical power of Reason—is at home, is the ideological counterpart to the very material process in which advanced industrial society silences and reconciles the opposition. The impact of progress turns Reason into submission to the facts of life, and to the dynamic capability of producing more and bigger facts of the same sort of life. The efficiency of the system blunts the individuals' recognition that it contains no facts which do not communicate the repressive power of the whole. If the individuals find themselves in the things which shape their life, they do so, not by giving, but by accepting the law of things—not the law of physics but the law of their society.

I have just suggested that the concept of alienation seems to become questionable when the individuals identify themselves with the existence which is imposed upon them and have in it their own development and satisfaction. This identification is not illusion but reality. However, the reality constitutes a more progressive stage of alienation. The latter has become entirely objective; the subject which is alienated is swallowed up by its alienated existence. There is only one dimension, and it is everywhere and in all forms. The achievements of progress defy ideological indictment as well as justification; before their tribunal, the "false consciousness" of their rationality becomes the true consciousness.

This absorption of ideology into reality does not, however, signify the "end of ideology." On the contrary, in a specific sense advanced industrial culture is more ideological than its predecessor, inasmuch as today the ideology is in the process of production itself. In a provocative form, this proposition reveals the political aspects of the prevailing technological rationality. The productive apparatus and the goods and services which it produces "sell" or impose the social system as a whole. The means of mass transportation and communication, the commodities of lodging, food, and clothing, the irresistible output of the entertainment and information industry carry with the prescribed attitudes and habits, certain intellectual and emotional reactions which bind the consumers more or less pleasantly to the producers and, through the latter, to the whole. The products indoctrinate and manipulate; they promote a false consciousness which is immune against its falsehood. And as these beneficial products become available to more individuals in more social classes, the indoctrination they carry ceases to be publicity; it becomes a way of life. It is a good way of life—much better than before—and as a good way of life, it mitigates against qualitative change. Thus emerges a pattern of *one-dimensional thought and behavior* in which idea, aspirations, and objectives that, by their content, transcend the established universe of discourse and action are either repelled or reduced to terms of this universe. They are refined by the rationality of the given system and of its quantitative extension. . . .

One-dimensional thought is systematically promoted by the makers of politics and their purveyors of mass information. Their universe of discourse is populated by self-validating hypotheses which, incessantly and monopolistically repeated, become hypnotic definitions or dictations. For example, "free" are the institutions which operate (and are operated on) in the countries of the Free World; other transcending modes of freedom are by definition either anarchism, communism, or private enterprises not undertaken by private enterprise itself (or by government contracts), such as universal and comprehensive health insurance, or the protection of nature from all too sweeping commercialization, or the establishment of public services which may hurt private profit. This totalitarian logic of accomplished facts has its Eastern counterpart. There, freedom is the way of life instituted by a communist regime, and all other transcending modes of freedom are either capitalistic, or revisionist, or leftist sectarianism. In both camps, non-operational ideas are non-behavioral and subversive. The movement of thought is stopped at barriers which appear as the limits of Reason itself.

Such limitation of thought is certainly not new. Ascending modern rationalism, in its speculative as well as empirical form, shows a striking contrast between extreme critical radicalism in scientific and philosophic method on the one hand, and an uncritical quietism in the attitude toward established and functioning social institutions. Thus Descartes' ego cogitans was to leave the "great public bodies" untouched, and Hobbes held that "the present ought always to be preferred, maintained, and accounted best." Kant agreed with Locke in justifying revolution if and when it has succeeded in organizing the whole and in preventing subversion. . . .

With the gradual closing of this dimension by the society, the self-limitation of thought assumes a larger significance. The interrelation between scientific-philosophical and societal processes, between theoretical and practical Reason, asserts itself "behind the back" of the scientists and the philosophers. The society bars a whole type of oppositional operations and behavior; consequently, the concepts pertaining to them are rendered illusory or meaningless. Historical transcendence appears as metaphysical transcendence, not acceptable to science and scientific thought. The operational and behavioral point of view, practiced as a "habit of thought" at large, becomes the view of the established universe of discourse and action, needs and aspirations. The "cunning of Reason" works, as it so often did, in the interest of the powers that be. The insistence on operational and behavioral concepts turns against the efforts to free thought and behavior from the given reality and for the suppressed alternatives. Theoretical and practical Reason, academic and social behaviorism meet on common ground; that of an advanced society which makes scientific and technical process into an instrument of domination.

"Progress" is not a neutral term; it moves toward specific ends, and these ends are defined by the possibilities of ameliorating the human condition. Advanced industrial society is approaching the stage where continued progress would demand the radical subversion of the prevailing direction and organization of progress. This stage would be reached when material production (including the necessary services) becomes automated to the extent that all vital needs can be satisfied while necessary labor time is reduced to marginal time. From this point on, technical progress would transcend the realm of necessity, where it served as the instrument of domination and exploitation which thereby limited its rationality; technology would become subject to the free play of faculties in the struggle for the pacification of nature and of society. . . .

The most advanced areas of industrial society exhibit throughout these two features: a trend toward consummation of technological rationality, and intensive efforts to contain this trend within the established institutions. Here is the internal contradiction of this civilization: the irrational element in its rationality. It is the token of its achievements. The industrial society which makes technology and science its own is organized for the ever-more-effective domination of man and nature, for the ever-more-effective utilization of its resources. It becomes irrational when the success of these efforts opens new dimensions of human realization of war; the institutions which served the struggle for existence cannot serve the pacification of existence. Life as an end is qualitatively different from life as a means.

15

MATTHEW CAHN

Liberalism and Environmental Quality

Environmental concerns have become increasingly important over the last two decades. By now most people agree that measures must be taken to improve environmental quality. Environmental improvement, however, poses a difficult challenge to the American policy process. To understand environmental policy in the 1990s one must confront two distinct influences: the legacy of Lockean liberalism in American political culture; and the propensity of policy makers to "market" public policies through symbolic language.

Liberal society is fundamentally limited in its ability to resolve the problem of environmental degradation. There are two structural tensions between liberalism and environmental quality. First, liberalism's emphasis on individual self-interest creates a problematic concept of communal good. Society, as manifest in liberal contract theory, exists not to find some higher good, but to protect individual rights. Communal good is limited to providing a stable environment for individual rights. As a consequence, individual and corporate property rights have consistently overshadowed community claims on resource management. Second, capitalism, as a system of economic production and distribution, has been characterized by a constant drive for expansion in search of increased productivity and profit. The impact of that expansionary ethic has been overuse of limited resources and the degradation of our physical environment.

In the United States the tension between liberalism and environmental

From Matthew A. Cahn, *Environmental Deceptions: The Tension Between Liberalism and Environmental Quality in the United States* (Albany: State University of New York Press, 1995). Reprinted by permission of the State University of New York Press.

quality has been consistently understated in policy debates. Policy elites, seeking to resolve environmental problems while maintaining economic growth, have reduced complex environmental relationships to simple issues, suggesting that modest regulation will effect substantial improvement. In this sense, environmental policy has been largely symbolic. Environmental policies are consciously engineered both to create and to satisfy public demand. The public articulates vague needs, which are then adopted by policy makers who respond with specific goals, cuing public opinion into "attainable" policy options. Public demand is then satisfied with relatively soft regulation. . . .

Lockean Liberalism and Public Policy I: The Problem of Communal Good

American political culture has evolved from an awkward marriage of two disparate philosophical legacies: civic republicanism and Lockean liberalism. Several observers note that civic republicanism was favored by prerevolutionary thinkers (e.g., Wood 1969, Appleby 1984, Pocock 1975, Kann 1991). Wood (1969) argues that the American revolution was not merely economic, but philosophical, as colonists attempted to replace British autocracy with a federation of autonomous nation-states. As Kann suggests, "the ideal was that virtuous Americans would rise above self-interest, participate together to found state commonwealths, and balance liberty and authority for the public good" (1991:5). Civic republicanism, in this sense, placed public good before individual self-interest.

The republican potential, however, began to unfold as political and economic elites became less and less convinced that common people—e.g., non-elites—were virtuous enough to place public good ahead of individual passions. In this sense, Shays' Rebellion became emblematic of the Founders' fears. Daniel Shays, an army captain during the revolutionary war, led a group of farmers—most of whom were war veterans—in a rebellion intended to prevent foreclosures on their farms by keeping the western Massachusetts county courts from sitting until after the next election. In placing their self-interest before the interests of the state—and the financiers who stood to benefit—Shays and his colleagues shattered the republican model.

Civic virtue, in its classic sense, requires citizens to sublimate their individual passions for a common good. Early American political thinkers came to doubt that destructive individual passions (lust, greed, avarice) could be suppressed. Thus, if it was not possible to create a virtuous society, it was possible to create a society in which self-interest could be harnessed productively. If citizens could not sublimate their self-interest for a common interest, they could channel self-interest into economic productivity. The liberal self-interest model came to eclipse republican civic virtue with a social stability based on economic self-interest. But, as Pocock (1975) suggests, while the self-interest model may have replaced the civic republican model the discourse on civic virtue remained, albeit in a different context. Appleby (1984) points out that by the end of the 18th century the classical meaning of civic virtue—rising above private interests for some public good—was replaced with an alternate, even contrary meaning. Civic virtue became synonymous with individual industriousness and achievement. The result may be understood as a sort of latent civic virtue: economic self-interest as public interest.

This view permeates the liberal discourse. Schumpeter (1942) saw no public interest apart from individual self-interest. Citizens participate politically to the extent that they have self-interested goals and desires. Similarly, elected policymakers pursue public policy goals to satisfy the demands of the electorate, in the self-interested goal of re-election. Hartz (1955) and Macpherson (1962) argue that "possessive individualism" diverts the passions of men (laziness, self-indulgence) into a drive for economic gain, creating sober, productive citizens. Downs (1957) and other "Public Choice" scholars see self-interest as the primary motivation of all people.

The infusion of this latent civic virtue into Lockean liberalism creates a uniquely American liberalism where public good is defined by incrementally increasing individual good. In this sense American liberalism remains true to its utilitarian roots: the common good is the aggregate sum of individual good. Thus, the role of the community is to provide the infrastructure to make the pursuit and enjoyment of individual rights possible. In Lockean terms, the public good is provided through the creation of a stable environment for the acquisition, use, and disposition of private property. As a consequence, liberal society is fundamentally organized around economic interaction. The policy implications are twofold: liberal policy seeks to create independent economic actors; and, liberal policy demands that any communal need be evaluated in light of individual property rights. The primacy of liberal individualism creates a dilemma for public policy: Lockean individualism is nowhere manifest more strongly than in its commitment to individual property rights, and as a result, individual property rights limit the notion of communal rights, creating a problematic definition of communal good.

Self-Interest and the Public Good

Civic virtue has been alternately defined as altruism, self-control, sobriety, productivity, and love of country. In short, self-sacrifice in the public interest. As a tempering influence on self-interest, civic virtue succeeds in creating citizens who can live side by side in a stable political environment. The problem from a public policy perspective, however, is that liberal civic virtue, to the extent that it exists, remains privatized. What is missing is a notion of communal rights. There is no language of public interest apart from individual interest, leaving the scope of public policy choices severely limited.

The self-interest versus civic virtue debate in liberalism inevitably raises questions about altruism and examples of communitarianism. The nurturing of children and the elderly in families, volunteerism in church or organizational activities, contributing to charities, alumni support of schools, and participation in the civic operations of neighborhood communities and towns are all widespread in the American experience. Bellah et al. (1985), McWilliams (1973), and others present a vivid picture of the various communities Americans participate in in the search for social support networks. However, such communitarian participation takes place almost exclusively on the sub-national level. Family, church, union, school, town, and so forth, all offer identifiable community values with which members can identify; civic participation allows a sense of belonging. In this sense, self-sacrifice for the "good" of the community carries personal implications: improving the "community" directly improves one's immediate environment. As such, public interest and private interest are the same.

Communitarian involvement on the state and national level is much more difficult to identify. The only consistent self-sacrifice we see on the national level is military service. Yet, even military service provides a problematic form of civic virtue in the traditional sense. Historically, most soldiers came to "serve their country" through conscription, a not so subtle coercion. Perhaps today's all volunteer army is a result of civic mindedness. More likely, however, is the perception that military service provides some sort of personal opportunity. Individual self-interest may be a greater factor than civic virtue. College aid, job training, and veterans' benefits are major inducements. Military public service, then, may be conducive to self-interest. No one was more surprised by the U.S. deployment of 500,000 troops in the Persian Gulf than many of the soldiers themselves. Many had enlisted, not to become citizen soldiers, but to gain steady work (Wilkerson 1991).

The Search for a Common Good

Liberalism is based on individual self-interest as the foundation for preserving life. Society, as manifest in the social contract, exists not to find some higher collective good, but simply to ensure individual rights. The proper role of liberal government, then, is to protect a narrow scope of individual rights (self-preservation, liberty, and property). This definition of public good justifies the creation of an infrastructure which makes such protections possible: a police force and army; public laws which define a consistent system for the accumulation, use, and transfer of property; courts to arbitrate between competing interests; jails to house those who have violated the norms of liberal society; and ultimately, a structure to measure the aggregate individual good—elections to choose representatives for public office. Beyond this, liberal government has little authority.

In the absence of an explicit language of communal rights, there is little prospect of limiting concrete property rights for an abstract public good. The narrow liberal definition of communal good has consistently allowed individual and corporate claims of property rights to outweigh the need for serious environmental regulation. . . . As a consequence of the parameters imposed by the problematic liberal definition of communal good, the American policy process is fundamentally limited in its ability to confront environmental issues adequately.

The notion of communal good in American liberalism has evolved to accommodate specific problems that threaten the fabric of social stability. Public education programs evolved to encourage social integration (Peters 1993). New Deal liberalism, particularly through programs such as social security, developed as an accommodation to economic disintegration (Bowles and Gintis 1986). Yet, while traditional definitions of communal good remain narrow, environmental degradation may force a new approach. To the extent environmental destruction is understood to threaten social stability, American liberalism's latent civic virtue may resurface. Rawls's (1971) restatement of justice as a central liberal priority may provide the bridge.

Rawls accepts self-interest as the primary motivation in human society, but rejects the utilitarian influence that has come to characterize western liberalism. Rawls broadens the self-interest model to accommodate a communitarian ethic in the tradition of Kant. Rawls identifies two basic principles necessary for a just society:

> First: each person is to have an equal right to the most extensive basic liberty compatible with a similar liberty for others.
>
> Second: social and economic inequalities are to be arranged so that they are both (a) reasonably expected to be to everyone's advantage, and (b) attached to positions and offices open to all. (Rawls 1971:60)

In this sense, procedural justice exists when equal people give informed consent to the process by which decisions are made (Wenz 1988). In such cases, the decisions, regardless of outcome, are "fair."

Further, Rawls defines just policies as those that benefit the least advantaged within the society, in addition to anyone else. In this sense, "there is no injustice in the greater benefits earned by a few provided that the situation of persons not so fortunate is thereby improved" (Rawls 1971:15). This reflects Rawls's notion of *Pareto Optimality:* "a configuration is efficient whenever it is impossible to change it so as to make some persons (at least one) better off without at the same time making other persons (at least one) worse off" (Rawls 1971:67).

Rawls's concept of fairness and of *Pareto Optimality* are useful for expanding the traditionally narrow liberal self-interest model. Within the Rawlsian paradigm, self-interest itself must include minimizing social bads, because anyone of us may, at some time, be exposed to those bads. Self-interest is maintained, then, when individuals vote to finance greater fire protection services, since any one of us can suffer the tragedy of being in a burning building. By this logic, it is possible to argue that minimizing environmental degradation is a form of maintaining individual self-interest, because any one of us may find ourselves, for example, exposed to toxins that have seeped into aquifers. Wenz (1988) suggests that in establishing a common fund to clean up abandoned waste sites CERCLA (Superfund) is an example of just environmental policy—in the Rawlsian sense. Rawls reintegrates the language of civic virtue into a utilitarian liberal discourse.

The tension between public rights and private rights is nowhere felt more strongly than in environmental policy. Environmental policy is predicated on regulating the use and development of private property. Without redefining traditional Lockean property rights, environmental policy proposes to legislate what property owners can and cannot do with their property. Traditional concepts of liberal civic virtue say nothing to this dilemma. But, as Rawls suggests, it may be possible to accommodate communal challenges by redefining self-interest. . . .

The Tension Between Liberalism and Environmental Quality

[Liberal] capitalism, as an economic system establishing supply and distribution of goods, is largely inconsistent with the collective good of maintaining environmental quality. Liberalism equates liberty with the ability to acquire, use, and dispose of private property free of government intrusion. Capitalism encourages environmental degradation in several ways. As the Marshall Court articulated, liberal society is based upon the rights of private property (economic liberty). As such, the state has limited authority to mandate how citizens use their property. Environmental policy, on the other hand, is predicated on the regulation of private resources and behaviors. If, in the view of liberalism, the chief end of civil society is the preservation and protection of property rights, environmental regulation challenges the ideological basis of political order.

Economic success in capitalism has historically been defined by economic growth. To maximize individual and corporate profit, and to minimize recessionary contractions, capitalism has relied on continual economic expansion. While one would expect the GNP to grow consistent with the growth of population, the drive to maximize profits pushes greater efficiency from available resources and expansion of markets to maximize productivity. As production increases ever greater materials are required, straining, and often destroying, environmental resources. And, extensive industrial and agricultural production has created vast amounts of waste, including sludge, heavy metals, salts, and toxic chemicals that are released into the air, water, and soil.

While population in the United States grew by 39 percent between 1960 and 1990, GNP rose by 150 percent. This greater productivity came as a result of new technologies that made industrial processes more efficient, and production materials cheaper. But, this was not without a cost. During the same time energy consumption increased by 85 percent, and municipal solid waste generation increased by 91 percent—more than twice the rate of population growth. Moreover, the demand for natural resources jumped, illustrated by a 75 percent increase in timber extraction. And, the reliance on toxic chemicals soared, as illustrated by a 60 percent increase in pesticide use. Environmental stress is a net result of unbridled economic growth.

Furthermore, as a system of individual economic actors (including corporate actors), capitalism encourages pollution by punishing those who would clean and reduce waste with a reduced profit margin. It is far cheaper and easier to simply dump waste than to reduce, reuse, or reprocess it. Even those manufacturers who wish to be good corporate citizens are slow to employ pollution reduction technologies voluntarily, because to do so unilaterally would put those corporations at a competitive disadvantage. Pollution is an economic externality in that polluters are able to shift the cost of polluting to the society as a whole. While environmental degradation is certainly not unique to capitalist economies, as a system based on maximizing profit, capitalism is inconsistent with maintaining environmental quality. . . .

References

Appleby, Joyce. 1984. *Capitalism and a New Social Order.* New York: New York University Press.

Bellah, Robert, Richard Madsen, William Sullivan, Ann Swidler, and Steven Tipton. 1985. *Habits of the Heart: Individualism and Commitment in American Life*. Berkeley: University of California Press.
Downs, Anthony. 1957. *An Economic Theory of Democracy*. New York: Harper and Row.
Dye, Thomas R. 1986. *Who's Running America?* The Conservative Years. 4th edition. Englewood Cliffs, NJ: Prentice-Hall, Inc.
Hartz, Louis. 1955. *The Liberal Tradition in America*. New York: Harcourt Brace Jovanovich.
Kann, Mark E. 1991. *On the Man Question: Gender and Civic Virtue in America*. Philadelphia: Temple University Press.
Macpherson, C.B. 1962. *The Political Theory of Possessive Individualism: Hobbes to Locke*. London: Oxford University Press.
McWilliams, Wilson Cary. 1973. *The Idea of Fraternity in America*. Berkeley: University of California Press.
Mills, C.W. 1956. *The Power Elite*. Oxford: Oxford University Press.
Peters, B. Guy. 1993. *American Public Policy: Promise and Performance*. 3rd edition. Chatham, NJ: Chatham House Publishers.
Pocock, J.G.A. 1975. *The Machiavellian Moment: Florentine Political Thought and the Republican Tradition*. Princeton: Princeton University Press.
Rawls, John. 1971. *A Theory of Justice*. Cambridge, MA: The Belknap Press of Harvard University Press.
Schumpeter, Joseph. 1942. *Capitalism, Socialism, and Democracy*. New York: Harper and Row.
Wenz, Peter S. 1988. *Environmental Justice*. Albany: State University of New York Press.
Wilkerson, Isabel. 1991. "Blacks Wary of Their Big Role in the Military," *New York Times*. 25 December. A1.
Wood, Gordon. 1969. *The Creation of the American Republic, 1776–1787*. New York: W.W. Norton and Company.

Part III

The Green Critique

16

MATTHEW CAHN

The Green Critique: An Introduction

The emergence of green criticism did not begin with the environmental writers. Rather, as the earlier chapters illustrate, there has been a slow evolution of thought on nature and the physical world. Yet, there was a turning point in the mid-nineteenth century when a uniquely naturalist critique of the relationship between human civilization and the physical world emerged. The green critique reflects a nostalgia for a time that may never have existed but, like Locke's state of nature, provides a conceptual tool for assessing our current position. If early writers pondered uninhibitedly the human role in the physical world, it was a result of the unbridled optimism of an as yet undiscovered universe. As nature was subdued for human consumption, the issues of property and ownership became natural dilemmas. And, as industrial development unfolded, the contemporary environmental problematic emerged: identifying the ideal equilibrium between controlling nature and preserving nature. The environmental problematic only becomes more complex as knowledge of our physical world increases.

The Evolution of the Environmental Ethic

As early as 1851 Thoreau called for a reinterpretation of the significance of nature. As a transcendentalist, Thoreau saw the physical world—nature—as a reflection of spiritual truth and moral law (Nash 1990). In this sense nature, specifically wilderness, provides an antidote to the sterility, conformity, and predictability of "civilized" life: "I derive more of my subsistence from the swamps which surround my native town than from the cultivated gardens in the village. . . ." (Thoreau 1851). Thoreau's writings express the shortsightedness and ultimate vacuity of treasuring only the material potential of the natural environment. In this way Thoreau provides the intellectual foundation for the emerging preservationist movement. Emerson similarly saw the rejuvenating value of nature: "At the gates of the forest, the surprised man of the world is forced to leave his city estimates of great and small, wise and foolish. . . . Here is sanctity which shames our religions, and reality which discredits our heros" (Emerson 1985).

The systematic concern for environmental protection has evolved through the efforts of an intellectual tradition that traces its roots back a century and a half. As early as the 1860s, the need for sustaining forest resources was broadly discussed. Basic forest preservation was introduced through limited forest reserves in 1891, and selective cutting programs in 1897 (Caulfield 1989). The appearance of preservationism as distinct from traditional conservationism emerged during the presidency of Theodore Roosevelt. Conservationists have traditionally sought the development and regulation of natural resources, to ensure long-term resource extraction. On the other hand, the emerging preservationist movement sought to protect specific resources by banning development and resource extraction altogether. It was the preservationist movement that succeeded in setting aside Yosemite Valley as a state park in 1860 (designated as a national park in 1890), as well as the creation of Yellowstone National Park in 1872 (Cahn 1995).

The preservationist movement began in the West. Led by the San Francisco–based Sierra Club (established in 1892 by John Muir), preservationists met stiff resistance from ranching and mining interests who favored conservationists, but it managed to win the creation of the National Park Service in 1916. This was significant because it allowed for the transfer of public land from the Forest Service, a strictly conservationist agency, to the Park Service, an agency whose mandate was to preserve public lands. By the 1940s and 1950s public sentiment was strong enough to allow Congress to pass the federal water protection acts over the vetoes of presidents Truman and Eisenhower. And, by 1961, the Senate Select Committee on National Water Resources sought federal plain regulation as an alternative to flood control dams (Caulfield 1989).

The contemporary environmental movement coincided with the "new politics" of the Kennedy administration, bringing together preservationists and those concerned with the degrading urban environment. In his "Special Message to the Congress on Natural Resources," Kennedy articulated a concern with depleting resources. The message outlined the need for federal legislation protecting air, water, forests, topsoil, wildlife, seashores, and public lands for recreational use. Kennedy's secretary of the interior, Stewart Udall, became the administration's environmental torchbearer. He sought an increase in federal parklands, ordered the Fish and Wildlife Service to draft an endangered species act, and by 1964 turned the dull annual reports of the Interior Department into unusually colorful publications with a wide readership. Udall himself traveled the country giving speeches on behalf of his preservationist policies.

President Lyndon Johnson remained sensitive to the growing environmental constituency. In September 1964 the Land and Water Conservation Fund Act and the Wilderness Act were signed into law. The Water Quality Act establishing the Federal Water Pollution Control Administration was signed in 1965. The first Clean Air Act was adopted in 1965, and the Air Quality Act in 1967. The Endangered Species Act was signed in 1966 (and a revised act in 1969). And, finally, in October 1968, Johnson signed the Wild and Scenic Rivers Act and the National Trails System Act, and established the North Cascades National Park and Redwood National Park (Caulfield 1989).

Nixon's election to office slowed the early environmental momentum. His appointment to secretary of the interior was Walter Hickel, a former governor of Alaska who was more concerned with development than with environmental protection. In order to satisfy the Senate Interior Committee, Nixon ultimately appointed Russell Train, president of the Conservation Foundation, as undersecretary of the interior. Though Nixon was by no means an environmentalist, he was not prepared to fight a Congress aware of the growing environmental concern among the public. Hesitantly, the Nixon administration carried on the policies of his predecessors (Cahn 1995).

The growing strength of the grassroots environmental movement in the late 1960s came as a result of increasing urban pollution and numerous environmental mishaps, including the massive Santa Barbara oil spill in 1969. With the waning urgency of the anti–Vietnam War movement, much of the energy of the counterculture was retained by the growing environmental movement. Popular concern culminated on Earth Day (1970), observed on university campuses throughout the country. Earth Day was a celebration of the nurturance and beauty of the natural environment, and a day of education focusing on the difficult issues of environmental degradation. This growing salience was illustrated in the popularity of a number of books that held broad appeal, including Rachel Carson's *Silent Spring* (1962), Paul Erlich's *The Population Bomb* (1968), Charles Reich's *The Greening of America* (1970), and Barry Commoner's *The Closing Circle—Man, Nature, and Technology* (1971). Clearly, the environmental issue had become a permanent feature on the national agenda.

The Modern Environmental Critique

Silent Spring (1962) sounded the contemporary environmental siren. Rachel Carson, a noted naturalist writer, published several articles on the dangers of widespread insecticide use in the *New Yorker.* Following publication of *Silent Spring,* a palpable public concern emerged: "The most alarming of man's assaults upon the environment is the contamination of air, earth, rivers, and sea with dangerous and even lethal materials. . . . Chemicals are the sinister and little-recognized partners of radiation in changing the very nature of the world—the very nature of its life." Carson exposed the dangers of DDT, strontium 90, and a host of commonly used chemical pesticides and fertilizers. Her warnings had particular salience as urban air pollution reached unprecedented levels and the nation's most polluted waterways seemed to actually catch fire with increasing frequency. The public had a vague anxiety about environmental degradation that Carson gave language to. Pollution, ecology, and environmentalism merged into the 1960s vernacular, and concern for environmental degradation merged into our political culture.

As environmentalism became increasingly prominent, writers and scholars searched for causes and solutions. In *The Population Bomb* (1968) Ehrlich resurrected the Malthusian analysis that overpopulation leads to disaster. Thomas Malthus (1766–1834) wrote that population would inevitably increase faster than the food supply, leading to certain starvation unless birth control was widely used. Erhlich extends the Malthusian dilemma beyond mere famine to the environment generally: "In the United States . . . we hear constantly of the headaches caused by overpopulation: not just garbage in our environment, but overcrowded highways, burgeoning slums, deteriorating school systems, rising crime rates, riots. . . ." And, like many population theorists, Ehrlich extends greater responsibility for the problem to countries with high population rates.

Barry Commoner put the environmental message into a broader context, connecting environmental degradation and technology:

> We have long known that ours is a technological society, a society in which the knowledge generated by science is a chief source of wealth and power. But what the environmental crisis tells us is that the future of our society now depends on new, profoundly fundamental judgements of how this knowledge, and the power that it endows, is to be used. (Commoner 1970)

But it was *The Closing Circle* (1971) that brought greater public attention. Mystified by the sudden rediscovery of environmental degradation, Commoner reminded the public that, in fact, we are all responsible. Quoting Pogo, Commoner put it squarely: "We have met the enemy and he is us."

As with all movements, the emerging environmental movement did not speak with one voice. The deepest rift was seen between liberal environmentalists and their radical counterparts.[1] Arne Naess distinguished between these elements as shallow ecology and deep ecology. Shallow ecology fights against pollution but maintains a central focus on maintaining the health and affluence of those in developed nations. Deep ecology is an organic philosophy based on changing the entire relationship between human civilization and the natural world. Thus, in addition to fighting pollution and resource depletion, deep ecology asserts a "biospherical egalitarianism," based on the mutual respect of all species of plants and animals—the principle of ecological diversity. Further, deep ecology takes an anticlass posture, favoring instead economies that are small, local, and autonomous. Thus, while shallow ecology strives to improve our current lifestyle, deep ecology strives to change social interaction at its roots. In short, where shallow ecology remains anthropocentric, deep ecology is ecocentric.

Garrett Hardin sees causality in rational self-interest. Since each person is self-interested, he or she will act in a manner that maximizes self-benefit. This, more often than not, Hardin argues, is at the expense of the common good. Using the classic discourse on the commons, Hardin illustrates the inevitability of ecological destruction in an unregulated environment. The commons are those resources which all members of a society hold in common. Hardin supposes a large grassland commons, in which many people graze sheep. Self-interested shepherds recognize that they will enjoy individual benefits (more sheep to sell) by grazing greater numbers of sheep while the costs of grazing additional sheep (e.g., overgrazing) will be shared among all users of the commons. Eventually, of course, the commons will be destroyed through overgrazing. But this long-range consequence is inadequate to deny the short-term gains: "Ruin is the destination to which all men rush, each pursuing his own best interest in a society that believes in the freedom of the commons. Freedom in a commons brings ruin to all" (Hardin 1977). The tragedy of the commons extends in the contemporary discourse to air, water, national forests, and all public lands. Lacking external controls, rational, self-interested users will deplete such resources in a quest for personal gain.

Ynestra King offers a more complex analysis, arguing that ecology is a feminist issue. Feminism, at its core, negates patriarchal domination of society and of nature: "Either we take the anthropocentric position that nature exists solely to serve the needs of the male bourgeois who has crawled out of the slime to be lord and master of everything, or we take the naturalist position that nature has a purpose of its own apart from serving 'man' "(King 1981). This is not to say that "men" are responsible for all environmental destruction, but that patriarchy—the systematic domination of society by a hierarchically structured network of men—is incompatible with environmental sustenance.

In *The Ecology of Freedom* (1982) Murray Bookchin identifies a holistic ecology. Environmental degradation is a result, Bookchin reminds us, not only of misused technology, but of social dysfunction as well:

> ... social ecology provides more than a critique of the split between humanity and nature; it also poses the need to heal them. Indeed, it poses the need to radically transform them. ... In conceiving them holistically, that is to say, in terms of their mutual interdependence, social ecology seeks to unravel the forms and patterns of interrelationships that give intelligibility to a community, be it natural or social.

In this sense, social ecology seeks to heal the alienation within society, so as to make a more ecosensitive civilization possible.

Ultimately, however, the critical question remains: Why should we care about environmental degradation and biodiversity? Biologist E. O. Wilson comes right to the point:

> What difference does it make if some species are extinguished, if even half of all the species on earth disappear? Let me count the ways. New sources of information will be lost. Vast potential biological wealth will be destroyed. Still undeveloped medicines, crops, pharmaceuticals, timber, fibers, pulp, soil-restoring vegetation, petroleum substitutes, and other products and amenities will never come to light. (Wilson 1993, 347)

Life in this physical world is interdependent on all other species. Environmental quality and biodiversity, therefore, are not just a moral question or ethical dilemma but are a requisite for sustaining life.

The cost of environmental degradation is heavy. And, as Robert Bullard points out in *Confronting Environmental Racism* (1993), it is not shared equally. Technology and modern industrial processes create goods and services, as well as toxins and degradation. The traditional environmental debate focuses on finding a balance between the costs and the benefits. But what if the costs and the benefits are not shared equitably? Does this shift the context of the environmental discourse? Bullard argues that it does: "Whether by conscious design or institutional neglect, communities of color in urban ghettos, in rural 'poverty pockets,' or on economically impoverished Native-American reservations face some of the worst environmental devastation in the nation" (Bullard 1993). The disproportionate burden on minority communities is not only ethically unsustainable, but environmentally unsustainable. Bullard concludes that it is "unlikely that this nation will ever achieve lasting solutions to its environmental problems unless it also addresses the system of racial injustice that helps sustain the existence of powerless communities forced to bear disproportionate environmental costs."

The modern environmental critique expands the classical discourse on nature and the physical world—shifting from an equilibrium-based discourse to an ethical discourse. The earlier writers, reflected in the excerpts in Part I and Part II, are primarily concerned with the relationship between human civilization and the physical world, and ultimately between property rights and optimum resource allocation. In this sense, the early discourse remained within the anthropocentric paradigm. The environmental writers bring the discussion beyond the merely human-centered, to consider a host of material and ethical issues.

About This Section

The following chapters provide excerpts from these authors in an effort to provide the reader with tools for assessing the environmental problematic. Previous sections explored the role of nature and the physical world (Part I), and the evolving role of law and property (Part II). This section explores the environmental literature—the green critique (Part III). The final section explores strategies for resolving environmental degradation (Part IV: Accommodating the Future).

Note

1. The terms liberal and radical should not be misunderstood. Liberal, in this context, refers to the liberal capitalist tradition, as discussed at length in chapter 15. Radical, on the other hand, refers to those who see a problem at its roots.

References

Bookchin, Murray. 1982. *The Ecology of Freedom.* Palo Alto: Cheshire Books.
Bullard, Robert. 1993. *Confronting Environmental Racism.* Boston: South End Press.
Cahn, Matthew Alan. 1995. *Environmental Deceptions.* Albany: State University of New York Press.
Carson, Rachel. 1962. *Silent Spring.* Boston: Houghton Mifflin.
Caulfield, Henry. 1989. "The Conservation and Environmental Movements: An Historical Analysis." In *Environmental Politics and Policy: Theories and Evidence,* ed. James Lester. Durham, NC: Duke University Press.
Commoner, Barry. 1970. "Beyond the Teach-In," *Saturday Review* 53: 50–64.
———. 1971. *The Closing Circle—Man, Nature, and Technology.* New York: Knopf.
Emerson, Ralph Waldo. 1985. *Nature.* Boston: Beacon Press.
Erlich, Paul. 1968. *The Population Bomb.* New York: Ballantine.

Hardin, Garrett. 1977. "The Tragedy of the Commons." In *Managing the Commons,* ed. Garrett Hardin and John Baden. San Francisco: W.H. Freeman and Co.

King, Ynestra. 1981. "Feminism and the Revolt of Nature." *Heresies,* no. 13, 12–16.

Naess, Arne. 1973. "The Shallow and the Deep: The Long-Range Ecology Movement." *Inquiry* 16: 95–100.

Nash, Roderick Frazier. 1990. *American Environmentalism: Readings in Conservation History.* New York: McGraw-Hill Publishing Co.

Reich, Charles. 1970. *The Greening of America.* New York: Random House.

Thoreau, Henry David. [1851] 1893. "Walking." In *Excursions, The Writings of Henry David Thoreau.* Vol. 9. Riverside Edition. Boston: Houghton Mifflin.

Wilson, Edward O. 1993. *The Diversity of Life.* New York: W.W. Norton and Company.

17

Henry David Thoreau

Higher Laws

As I came home through the woods with my string of fish, trailing my pole, it being now quite dark, I caught a glimpse of a woodchuck stealing across my path, and felt a strange thrill of savage delight, and was strongly tempted to seize and devour him raw; not that I was hungry then, except for that wildness which he represented. Once or twice, however, while I lived at the pond, I found myself ranging the woods, like a half-starved hound, with a strange abandonment, seeking some kind of venison which I might devour, and no morsel could have been too savage for me. The wildest scenes had become unaccountably familiar. I found in myself, and still find, an instinct toward a higher, or, as it is named, spiritual life, as do most men, and another toward a primitive rank and savage one, and I reverence them both. I love the wild not less than the good. The wildness and adventure that are in fishing still recommended it to me. I like sometimes to take rank hold on life and spend my day more as the animals do. Perhaps I have owed to this employment and to hunting, when quite young, my closest acquaintance with Nature. They early introduce us to and detain us in scenery with which otherwise, at that age, we should have little acquaintance. Fishermen, hunters, wood-choppers, and others, spending their lives in the fields and woods, in a peculiar sense a part of Nature themselves, are often in a more favorable mood for observing her, in the intervals of their pursuits, than philosophers or poets even, who approach her with expectation. She is not afraid to exhibit herself to them. The traveller on the prairie is naturally a hunter, on the head waters of the Missouri and Columbia a trapper, and at the Falls of St. Mary a fisherman. He who is only a traveller learns things at second-hand and by the halves, and is poor authority. We are most interested when science reports what those men already know practically or

---

From Henry David Thoreau, *Walden.*

instinctively, for that alone is a true *humanity*, or account of human experience.

They mistake who assert that the Yankee has few amusements, because he has not so many public holidays, and men and boys do not play so many games as they do in England, for here the more primitive but solitary amusements of hunting, fishing, and the like have not yet given place to the former. Almost every New England boy among my contemporaries shouldered a fowling-piece between the ages of ten and fourteen; and his hunting and fishing grounds were not limited, like the preserves of an English nobleman, but were more boundless even than those of a savage. No wonder, then, that he did not oftener stay to play on the common. But already a change is taking place, owing, not to an increased humanity, but to an increased scarcity of game, for perhaps the hunter is the greatest friend of the animals hunted, not excepting the Humane Society.

Moreover, when at the pond, I wished sometimes to add fish to my fare for variety. I have actually fished from the same kind of necessity that the first fishers did. Whatever humanity I might conjure up against it was all factitious, and concerned my philosophy more than my feelings. I speak of fishing only now, for I had long felt differently about fowling, and sold my gun before I went to the woods. Not that I am less humane than others, but I did not perceive that my feelings were much affected. I did not pity the fishes nor the worms. This was habit. As for fowling, during the last years that I carried a gun my excuse was that I was studying ornithology, and sought only new or rare birds. But I confess that I am now inclined to think that there is a finer way of studying ornithology than this. It requires so much closer attention to the habits of the birds, that, if for that reason only, I have been willing to omit the gun. Yet notwithstanding the objection on the score of humanity, I am compelled to doubt if equally valuable sports are ever substituted for these; and when some of my friends have asked me anxiously about their boys, whether they should let them hunt, I have answered, yes—remembering that it was one of the best parts of my education—make them hunters, though sportsmen only at first, if possible, mighty hunters at last, so that they shall not find game large enough for them in this or any vegetable wilderness—hunters as well as fishers of men. Thus far I am of the opinion of Chaucer's nun, who

> "yave not of the text a pulled hen
> That saith that hunters ben not holy men."

There is a period in the history of the individual, as of the race, when the hunters are the "best men," as the Algonquins called them. We cannot but pity the boy who has never fired a gun; he is no more humane, while his education has been sadly neglected. This was my answer with respect to those youths who were bent on this pursuit, trusting that they would soon outgrow it. No humane being, past the thoughtless age of boyhood, will want only to murder any creature which holds its life by the same tenure that he does. The hare in its extremity cries like a child. I warn you, mothers, that my sympathies do not always make the usual *philanthropic* distinctions.

Such is oftenest the young man's introduction to the forest, and the most original part of himself. He goes thither at first as a hunter and fisher, until at last, if he has the seeds of a better life in him, he distinguishes his proper objects, as a poet or naturalist it may be, and leaves the gun and fish-pole behind. The mass of men are still and always young in this respect. In some countries a hunting parson is no uncommon sight. Such a one might make a good shepherd's dog, but is far from being the Good Shepherd. I have been surprised to consider that the only obvious employment, except wood-chopping, ice-cutting, or the like business, which ever to my knowledge detained at Walden Pond for a whole half-day any of my fellow-citizens, whether fathers or children of the town, with just one exception, was fishing. Commonly they did not think that they were lucky, or well paid for their time, unless they got a long string of fish, though they had the opportunity of seeing the pond all the while. They might go there a thousand times before the sediment of fishing would sink to the bottom and leave their purpose pure; but no doubt such a clarifying process would be going on all the while. The Governor and his Council faintly remember the pond, for they went a-fishing there when they were boys; but now they are too old and dignified to go a-fishing, and so they know it no more forever. Yet even they expect to go to heaven at last. If the legislature regards it, it is chiefly to regulate the number of books to be used there; but they know nothing about the hook of hooks with which to angle for the pond itself, impaling the legislature for a bait. Thus, even in civilized communities, the embryo man passes through the hunter stage of development.

I have found repeatedly, of late years, that I cannot fish without falling a little in self-respect. I have tried it again and again. I have skill at it, and, like many of my fellows, a certain instinct for it, which revives from time to time, but always when I have done I feel that it would have been better if I had not fished. I think that I do not mistake. It is a faint intimation, yet so are the first streaks of morning. There is unquestionably this instinct in me which belongs to the lower orders of creation; yet with every year I am less a fisherman, though without more humanity or even wisdom; at present I am no fisherman at all. But I see that if I were to live in a wilderness I should again be tempted to become a fisher and hunter in earnest. Besides, there is something essentially unclean about this diet and all flesh, and I began to see where housework commences, and whence the endeavor, which costs too much, to wear a tidy and respectable appearance each day, to keep the house sweet and free from all ill odors and sights. Having been my own butcher and scullion and cook, as well as the gentleman for whom the dishes were served up, I can speak from an unusually complete experience. The practical objection to animal food in my case was its uncleanness; and besides, when I had caught and cleaned and cooked and eaten my fish, they seemed not to have fed me essentially. It was insignificant and unnecessary, and cost more than it came to. A little bread or a few potatoes would have done as well, with less trouble and filth. Like many of my contemporaries, I had rarely for many years used animal food, or tea, or coffee, etc.; not so much because of any ill effects which I had traced to them, as because they were not agreeable to my imagination. The repugnance to animal food is not the effect of experience, but is an instinct. It appeared more beautiful to live low and fare hard in many respects; and though I never did so, I went far enough to please my imagination. I believe that every man who has ever been earnest to preserve his higher or poetic faculties in the best condition has been particularly inclined to abstain from animal food, and from much food of any kind. It is a significant fact, stated by entomologists—I find it in Kirby and Spence—that "some insects in their perfect state, though furnished with organs of feeding, make no use of them"; and they lay it down a "general rule, that almost all insects in this state eat much less than in that of larvae. The voracious caterpillar when transformed into a butterfly . . . and the gluttonous maggot when become a fly" content themselves with a drop or two of honey or some other sweet liquid. The abdomen under the wings of the butterfly still represents the larva. This is the tidbit which tempts his insectivorous fate. The gross feeder is a man in the larva state; and there are whole nations in that condition, nations without fancy or imagination, whose vast abdomens betray them.

It is hard to provide and cook so simple and clean a diet as will not offend the imagination; but this, I think, is to be fed when we feed the body; they should both sit down at the same table. Yet perhaps this may be done. The fruits eaten temperately need not make us ashamed of our appetites, nor interrupt the worthiest pursuits. But put an extra condiment into your dish, and it will poison you. It is not worth the while to live by rich cookery. Most men would feel shame if caught preparing with their own hands precisely such a dinner, whether of animal or vegetable food, as is every day prepared for them by others. Yet till this is otherwise we are not civilized, and, if gentlemen and ladies, are not true men and women. This certainly suggests what change is to be made. It may be vain to ask why the imagination will not be reconciled to flesh and fat. I am satisfied that it is not. Is it not a reproach that man is a carnivorous animal? True, he can and does live, in a great measure, by preying on other animals; but this is a miserable way—as any one who will go to snaring rabbits, or slaughtering lambs, may learn—and he will be regarded as a benefactor of his race who shall teach man to confine himself to a more innocent and wholesome diet. Whatever my own practice may be, I have no doubt that it is a part of the destiny of the human race, in its gradual improvement, to leave off eating animals, as surely as the savage tribes have left off eating each other when they came in contact with the more civilized.

If one listens to the faintest but constant suggestions of his genius, which are certainly true, he sees not to what extremes, or even insanity, it may lead him; and yet that way, as he grows more resolute and faithful, his road lies. The faintest assured objection which one healthy man feels will at length prevail over the arguments and customs of mankind. No man ever followed his genius till it misled him. Though the result were bodily weakness, yet perhaps no one can say that the consequences were to be regretted, for these were a life in conformity to higher principles. If the day and the night are such that you greet them with joy, and life emits a fragrance like flowers and sweet-scented herbs, is more elastic, more starry, more immortal—that is your success. All nature is your congratulation, and you have cause momentarily to bless yourself. The greatest gains and values are farthest from being appreciated. We easily come to doubt if they exist. We soon forget them. They are the highest reality. Perhaps the facts most astounding and most real are never communicated by man to man. The true harvest of my daily life is somewhat as intangible and indescribable as the tints of morning or evening. It is a little star-dust caught, a segment of the rainbow which I have clutched.

Our whole life is startlingly moral. There is never an instant's truce between virtue and vice. Goodness is the only investment that never fails. In the music of the harp which trembles round the world it is the insisting on this which thrills us. The harp is the travelling patterer for the Universe's Insurance Company, recommending its law, and our little goodness is all the assessment that we pay. Though the youth at last grows indifferent, the laws of the universe are not indifferent, but are forever on the side of the most sensitive. Listen to every zephyr for some reproof, for it is surely there, and he is unfortunate who does not hear it. We cannot touch a string or move a stop but the charming moral transfixes us. Many an irksome noise, go a long way off, is heard as music, a proud, sweet satire on the meanness of our lives.

We are conscious of an animal in us, which awakens in proportion as our higher nature slumbers. It is reptile and sensual, and perhaps cannot be wholly expelled; like the worms which, even in life and health, occupy our bodies. Possibly we may withdraw from it, but never change its nature. I fear that it may enjoy a certain health of its own; that we may be well, yet not pure. The other day I picked up the lower jaw of a hog, with white and sound teeth and tusks, which suggested that there was an animal health and vigor distinct from the spiritual. This creature succeeded by other means than temperance and purity. "That in which men differ from brute beasts," says Mencius, "is a thing very inconsiderable; the common herd lose it very soon; superior men preserve it carefully." Who knows what sort of life would result if we had attained to purity? If I knew so wise a man he could teach me purity I would go to seek him forthwith. "A command over our passions, and over the external senses of the body, and good acts, are declared by the Ved to be indispensable in the mind's approximation to God." Yet the spirit can for the time pervade and control every member and function of the body, and transmute what in form is the grossest sensuality into purity and devotion. The generative energy, which, when we are loose, dissipates and makes us unclean, when we are continent invigorates and inspires us. Chastity is the flowering of man; and what are called Genius, Heroism, Holiness, and the like, are but various fruits which succeed it. Man flows at once to God when the channel of purity is open. By turns our purity inspires and our impurity casts us down. He is blessed who is assured that the animal is dying out in him day by day, and the divine being established. Perhaps there is none but has cause for shame on account of the inferior and brutish nature to which he is allied. I fear that we are such gods or demigods only as fauns and satyrs, the divine allied to beasts, the creatures of appetite, and that, to some extent, our very life is our disgrace.

> "How happy's he who hath due place assigned
> To his beasts and disafforested his mind!
> Can use his horse, goat, wolf, and ev'ry beast,
> And is not ass himself to all the rest!
> Else man not only is the herd of swine,
> But he's those devils too which did incline
> Them to a headlong rage, and made them worse."

All sensuality is one, though it takes many forms; all purity is one. It is the same whether a man eat, or drink, or cohabit, or sleep sensually. They are but one appetite, and we only need to see a person do any one of these things to know how great a sensualist he is. The impure can neither stand nor sit with purity. When the reptile is attacked at one mouth of his burrow, he shows himself at another. If you would be chaste, you must be temperate. What is chastity? How shall a man know if he is chaste? He shall not know it. We have heard of this virtue, but we know not what it is. We speak conformably to the rumor which we have heard. From exertion come wisdom and purity; from sloth ignorance and sensuality. In the student sensuality is a sluggish habit of mind. An unclean person is universally a slothful one, one who sits by a stove, whom the sun shines on prostrate, who reposes without being fatigued. If you would avoid uncleanness, and all the sins, work earnestly, though it be at cleaning a stable. Nature is hard to be overcome, but she must be overcome. What avails it that you are Christian, if you are not purer than the heathen, if you deny yourself no more, religious? I know of many systems of religion esteemed heathenish whose precepts fill the reader with shame, and provoke him to new endeavors, though it be to the performance of rites merely.

I hesitate to say these things, but it is not because of the subject—I care not how obscene my *words* are—but because I cannot speak of them without betraying my impurity. We discourse freely without shame of one form of sensuality, and are silent about another. We are so degraded that we cannot speak simply of the necessary functions of human nature. In earlier ages, in some countries, every function was reverently spoken of and regulated by law. Nothing was too trivial for the Hindoo lawgiver, however offensive it may be to modern taste. He teaches how to eat, drink, cohabit, void excrement and urine and the like, elevating what is mean, and does not falsely excuse himself by calling these things trifles.

Every man is the builder of a temple, called his body, to the god he worships, after a style purely his own, nor can he get off by hammering marble instead. We are all sculptors and painters, and our material is our own flesh and blood and bones. Any nobleness begins at once to refine a man's features, any meanness or sensuality to imbrute them.

John Farmer sat at his door one September evening, after a hard day's works, his mind still running on his labor more or less. Having bathed, he sat down to re-create his intellectual man. It was a rather cool evening, and some of his neighbors were apprehending a frost. He had not attended to the train of his thoughts long when he heard some one playing on a flute, and that sound harmonized with his mood. Still he thought of his work; but the burden of his thought was, that though this kept running in his head, and he found himself planning and contriving it against his will, yet it concerned him very little. It was no more than the scurf of his skin, which was constantly shuffled off. But the notes of the flute came home to his ears out of a different sphere from that he worked in, and suggested work for certain faculties which slumbered in him. They gently did away with the street, and the village, and the state in which he lived. A voice said to him—Why do you stay here and live this mean moiling life, when a glorious existence is possible for you? Those same stars twinkle over other fields than these. But how to come out of his condition and actually migrate thither? All that he could think of was to practise some new austerity, to let his mind descend into his body and redeem it, and treat himself with ever increasing respect.

18

Ralph Waldo Emerson

Nature

There are days which occur in this climate, at almost any season of the year, wherein the world reaches its perfection, when the air, the heavenly bodies, and the earth, make a harmony, as if nature would indulge her offspring; when, in these bleak upper sides of the planet, nothing is to desire that we have heard of the happiest latitudes, and we bask in the shining hours of Florida and Cuba; when everything that has life gives sign of satisfaction, and the cattle that lie on the ground seem to have great and tranquil thoughts. These halcyons may be looked for with a little more assurance in that pure October weather, which we distinguish by the name of the Indian Summer. The day, immeasurably long, sleeps over the broad hills and warm wide fields. To have lived through all its sunny hours, seems longevity enough. The solitary places do not seem quite lonely. At the gates of the forest, the surprised man of the world is forced to leave his city estimates of great and small, wise and foolish. The knapsack of custom falls off his back with the first step he makes into these precincts. Here is sanctity which shames our religions, and reality which discredits our heroes. Here we find nature to be the circumstance which dwarfs every other circumstance, and judges like a god all men that come to her. . . .

These enchantments are medicinal, they sober and heal us. These are plain pleasures, kindly and native to us. We come to our own, and make friends with matter, which the ambitious chatter of the schools would persuade us to despise. We never can part with it; the mind loves its old home: as water to our thirst, so is the rock, the ground, to our eyes, and hands, and feet. It is firm water: it is cold flame: what health, what affinity! Ever an old

From Ralph Waldo Emerson, *Emerson's Essays.*

friend, ever like a dear friend and brother, when we chat affectedly with strangers, comes in this honest face, and takes a grave liberty with us, and shames us out of our nonsense. Cities give not the human senses room enough. We go out daily and nightly to feed the eyes on the horizon, and require so much scope, just as we need water for our bath. There are all degrees of natural influence, from these quarantine powers of nature, up to her dearest and gravest ministrations to the imagination and the soul. There is the bucket of cold water from the spring, the wood-fire to which the chilled traveler rushes for safety—and there is the sublime moral of autumn and of noon. We nestle in nature, and draw our living as parasites from her roots and grains, and we receive glances from the heavenly bodies, which call us to solitude, and foretell the remotest future. . . .

My house stands in low land, with limited outlook, and on the skirt of the village. But I go with my friend to the shore of our little river; and with one stroke of the paddle, I leave the village politics and personalities, yes, and the world of villages and personalities behind, and pass into a delicate realm of sunset and moonlight, too bright almost for spotted man to enter without noviciate and probation. . . .

Nature is always consistent, though she feigns to contravene her own laws. She keeps her laws, and seems to transcend them. She arms and equips an animal to find its place and living in the earth, and, at the same time, she arms and equips another animal to destroy it. Space exists to divide creatures; but by clothing the sides of a bird with a few feathers, she gives him a petty omnipresence. The direction is forever onward, but the artist still goes back for materials, and begins again with the first elements on the most advanced stage: otherwise, all goes to ruin. Plants are the young of the world, vessels of health and vigor; but they grope ever upward toward consciousness; the trees are imperfect men, and seem to bemoan their imprisonment, rooted in the ground. The animal is the novice and probationer of a more advanced order. The men, though young, having tasted the first drop from the cup of thought, are already dissipated: the maples and ferns are still uncorrupt; yet no doubt, when they come to consciousness, they too will curse and swear. Flowers so strictly belong to youth, that we adult men soon come to feel, that their beautiful generations concern not us: we have had our day; now let the children have theirs. The flowers jilts us, and we are old bachelors with our ridiculous tenderness.

There is throughout nature something mocking, something that leads us on and on, but arrives nowhere, keeps no faith with us. All promise outruns the performance. We live in a system of approximations. Every end is prospective of some other end, which is also temporary; a round and final success nowhere. We are encamped in nature, not domesticated. Hunger and thirst lead us on to eat and to drink; but bread and wine, mix and cook them how you will, leave us hungry and thirsty, after the stomach is full. It is the same with all our arts and performances. Our music, our poetry, our language itself are not satisfactions, but suggestions. The hunger for wealth, which reduces the planet to a garden, fools the eager pursuer.

19

Rachel Carson

Silent Spring

The history of life on earth has been a history of interaction between living things and their surroundings. To a large extent, the physical form and the habits of the earth's vegetation and its animal life have been molded by the environment. Considering the whole span of earthly time, the opposite effect, in which life actually modifies its surroundings, has been relatively slight. Only within the moment of time represented by the present century has one species—man—acquired significant power to alter the nature of his world.

During the past quarter century this power has not only increased to one of disturbing magnitude but it has changed in character. The most alarming of all man's assaults upon the environment is the contamination of air, earth, rivers, and sea with dangerous and even lethal materials. This pollution is for the most part irrecoverable; the chain of evil it initiates not only in the world that must support life but in living tissues is for the most part irreversible. In this now universal contamination of the environment, chemicals are the sinister and little-recognized partners of radiation in changing the very nature of the world—the very nature of its life. Strontium 90, released through nuclear explosions into the air, comes to earth in rain or drifts down as fallout, lodges in soil, enters into the grass or corn or wheat grown there, and in time takes up its abode in the bones of a human being, there to remain until his death. Similarly, chemicals sprayed on croplands or forests or gardens lie long in soil, entering into living organisms, passing from one to another in a chain of poisoning and death. Or they pass mysteriously by underground streams until they emerge and, through the alchemy of air and sunlight, combine into new forms that kill vegetation, sicken

---

cattle, and work unknown harm on those who drink from once pure wells. As Albert Schweitzer has said, "Man can hardly even recognize the devils of his own creation."

It took hundreds of millions of years to produce the life that now inhabits the earth—eons of time in which that developing and evolving and diversifying life reached a state of adjustment and balance with its surroundings. The environment, rigorously shaping and directing the life it supported, contained elements that were hostile as well as supporting. Certain rocks gave out dangerous radiation; even within the light of the sun, from which all life draws its energy, there were short-wave radiations with power to injure. Given time—time not in years but in millennia—life adjusts, and a balance has been reached. For time is the essential ingredient; but in the modern world there is no time.

The rapidity of change and the speed with which new situations are created follow the impetuous and heedless pace of man rather than the deliberate pace of nature. Radiation is no longer merely the background radiation of rocks, the bombardment of cosmic rays, the ultraviolet of the sun that have existed before there was any life on earth; radiation is now the unnatural creation of man's tampering with the atom. The chemicals to which life is asked to make its adjustment are no longer merely the calcium and silica and copper and all the rest of the minerals washed out of the rocks and carried in rivers to the sea; they are the synthetic creations of man's inventive mind, brewed in his laboratories, and having no counterparts in nature.

To adjust to these chemicals would require time on the scale that is nature's; it would require not merely the years of a man's life but the life of generations. And even this, were it by some miracle possible, would be futile, for the new chemicals come from our laboratories in endless stream; almost 500 annually find their way into actual use in the United States alone. The figure is staggering and its implications are not easily grasped—500 new chemicals to which the bodies of men and animals are required somehow to adapt each year, chemicals totally outside the limits of biologic experience.

Among them are many that are used in man's war against nature. Since the mid-1940s over 200 basic chemicals have been created for use in killing insects, weeds, rodents, and other organisms described in the modern vernacular as "pests"; and they are sold under several thousand different brand names.

These sprays, dusts, and aerosols are now applied almost universally to farms, gardens, forests, and homes—nonselective chemicals that have the power to kill every insect, the "good" and the "bad," to still the song of birds and the leaping of fish in the streams, to coat the leaves with a deadly film, and to linger on in soil—all this though the intended target may be only a few weeds or insects. Can anyone believe it is possible to lay down such a barrage of poisons on the surface of the earth without making it unfit for all life? They should not be called "insecticides," but "biocides."

The whole process of spraying seems caught up in an endless spiral. Since DDT was released for civilian use, a process of escalation has been going on in which ever more toxic materials must be found. This has happened because insects, in a triumphant vindication of Darwin's principle of the survival of the fittest, have evolved super races immune to the particular insecticide used, hence a deadlier one has always to be developed—and then a deadlier one than that. It has happened also because for reasons to be described later, destructive insects often undergo a "flareback," or resurgence, after spraying, in numbers greater than before. Thus the chemical war is never won, and all life is caught in its violent crossfire.

Along with the possibility of the extinction of mankind by nuclear war, the central problem of our age has therefore become the contamination of man's total environment with such substances of incredible potential for harm—substances that accumulate in the tissues of plants and animals and even penetrate the germ cells to shatter or alter the very material of heredity upon which the shape of the future depends.

Some would-be architects of our future look toward a time when it will be possible to alter the human germ plasm by design. But we may easily be doing so now by inadvertence, for many chemicals, like radiation, bring about gene mutations. It is ironic to think that man might determine his own future by something so seemingly trivial as the choice of an insect spray.

All this has been risked—for what? Future historians may well be amazed by our distorted sense of proportion. How could intelligent beings seek to control a few unwanted species by a method that contaminated the entire environment and brought the threat of disease and death even to their own kind? Yet this is precisely what we have done. We have done it, moreover, for reasons that collapse the moment we examine them. We are told that the enormous and expanding use of pesticides is necessary to maintain farm production. Yet is our real problem not one of *overproduction?* Our farms, despite measures to remove acreages from production and to pay farmers *not* to produce, have yielded such a staggering excess of crops that the American taxpayer in 1962 is paying out more than one billion dollars a year as the total carrying cost of the surplus-food storage program. And is the situation helped when one branch of the Agriculture Department tries to reduce production while another states, as it did in

1958, "It is believed generally that reduction of crop acreages under provisions of the Soil Bank will stimulate interest in use of chemicals to obtain maximum production on the land retained in crops."

All this is not to say there is no insect problem and no need of control. I am saying, rather, that control must be geared to realities, not to mythical situations, and that the methods employed must be such that they do not destroy us along with the insects.

The problem whose attempted solution has brought such a train of disaster in its wake is an accompaniment of our modern way of life. Long before the age of man, insects inhabited the earth—a group of extraordinarily varied and adaptable beings. Over the course of time since man's advent, a small percentage of the more than half a million species of insects have come into conflict with human welfare in two principal ways: as competitors for the food supply and as carriers of human disease.

Disease-carrying insects become important where human beings are crowded together, especially under conditions where sanitation is poor, as in time of natural disaster or war or in situations of extreme poverty and deprivation. Then control of some sort becomes necessary. It is a sobering fact, however, as we shall presently see, that the method of massive chemical control has had only limited success, and also threatens to worsen the very conditions it is intended to curb.

Under primitive agricultural conditions the farmer had few insect problems. These arose with the intensification of agriculture—the devotion of immense acreages to a single crop. Such a system set the stage for explosive increases in specific insect populations. Single-crop farming does not take advantage of the principles by which nature works; it is agriculture as an engineer might conceive it to be. Nature has introduced great variety into the landscape, but man has displayed a passion for simplifying it. Thus he undoes the built-in checks and balances by which nature holds the species within bounds. One important natural check is a limit on the amount of suitable habitat for each species. Obviously then, an insect that lives on wheat can build up its population to much higher levels on a farm devoted to wheat than on one in which wheat is intermingled with other crops to which the insect is not adapted.

The same thing happens in other situations. A generation or more ago, the towns of large areas of the United States lined their streets with the noble elm tree. Now the beauty they hopefully created is threatened with complete destruction as disease sweeps through the elms, carried by a beetle that would have only limited chance to build up large populations and to spread from tree to tree if the elms were only occasional trees in a richly diversified planting.

Another factor in the modern insect problem is one that must be viewed against a background of geologic and human history: the spreading of thousands of different kinds of organisms from their native homes to invade new territories. This worldwide migration has been studied and graphically described by the British ecologist Charles Elton in his recent book *The Ecology of Invasions*. During the Cretaceous Period, some hundred million years ago, flooding seas cut many land bridges between continents and living things found themselves confined in what Elton calls "colossal separate nature reserves." There, isolated from others of their kind, they developed many new species. When some of the land masses were joined again, about 15 million years ago, these species began to move out into new territories—a movement that is not only still in progress but is now receiving considerable assistance from man.

The importation of plants is the primary agent in the modern spread of species, for animals have almost invariably gone along with the plants, quarantine being a comparatively recent and not completely effective innovation. The United States Office of Plant Introduction alone has introduced almost 200,000 species and varieties of plants from all over the world. Nearly half of the 180 or so major insect enemies of plants in the United States are accidental imports from abroad, and most of them have come as hitchhikers on plants.

In new territory, out of reach of the restraining hand of the natural enemies that kept down its numbers in its native land, an invading plant or animal is able to become enormously abundant. Thus it is no accident that our most troublesome insects are introduced species.

These invasions, both the naturally occurring and those dependent on human assistance, are likely to continue indefinitely. Quarantine and massive chemical campaigns are only extremely expensive ways of buying time. We are faced, according to Dr. Elton, "with a life-and-death need not just to find new technological means of suppressing this plant or that animal"; instead we need the basic knowledge of animal populations and their relations to their surroundings that will "promote an even balance and damp down the explosive power of outbreaks and new invasions."

Much of the necessary knowledge is now available but we do not use it. We train ecologists in our universities and even employ them in our governmental agencies but we seldom take their advice. We allow the chemical death rain to fall as though there were no alternative, whereas in fact there are many, and our ingenuity could soon discover many more if given opportunity.

Have we fallen into a mesmerized state that makes us accept as inevitable that which is inferior or detrimental, as though having lost the will or the vision to demand that which is good? Such thinking, in the words of the ecologist Paul Shepard, "idealizes life with only its head out of water, inches above the limits of toleration of the corruption of its own environment. . . . Why should we tolerate a diet of weak poisons, a home in insipid surroundings, a circle of acquaintances who are not quite our enemies, the noise of motors with just enough relief to prevent insanity? Who would want to live in a world which is just not quite fatal?"

Yet such a world is pressed upon us. The crusade to create a chemically sterile, insect-free world seems to have engendered a fanatic zeal on the part of many specialists and most of the so-called control agencies. On every hand there is evidence that those engaged in spraying operations exercise a ruthless power. "The regulatory entomologists . . . function as prosecutor, judge and jury, tax assessor and collector and sheriff to enforce their own orders," said Connecticut entomologist Neely Turner. The most flagrant abuses go unchecked in both state and federal agencies.

It is not my contention that chemical insecticides must never be used. I do contend that we have put poisonous and biologically potent chemicals indiscriminately into the hands of persons largely or wholly ignorant of their potentials for harm. We have subjected enormous numbers of people to contact with these poisons, without their consent and often without their knowledge. If the Bill of Rights contains no guarantee that a citizen shall be secure against lethal poisons distributed either by private individuals or by public officials, it is surely only because our forefathers, despite their considerable wisdom and foresight, could conceive of no such problem.

I contend, furthermore, that we have allowed these chemicals to be used with little or no advance investigation of their effect on soil, water, wildlife, and man himself. Future generations are unlikely to condone our lack of prudent concern for the integrity of the natural world that supports all life.

There is still very limited awareness of the nature of the threat. This is an era of specialists, each of whom sees his own problem and is unaware of or intolerant of the larger frame into which it fits. It is also an era dominated by industry, in which the right to make a dollar at whatever cost is seldom challenged. When the public protests, confronted with some obvious evidence of damaging results of pesticide applications, it is fed little tranquilizing pills of half truth. We urgently need an end to these false assurances, to the sugar coating of unpalatable facts. It is the public that is being asked to assume the risks that the insect controllers calculate. The public must decide whether it wishes to continue on the present road, and it can do so only when in full possession of the facts. In the words of Jean Rostand, "The obligation to endure gives us the right to know."

20

PAUL EHRLICH

The Population Bomb

Americans are beginning to realize that the undeveloped countries of the world face an inevitable population–food crisis. Each year food production in undeveloped countries falls a bit further behind burgeoning population growth, and people go to bed a little bit hungrier. While there are temporary or local reversals of this trend, it now seems inevitable that it will continue to its logical conclusion: mass starvation. The rich are going to get richer, but the more numerous poor are going to get poorer. Of these poor, a minimum of three and one-half million will starve to death this year, mostly children. But this is a mere handful compared to the numbers that will be starving in a decade or so. And it is now too late to take action to save many of those people.

In a book about population there is a temptation to stun the reader with an avalanche of statistics. I'll spare you most, but not all, of that. After all, no matter how you slice it, population is a numbers game. Perhaps the best way to impress you with numbers is to tell you about the "doubling time"—the time necessary for the population to double in size.

It has been estimated that the human population of 6000 B.C. was about five million people, taking perhaps one million years to get there from two and a half million. The population did not reach 500 million until almost 8,000 years later—about 1650 A.D. This means it doubled roughly once every thousand years or so. It reached a billion people around 1850, doubling in some 200 years. It took only 80 years or so for the next doubling, as the population reached two billion around 1930. We have not completed the next doubling to four billion yet, but we now have well over three billion people. The doubling time at present seems to be about 37 years.

Quite a reduction in doubling time: 1,000,000 years, 1,000 years, 200 years, 80 years, 37 years. Perhaps the meaning of a doubling time of around 37 years is best brought home by a theoretical exercise. Let's examine what might happen on the absurd assumption that the population continued to double every 37 years into the indefinite future.

If growth continued at that rate for about 900 years, there would be some 6,000,000,000,000,000 people on the face of the earth. Sixty million billion people. This is about 100 persons for each square yard of the Earth's surface, land and sea. A British physicist, J.H. Fremlin, guessed that such a multitude might be housed in a continuous 2,000-story building covering our entire planet. The upper 1,000 stories would contain only the apparatus for running this gigantic warren. Ducts, pipes, wires, elevator shafts, etc., would occupy about half of the space in the bottom 1,000 stories. This would leave three or four yards of floor space for each person. I will leave to your imagination the physical details of existence in this ant heap, except to point out that all would not be black. Probably each person would be limited in his travel. Perhaps he could take elevators through all 1,000 residential stories but could travel only within a circle of a few hundred yards' radius on any floor. This would permit, however, each person to choose his friends from among some ten million people! And, as Fremlin points out, entertainment on the worldwide TV should be excellent, for at any time "one could expect some ten million Shakespeares and rather more Beatles to be alive."

Could growth of the human population of the Earth continue beyond that point? Not according to Fremlin. We would have reached a "heat-limit." People themselves, as well as their activities, convert other forms of energy into heat which must be dissipated. In order to permit this excess heat to radiate directly from the top of the "world building" directly into space, the atmosphere would have been pumped into flasks under the sea well before the limiting population size was reached. The precise limit would depend on the technology of the day. At a population size of one billion people, the temperature of the "world roof" would be kept around the melting point of iron to radiate away the human heat generated.

But, you say, surely Science (with a capital "S") will find a way for us to occupy the other planets of our solar system and eventually of other stars before we get all that crowded. Skip for a moment the virtual certainty that those planets are uninhabitable. Forget also the insurmountable logistic problems of moving billions of people off the Earth. Fremlin has made some interesting calculations on how much time we could buy by occupying the planets of the solar system. For instance, at any given time it would take only about 50 years to populate Venus, Mercury, Mars, the moon, and the moons of Jupiter and Saturn to the same population density as Earth.

What if the fantastic problems of reaching and colonizing the other planets of the solar system, such as Jupiter and Uranus, can be solved? It would take only about 200 years to fill them "Earth-full." So we could perhaps gain 250 years of time for population growth in the solar system after we had reached an absolute limit on Earth. What then? We can't ship our surplus to the stars. Professor Garrett Hardin of the University of California at Santa Barbara has dealt effectively with this fantasy. Using extremely optimistic assumptions, he has calculated that Americans, by cutting their standard of living down to 18 percent of its present level, could in one year set aside enough capital to finance the exportation to the stars of *one day's* increase in the population of the world.

Interstellar transport for surplus people presents an amusing prospect. Since the ships would take generations to reach most stars, the only people who could be transported would be those willing to exercise strict birth control. Population explosions on space ships would be disastrous. Thus we would have to export our responsible people, leaving the irresponsible at home on Earth to breed.

Enough of fantasy. Hopefully, you are convinced that the population will have to stop growing sooner or later and that the extremely remote possibility of expanding into outer space offers no escape from the laws of population growth. If you still want to hope for the stars, just remember that, at the current growth rate, in a few thousand years everything in the visible universe would be converted into people, and the ball of people would be expanding with the speed of light! Unfortunately, even 900 years is much too far in the future for those of us concerned with the population explosion. As you shall see, the next nine years will probably tell the story.

Of course, population growth is not occurring uniformly over the face of the Earth. Indeed, countries are divided rather neatly into two groups: those with rapid growth rates, and those with relatively slow growth rates. The first group, making up about two-thirds of the world population, coincides closely with what are known as the "underdeveloped countries" (UDCs). The UDCs are not industrialized, tend to have inefficient agriculture, very small gross national products, high illiteracy rates, and related problems. That's what UDCs are technically, but a short definition of undeveloped is "starving." Most Latin American, African, and Asian countries fall into this category. The second group consists, in essence, of the "developed countries" (DCs). DCs are modern, industrial nations, such as the United States, Canada, most European countries, Israel, Russia, Japan, and Australia. Most people in these countries are adequately nourished.

Doubling times in the UDCs range around 20 to 35 years. Examples of these times (from the 1968 figures just released by the Population Reference Bureau) are Kenya, 24 years; Nigeria, 28; Turkey, 24; Indonesia, 31: Philippines, 20; Brazil, 22; Costa Rica, 20; and El Salvador, 19. Think of what it means for the population of a country to double in 25 years. In order just to keep living standards at the present inadequate level, the food available for the people must be doubled. Every structure and road must be duplicated. The amount of power must be doubled. The capacity of the transport system must be doubled. The number of trained doctors, nurses, teachers, and administrators must be doubled. This would be a fantastically difficult job in the United States—a rich country with a fine agricultural system, immense industries, and rich natural resources. Think of what it means to a country with none of these. Remember also that in virtually all UDCs, people have gotten the word about the better life it is possible to have. They have seen colored pictures in magazines of the miracles of Western technology. They have seen automobiles and airplanes. They have seen American and European movies. Many have seen refrigerators, tractors, and even TV sets. Almost all have heard transistor radios. They *know* that a better life is possible. They have what we like to call "rising expectations." If twice as many people are to be happy, the miracle of doubling what they now have will not be enough. It will only maintain today's standard of living. There will have to be tripling or better. Needless to say, they are not going to be happy.

Doubling times for the populations of the DCs tend to be in the 50-to-200-year range. Examples of 1968 doubling times are the United States, 63 years; Austria, 175; Denmark, 88; Norway, 88; United Kingdom, 140; Poland, 88; Russia, 63; Italy, 117; Spain, 88; and Japan, 63. These are industrialized countries that have undergone the so-called demographic transition—a transition from high to low growth rate. As industrialization progressed, children became less important to parents as extra hands to work on the farm and as support in old age. At the same time they became a financial drag—expensive to raise and educate. Presumably these are the reasons for a slowing of population growth after industrialization. They boil down to a simple fact—people just want to have fewer children.

This is not to say, however, that population is not a problem for the DCs. First of all, most of them are overpopulated. They are overpopulated by the simple criterion that they are not able to produce enough food to feed their populations. It is true that they have the money to buy food, but when food is no longer available for sale they will find the money rather indigestible. Then, too, they share with the UDCs a serious problem of population distribution. Their urban centers are getting more and more crowded relative to the countryside. This problem is not as severe as it is in the UDCs (if current trends should continue, which they cannot, Calcutta could have 66 million inhabitants in the year 2000). As you are well aware, however, urban concentrations are creating serious problems even in America. In the United States, one of the more rapidly growing DCs, we hear constantly of the headaches caused by growing population: not just garbage in our environment, but overcrowded highways, burgeoning slums, deteriorating school systems, rising crime rates, riots, and other related problems.

From the point of view of a demographer, the whole problem is quite simple. A population will continue to grow as long as the birth rate exceeds the death rate—if immigration and emigration are not occurring. It is, of course, the balance between birth rate and death rate that is critical. . . .

21

BARRY COMMONER

The Closing Circle: Nature, Man, and Technology

The environment has just been rediscovered by the people who live in it. In the United States the event was celebrated in April 1970, during Earth Week. It was a sudden, noisy awakening. School children cleaned up rubbish; college students organized huge demonstrations; determined citizens recaptured the streets from the automobile, at least for a day. Everyone seemed to be aroused to the environmental danger and eager to do something about it.

They were offered lots of advice. Almost every writer, almost every speaker, on the college campuses, in the streets and on television and radio broadcasts, was ready to fix the blame and pronounce a cure for the environmental crisis. Some regarded the environmental issue as politically innocuous:

> Ecology has become the political substitute for the word "motherhood."
>
> —Jesse Unruh, Democratic Leader of the State of California Assembly

But the FBI took it more seriously:

> On April 22, 1970, representatives of the FBI observed about two hundred persons on the Playing Fields shortly after 1:30 P.M. They were joined a few minutes later by a contingent of George Washington University students who arrived chanting "Save Our Earth.". . . A sign was noted which read "God Is Not Dead; He Is Polluted on Earth.". . . Shortly after 8:00 P.M. Senator Edmund Muskie (D), Maine, arrived and gave a short anti-pollution speech.

Senator Muskie was followed by journalist I.F. Stone, who spoke for twenty minutes on the themes of anti-pollution, anti-military, and anti-administration.

—FBI Report entered into Congressional Record
by Senator Muskie on April 14, 1971

Some blamed pollution on the rising population:

The pollution problem is a consequence of population. It did not much matter how a lonely American frontiersman disposed of his waste. . . . But as population became denser, the natural chemical and biological recycling processes became overloaded. . . . Freedom to breed will bring ruin to all.

—Garrett Hardin, biologist

The causal chain of the deterioration [of the environment] is easily followed to its source. Too may cars, too many factories, too much detergent, too much pesticide, multiplying contrails, inadequate sewage treatment plants, too little water, too much carbon dioxide—all can be traced easily to *too many people.*

—Paul R. Ehrlich, biologist

Some blamed affluence:

The affluent society has become an effluent society. The 6 percent of the world's population in the United States produces 70 percent or more of the world's solid wastes.

—Walter S. Howard, biologist

And praised poverty:

Blessed be the starving blacks of Mississippi with their outdoor privies, for they are ecologically sound, and they shall inherit a nation.

—Wayne H. Davis, biologist

But not without rebuttal from the poor:

You must not embark on programs to curb economic growth without placing a priority on maintaining income, so that the poorest people won't simply be further depressed in their condition but will have a share, and be able to live decently.

—George Wiley, chemist and chairman,
National Welfare Rights Organization

And encouragement from industry:

It is not industry *per se,* but the demands of the public. And the public's demands are increasing at a geometric rate, because of the increasing standard of living and the increasing growth of population. . . . If we can convince the national and local leaders in the environmental crusade of this basic logic, that population causes pollution, then we can help them focus their attention on the major aspect of the problem.

—Sherman R. Knapp, chairman of the board, Northeast Utilities

Some blamed man's innate aggressiveness:

The first problem, then, is people. . . . The second problem, a most fundamental one, lies within us—our basic aggressions. . . . As Anthony Storr has said: "The sombre fact is that we are the cruelest and most ruthless species that has ever walked the earth."

—William Roth, director, Pacific Life Assurance Company

While others blamed what man had learned:

People are afraid of their humanity because systematically they have been taught to become inhuman. . . . They have no understanding of what it is to love nature. And so our airs are being polluted, our rivers are being poisoned, and our land is being cut up.

—Arturo Sandoval, student, Environmental Action

A minister blamed profits:

Environmental rape is a fact of our national life only because it is more profitable than responsible stewardship of earth's limited resources.

—Channing E. Phillips, Congregationalist Minister

While a historian blamed religion:

Christianity bears a huge burden of guilt. . . . We shall continue to have a worsening ecologic crisis until we reject the Christian axiom that nature has no reason for existence save to serve man.

—Lynn White, Historian

A politician blamed technology:

A runaway technology, whose only law is profit, has for years poisoned our air, ravaged our soil, stripped our forests bare, and corrupted our water resources.

—Vance Hartke, Senator from Indiana

While an environmentalist blamed politicians:

There is a peculiar paralysis in our political branches of government, which are primarily responsible for legislating and executing the policies environmentalists are urging. . . . Industries who profit by the rape of our environ-

> ment see to it that legislators friendly to their attitudes are elected, and that bureaucrats of similar attitude are appointed.
>
> —Roderick A. Cameron, of the Environmental Defense Fund

Some blamed capitalism:

> Yes, it's official—the conspiracy against pollution. And we have a simple program—arrest Agnew and smash capitalism. We make only one exception to our pollution stand—everyone should light up a joint and get stoned. . . . We say to Agnew country that Earth Day is for the sons and daughters of the American Revolution who are going to tear this capitalism down and set us free.
>
> —Rennie Davis, a member of the Chicago Seven

While capitalists counterattacked:

> The point I am trying to make is that we are solving most of our problems . . . that conditions are getting better not worse . . . that American industry is spending over three billion dollars a year to clean up the environment and additional billions to develop products that will *keep* it clean . . . and that the real danger is *not* from the free-enterprise Establishment that has made ours the most prosperous, most powerful and most charitable nation on earth. No, the danger today resides in the Disaster Lobby—those crepe-hangers who, for personal gain or out of sheer ignorance, are undermining the American system and threatening the lives and fortunes of the American people. Some people have let the gloom-mongers scare them beyond rational response with talk about atomic annihilation. . . . Since World War II over one *billion* human beings who worried about A-bombs and H-bombs died of other causes. They worried for nothing.
>
> —Thomas R. Shepard, Jr., publisher, Look Magazine

And one keen observer blamed everyone:

> We have met the enemy and he is us.
>
> —Pogo

Earth Week and the accompanying outburst of publicity, preaching, and prognostication surprised most people, including those of us who had worked for years to generate public recognition of the environmental crisis. What surprised me most were the numerous, confident explanations of the cause and cure of the crisis. For having spent some years in the effort simply to detect and describe the growing list of environmental problems—radioactive fallout, air and water pollution, the deterioration of the soil—and in tracing some of the links to social and political processes, the identification of a single cause and cure seemed a rather bold step. . . .

After the excitement of Earth Week, I tried to find some meaning in the welter of contradictory advice that it produced. It seemed to me that the confusion of Earth Week was a sign that the situation was so complex and ambiguous that people could read whatever conclusions their own beliefs—about human nature, economics, and politics—suggested. Like a Rorschach ink blot, Earth Week mirrored personal convictions more than objective knowledge.

Earth Week convinced me of the urgency of a deeper public understanding of the origins of the environmental crisis. . . . [They] can be organized into a kind of informal set of "laws of ecology." These are described in what follows.

The First Law of Ecology: Everything Is Connected to Everything Else

Some of the evidence that leads to this generalization has already been discussed. It reflects the existence of the elaborate network of interconnections in the ecosphere: among different living organisms, and between populations, species, and individual organisms and their physicochemical surroundings.

The single fact that an ecosystem consists of multiple interconnected parts, which act on one another, has some surprising consequences. . . .

The Second Law of Ecology: Everything Must Go Somewhere

This is, of course, simply a somewhat informal restatement of a basic law of physics—that matter is indestructible. Applied to ecology, the law emphasizes that in nature there is no such thing as "waste." In every natural system, what is excreted by one organism as waste is taken up by another as food. Animals release carbon dioxide as a respiratory waste; this is an essential nutrient for green plants. Plants excrete oxygen, which is used by animals. Animal organic wastes nourish the bacteria of decay. Their wastes, inorganic materials such as nitrate, phosphate, and carbon dioxide, become algal nutrients.

A persistent effort to answer the question "Where does it go?" can yield a surprising amount of valuable information about an ecosystem. Consider, for example, the fate of a household item which contains mercury—a substance with serious environmental effects that have just recently surfaced. A dry-cell battery containing mercury is purchased, used to the point of exhaustion, and then "thrown out." But where does it really go? First it is placed in a container of rubbish; this is collected and taken to an incinerator. Here the mercury is heated; this produces mercury vapor which is emitted by the incinerator stack, and mercury *vapor* is toxic. Mercury vapor is carried by the wind, eventually brought to earth in rain or snow. Entering a mountain lake, let us say, the mercury condenses and sinks to the bottom. Here it is acted on by bacteria which convert it to methyl mercury. This is soluble and taken up by fish; since it is not metabolized, the mercury accumulates in the organs and flesh of the fish. The fish is caught and eaten by a man and the mercury becomes deposited in his organs, where it might be harmful. And so on . . .

The Third Law of Ecology: Nature Knows Best

In my experience this principle is likely to encounter considerable resistance, for it appears to contradict a deeply held idea about the unique competence of human beings. One of the most pervasive features of modern technology is the notion that it is intended to "improve on nature"—to provide food, clothing, shelter, and means of communication and expression which are superior to those available to man in nature. Stated baldly, the third law of ecology holds that any major man-made change in a natural system is likely to be *detrimental* to that system. . . .

The Fourth Law of Ecology: There Is No Such Thing as a Free Lunch

In my experience, this idea has proven so illuminating for environmental problems that I have borrowed it from its original source, economics. The "law" derives from a story that economists like to tell about an oil-rich potentate who decided that his new wealth needed the guidance of economic science. Accordingly he ordered his advisers, on pain of death, to produce a set of volumes containing all the wisdom of economics. When the tomes arrived, the potentate was impatient and again issued an order—to reduce all the knowledge of economics to a single volume. The story goes on in this vein, as such stories will, until the advisers are required, if they are to survive, to reduce the totality of economic science to a single sentence. This is the origin of the "free lunch" law.

In ecology, as in economics, the law is intended to warn that every gain is won at some cost. In a way, this ecological law embodies the previous three laws. Because the global ecosystem is a connected whole, in which nothing can be gained or lost and which is not subject to over-all improvement, anything extracted from it by human effort must be replaced. Payment of this price cannot be avoided; it can only be delayed. The present environmental crisis is a warning that we have delayed nearly too long.

22

ARNE NAESS

Ecology: The Shallow and the Deep

Ecologically responsible policies are concerned only in part with pollution and resource depletion. There are deeper concerns which touch upon principles of diversity, complexity, autonomy, decentralization, symbiosis, egalitarianism, and classlessness.

The emergence of ecologists from their former relative obscurity marks a turning-point in our scientific communities. But their message is twisted and misused. A shallow, but presently rather powerful movement, and a deep, but less influential movement, compete for our attention. I shall make an effort to characterize the two.

1. The Shallow Ecology Movement

Fight against pollution and resource depletion. Central objective: the health and affluence of people in the developed countries.

2. The Deep Ecology Movement

(1) Rejection of the man-in-environment image in favour of *the relational, total-field image*. Organism as knots in the biospherical net or field of intrinsic relations. An intrinsic relation between two things *A* and *B* is such that the relation belongs to the definitions or basic constitutions of *A* and *B*, so that without the relation, *A* and *B* are no longer the same things. The total-field model dissolves not only the man-in-environment concept, but

Reprinted from Arne Naess, "The Shallow and the Deep, Long-Range Ecology Movement," *Inquiry* 1973 (16), pp. 95–100, by permission of Scandinavian University Press, Oslo, Norway.

every compact thing-in-milieu concept—except when talking at a superficial or preliminary level of communication.

(2) *Biospherical egalitarianism*—in principle. The "in principle" clause is inserted because any realistic praxis necessitates some killing, exploitation, and suppression. The ecological field-worker acquires a deep-seated respect, or even veneration, for ways and forms of life. He reaches an understanding from within, a kind of understanding that others reserve for fellow men and for a narrow section of ways and forms of life. To the ecological field-worker, *the equal right to live and blossom* is an intuitively clear and obvious value axiom. Its restriction to humans is an anthropocentrism with detrimental effects upon the life quality of humans themselves. This quality depends in part upon the deep pleasure and satisfaction we receive from close partnership with other forms of life. The attempt to ignore our dependence and to establish a master-slave role has contributed to the alienation of man from himself.

Ecological egalitarianism implies the reinterpretation of the future-research variable, "level of crowding," so that *general* mammalian crowding and loss of life-equality is taken seriously, not only human crowding. (Research on the high requirements of free space of certain mammals has, incidentally, suggested that theorists of human urbanism have largely underestimated human life-space requirements. Behavioural crowding symptoms [neuroses, aggressiveness, loss of traditions] are largely the same among mammals.)

(3) *Principles of diversity and of symbiosis.* Diversity enhances the potentialities of survival, the chances of new modes of life, the richness of forms. And the so-called struggle of life, and survival of the fittest, should be interpreted in the sense of ability to coexist and cooperate in complex relationships, rather than ability to kill, exploit, and suppress. "Live and let live" is a more powerful ecological principle than "Either you or me."

The latter tends to reduce the multiplicity of kinds of forms of life, and also to create destruction within the communities of the same species. Ecologically inspired attitudes therefore favour diversity of human ways of life, of cultures, of occupations, of economies. They support the fight against economic and cultural, as much as military, invasion and domination, and they are opposed to the annihilation of seals and whales as much as to that of human tribes or cultures.

(4) *Anti-class posture.* Diversity of human ways of life is in part due to (intended or unintended) exploitation and suppression on the part of certain groups. The exploiter lives differently from the exploited, but both are

adversely affected in their potentialities of self-realization. The principle of diversity does not cover differences due merely to certain attitudes or behaviours forcibly blocked or restrained. The principles of ecological egalitarianism and of symbiosis support the same anti-class posture. The ecological attitude favours the extension of all three principles to any group conflicts, including those of today between developing and developed nations. The three principles also favour extreme caution towards any over-all plans for the future, except those consistent with wide and widening classless diversity.

(5) Fight against *pollution and resource depletion.* In this fight ecologists have found powerful supporters, but sometimes to the detriment of their total stand. This happens when attention is focused on pollution and resource depletion rather than on the other points, or when projects are implemented which reduce pollution but increase evils of the other kinds. Thus, if prices of life necessities increase because of the installation of anti-pollution devices, class differences increase too. An ethics of responsibility implies that ecologists do not serve the shallow, but the deep ecological movement. That is, not only point (5), but all seven points must be considered together.

Ecologists are irreplaceable informants in any society, whatever their political colour. If well organized, they have the power to reject jobs in which they submit themselves to institutions or to planners with limited ecological perspectives. As it is now, ecologists sometimes serve masters who deliberately ignore the wider perspectives.

(6) *Complexity, not complication.* The theory of ecosystems contains an important distinction between what is complicated without any Gestalt or unifying principles—we may think of finding our way through a chaotic city—and what is complex. A multiplicity of more or less lawful, interacting factors may operate together to form a unity, a system. We make a shoe or use a map or integrate a variety of activities into a workaday pattern. Organisms, ways of life, and interactions in the biosphere in general, exhibit complexity of such an astoundingly high level as to colour the general outlook of ecologists. Such complexity makes thinking in terms of vast systems inevitable. It also makes for a keen, steady perception of the profound *human ignorance* of biospherical relationships and therefore of the effect of disturbances.

Applied to humans, the complexity-not-complication principle favours division of labour, *not fragmentation of labour.* It favours integrated actions in which the whole person is active, not mere reactions. It favours complex economies, an integrated variety of means of living. (Combinations of industrial and agricultural activity, of intellectual and manual work, of specialized and non-specialized occupations, of urban and non-urban activity, of work in city and recreation in nature with recreation in city and work in nature. . . .)

It favours soft technique and "soft future-research," less prognosis, more clarification of possibilities. More sensitivity towards continuity and live traditions, and—most importantly—towards our state of ignorance.

The implementation of ecologically responsible policies requires in this century an exponential growth of technical skill and invention—but in new directions, directions which today are not consistently and liberally supported by the research policy organs of our nation-states.

(7) *Local autonomy and decentralization.* The vulnerability of a form of life is roughly proportional to the weight of influences from afar, from outside the local region in which that form has obtained an ecological equilibrium. This lends support to our efforts to strengthen local self-government and material and mental self-sufficiency. But these efforts presuppose an impetus towards decentralization. Pollution problems, including those of thermal pollution and recirculation of materials, also lead us in this direction, because increased local autonomy, if we are able to keep other factors constant, reduces energy consumption. (Compare an approximately self-sufficient locality with one requiring the importation of foodstuff, materials for house construction, fuel and skilled labour from other continents. The former may use only five per cent of the energy used by the latter.) Local autonomy is strengthened by a reduction in the number of links in the hierarchical chains of decision. (For example a chain consisting of local board, municipal council, highest sub-national decision-maker, a state-wide institution in a state federation, a federal national government institution, a coalition of nations, and of institutions, e.g. E.E.C. top levels, and a global institution, can be reduced to one made up of local board, nation-wide institution, and global institution.) Even if a decision follows majority rules at each step, many local interests may be dropped along the line, if it is too long.

Summing up, then, it should, first of all, be borne in mind that the norms and tendencies of the Deep Ecology movement are not derived from ecology by logic or induction. Ecological knowledge and the life-style of the ecological field-worker have *suggested, inspired, and fortified* the perspectives of the Deep Ecology movement. Many of the formulations in the above seven-point survey are rather vague generalizations, only tenable if made more precise in certain directions.

But all over the world the inspiration from ecology has shown remarkable convergencies. The survey does not pretend to be more than one of the possible condensed codifications of these convergencies.

Second, it should be fully appreciated that the significant tenets of the Deep Ecology movement are clearly and forcefully *normative*. They express a value priority system only in part based on results (or lack of results, cf. Point [6]) of scientific research. Today, ecologists try to influence policy-making bodies largely through threats, through predictions concerning pollutants and resource depletion, knowing that policy-makers accept at least certain minimum *norms* concerning health and just distribution. But it is clear that there is a vast number of people in all countries, and even a considerable number of people in power, who accept as valid the wider norms and values characteristic of the Deep Ecology movement. There are political potentials in this movement which should not be overlooked and which have little to do with pollution and resource depletion. In plotting possible futures, the norms should be freely used and elaborated.

Third, in so far as ecology movements deserve our attention, they are *ecosophical* rather than ecological. Ecology is a *limited* science which makes *use* of scientific methods. Philosophy is the most general forum of debate on fundamentals, descriptive as well as prescriptive, and political philosophy is one of its subsections. By an *ecosophy* I mean a philosophy of ecological harmony or equilibrium. A philosophy as a kind of *sofia* wisdom is openly normative, it contains *both* norms, rules, postulates, value priority announcements *and* hypotheses concerning the state of affairs in our universe. Wisdom is policy wisdom, prescription, not only scientific description and prediction.

The details of an ecosophy will show many variations due to significant differences concerning not only "facts" of pollution, resources, population, etc., but also value priorities. Today, however, the seven points listed provide one unified framework for ecosophical systems.

In general system theory, systems are mostly conceived in terms of causally or functionally interacting or interrelated items. An ecosophy, however, is more like a system of the kind constructed by Aristotle or Spinoza. It is expressed verbally as a set of sentences with a variety of functions, descriptive and prescriptive. The basic relation is that between subsets of premisses and subsets of conclusions, that is, the relation of derivability. The relevant notions of derivability may be classed according to rigour, with logical and mathematical deductions topping the list, but also according to how much is implicitly taken for granted. An exposition of an ecosophy must necessarily be only moderately precise considering the vast scope of relevant ecological and normative (social, political, ethical) material. At the moment, ecosophy might profitably use models of systems, rough approximations of global systematizations. It is the global character, not preciseness in detail, which distinguishes an ecosophy. It articulates and integrates the efforts of an ideal ecological team, a team comprising not only scientists from an extreme variety of disciplines, but also students of politics and active policy-makers.

Under the name of *ecologism,* various deviations from the deep movement have been championed—primarily with a one-sided stress on pollution and resource depletion, but also with a neglect of the great differences between under- and over-developed countries in favour of a vague global approach. The global approach is essential, but regional differences must largely determine policies in the coming years.

23

GARRETT HARDIN

The Tragedy of the Commons

At the end of a thoughtful article on the future of nuclear war, J.B. Wiesner and H.F. York concluded that: "both sides in the arms race are . . . confronted by the dilemma of steadily increasing military power and steadily decreasing national security. *It is our considered professional judgement that this dilemma has no technical solution.* If the great powers continue to look for solutions in the area of science and technology only, the result will be to worsen the situation."

I would like to focus your attention not on the subject of the article (national security in a nuclear world) but on the kind of conclusion they reached, namely that there is no technical solution to the problem. An implicit and almost universal assumption of discussions published in professional and semipopular scientific journals is that the problem under discussion has a technical solution. A technical solution may be defined as one that requires a change only in the techniques of the natural sciences, demanding little or nothing in the way of change in human values or ideas of morality.

In our day (though not in earlier times) technical solutions are always welcome. Because of previous failures in prophecy, it takes courage to assert that a desired technical solution is not possible. Wiesner and York exhibited this courage; publishing in a science journal, they insisted that the solution to the problem was not to be found in the natural sciences. They cautiously qualified their statement with the phrase, "It is our considered professional judgment. . . ." Whether they were right or not is not the concern of the present article. Rather, the concern here is with the important concept of a class of human problems which can be called "no technical solution problems," and more specifically, with the identification and discussion of one of these.

It is easy to show that the class is not a null class. Recall the game of tick-tack-toe. Consider the problem, "How can I win the game of tick-tack-toe?" It is well known that I cannot, if I assume (in keeping with the conventions of game theory) that my opponent understands the game perfectly. Put another way, there is no "technical solution" to the problem. I can win only by giving a radical meaning to the word "win." I can hit my opponent over the head; or I can falsify the records. Every way in which I "win" involves, in some sense, an abandonment of the game, as we intuitively understand it. (I can also, of course, openly abandon the game—refuse to play it. This is what most adults do.)

The class of "no technical solution problems" has members. My thesis is that the "popular problem," as conventionally conceived, is a member of this class. How it is conventionally conceived needs some comment. It is fair to say that most people who anguish over the population problem are trying to find a way to avoid the evils of overpopulation without relinquishing any of the privileges they now enjoy. They think that farming the seas or developing new strains of wheat will solve the problem—technologically. I try to show here that the solution they seek cannot be found. The population problem cannot be solved in a technical way, any more than can the problem of winning the game of tick-tack-toe.

What Shall We Maximize?

Population, as Malthus said, naturally tends to grow "geometrically," or, as we would now say, exponentially. In a finite world this means that the per-capita share of the world's goods must decrease. Is ours a finite world?

A fair defense can be put forward for the view that the world is infinite; or that we do not know that it is not. But, in terms of the practical problems that we must face in the next few generations with the foreseeable technology, it is clear that we will greatly increase human misery if we do not, during the immediate future, assume that the world available to the terrestrial human population is finite. "Space" is no escape.

A finite world can support only a finite population; therefore, population growth must eventually equal zero. (The case of perpetual wide fluctuations above and below zero is a trivial variant that need not be discussed.) When this condition is met, what will be the situation of mankind? Specifically, can Bentham's goal of "the greatest good for the greatest number" be realized?

No—for two reasons, each sufficient by itself. The first is a theoretical one. It is not mathematically possible to maximize for two (or more) variables at the same time. This was clearly stated by von Neumann and Morgenstern, but the principle is implicit in the theory of partial differential equations, dating back at least to D'Alembert (1717–1783).

The second reason springs directly from biological facts. To live, any organism must have a source of energy (for example, food). This energy is utilized for two purposes: mere maintenance and work. For man, maintenance of life requires about 1600 kilocalories a day ("maintenance calories"). Anything that he does over and above merely staying alive will be defined as work, and is supported by "work calories" which he takes in. Work calories are used not only for what we call work in common speech; they are also required for all forms of enjoyment, from swimming and automobile racing to playing music and writing poetry. If our goal is to maximize population it is obvious what we must do: We must make the work calories per person approach as close to zero as possible. No gourmet meals, no vacations, no sports, no music, no literature, no art.

. . . I think that everyone will grant, without argument or proof, that maximizing population does not maximize goods. Bentham's goal is impossible.

In reaching this conclusion I have made the usual assumption that it is the acquisition of energy that is the problem. The appearance of atomic energy has led some to question this assumption. However, given an infinite source of energy, population growth still produces an inescapable problem. The problem of the acquisition of energy is replaced by the problem of its dissipation, as J.H. Fremlin has so wittily shown. The arithmetic signs in the analysis are, as it were, reversed; but Bentham's goal is unobtainable.

The optimum population is, then, less than the maximum. The difficulty of defining the optimum is enormous; so far as I know, no one has seriously tackled this problem. Reaching an acceptable and stable solution will surely require more than one generation of hard analytical work—and much persuasion.

We want the maximum good per person; but what is good? To one person it is wilderness, to another it is ski lodges for thousands. To one it is estuaries to nourish ducks for hunters to shoot; to another it is factory land. Comparing one good with another is, we usually say, impossible because goods are incommensurable. Incommensurables cannot be compared.

Theoretically this may be true; but in real life incommensurables are commensurable. Only a criterion of judgment and a system of weighting are needed. In nature the criterion is survival. Is it better for a species to be small and hideable, or large and powerful? Natural selection commensurates the incommensurables. The compromise achieved depends on a natural weighting of the values of the variables.

Man must imitate this process. There is no doubt that in fact he already does, but unconsciously. It is when the hidden decisions are made explicit that the arguments begin. The problem for the years ahead is to work out an acceptable theory of weighting. Synergistic effects, nonlinear variation, and difficulties in discounting the future make the intellectual problem difficult, but not (in principle) insoluble.

Has any cultural group solved this practical problem at the present time, even on an intuitive level? One simple fact proves that none has: there is no prosperous population in the world today that has, and has had for some time, a growth rate of zero. Any people that has intuitively identified its optimum point will soon reach it, after which its growth rate becomes and remains zero.

Of course, a positive growth rate might be taken as evidence that a population is below its optimum. However, by any reasonable standards, the most rapidly growing populations on earth today are (in general) the most miserable. This association (which need not be invariable) casts doubt on the optimistic assumption that the positive growth rate of a population is evidence that it has yet to reach its optimum.

We can make little progress in working toward optimum population size until we explicitly exorcise the spirit of Adam Smith in the field of practical demography. In economic affairs, *The Wealth of Nations* (1776) popularized the "invisible hand," the idea that an individual who "intends only his own gain," is, as it were, "led by an invisible hand to promote . . . the public interest." Adam Smith did not assert that this was invariably true, and perhaps neither did any of his followers. But he contributed to a dominant tendency of thought that has ever since interfered with positive action based on rational analysis, namely, the tendency to assume that decisions reached individually will, in fact, be the best decisions for an entire society. If this assumption is correct it justifies the continuance of our present policy of *laissez faire* in reproduction. If it is correct we can assume that men will control their individual fecundity so as to produce the optimum population. If the assumption is not correct, we need to reexamine our individual freedoms to see which ones are defensible.

Tragedy of Freedom in a Commons

The rebuttal to the invisible hand in population control is to be found in a scenario first sketched in a little-known pamphlet in 1833 by a mathematical amateur named William Forster Lloyd (1794–1852). We may well call it "the tragedy of the commons," using the word "tragedy" as the philosopher Whitehead used it. "The essence of dramatic tragedy is not unhappiness. It resides in the solemnity of the remorseless working of things." He then goes on to say, "This inevitableness of destiny can only be illustrated in terms of human life by incidents which in fact involve unhappiness. For it is only by them that the futility of escape can be made evident in the drama."

The tragedy of the commons develops in this way. Picture a pasture open to all. It is to be expected that each herdsman will try to keep as many cattle as possible on the commons. Such an arrangement may work reasonably satisfactorily for centuries because tribal wars, poaching, and disease keep the numbers of both man and beast well below the carrying capacity of the land. Finally, however, comes the day of reckoning, that is, the day when the long-desired goal of social stability becomes a reality. At this point, the inherent logic of the commons remorselessly generates tragedy.

As a rational being, each herdsman seeks to maximize his gain. Explicitly or implicitly, more or less consciously, he asks, "What is the utility *to me* of adding one more animal to my herd?" This utility has one negative and one positive component.

1. The positive component is a function of the increment of one animal. Since the herdsman receives all the proceeds from the sale of the additional animal, the positive utility is nearly +1.

2. The negative component is a function of the additional overgrazing created by one more animal. Since, however, the effects of overgrazing are shared by all the herdsmen, the negative utility for any particular decision-making herdsman is only a fraction of –1.

Adding together the component partial utilities, the rational herdsman concludes that the only sensible course for him to pursue is to add another animal to his herd. And another. . . . But this is the conclusion reached by each and every rational herdsman sharing a commons. Therein is the tragedy. Each man is locked into a system that compels him to increase his herd without limit—in a world that is limited. Ruin is the destination toward which all men rush, each pursuing his own best interest in a society that believes in the freedom of the commons. Freedom in a commons brings ruin to all.

Some would say that this is a platitude. Would that it were! In a sense, it was learned thousands of years ago, but natural selection favors the forces of psychological denial. The individual benefits as an individual from his ability to deny the truth even though society as a whole, of which he is a part, suffers. Education can counteract the natural tendency to do the wrong thing, but the inexorable succession of generations requires that the basis for this knowledge be constantly refreshed.

A simple incident that occurred a few years ago in Leominster, Massachusetts, shows how perishable the knowledge is. During the Christmas shopping season the parking meters downtown were covered with plastic bags that bore tags reading: "Do not open until after Christmas. Free parking courtesy of the mayor and city council." In other words, facing the prospect of an increased demand for already scarce space, the city fathers reinstituted the system of the commons. (Cynically, we suspect that they gained more votes than they lost by this retrogressive act.)

In an approximate way, the logic of the commons has been understood for a long time, perhaps since the discovery of agriculture or the invention of private property in real estate. But it is understood mostly only in special cases which are not sufficiently generalized. Even at this late date, cattlemen leasing national land on the Western ranges demonstrate no more than an ambivalent understanding, in constantly pressuring federal authorities to increase the head count to the point where overgrazing produces erosion and weed-dominance. Likewise, the oceans of the world continue to suffer from the survival of the philosophy of the commons. Maritime nations still respond automatically to the shibboleth of the "freedom of the seas." Professing to believe in the "inexhaustible resources of the oceans," they bring species after species of fish and whales closer to extinction.

The National Parks present another instance of the working out of the tragedy of the commons. At present, they are open to all, without limit. The parks themselves are limited in extent—there is only one Yosemite Valley—whereas population seems to grow without limit. The values that visitors seek in the parks are steadily eroded. Plainly, we must soon cease to treat the parks as commons or they will be of no value to anyone.

What shall we do? We have several options. We might sell them off as private property. We might keep them as public property, but allocate the right to enter them. The allocation might be on the basis of wealth, by the use of an auction system. It might be on the basis of merit, as defined by some agreed-upon standards. It might be by lottery. Or it might be on a first-come, first-served basis, administered to long queues. These, I think, are all objectionable. But we must choose—or acquiesce in the destruction of the commons that we call our National Parks.

24

Ynestra King

Feminism and the Revolt of Nature

Ecology is a feminist issue. But why? Is it because women are more a part of nature than men? Is it because women are morally superior to men? Is it because ecological feminists are satisfied with the traditional female stereotypes and wish to be limited to the traditional concerns of women? Is it because the domination of women and the domination of nature are connected?

The feminist debate over ecology has gone back and forth and is assuming major proportions in the movement, but there is a talking-past-each-other, not-getting-to-what's-really-going-on quality to it. The differences derive from unresolved questions in our political and theoretical history, so the connection of ecology to feminism has met with radically different responses from the various feminisms.

Radical Feminism and Ecology

Radical feminists of one genre deplore the development of connections between ecology and feminism and see it as a regression which is bound to reinforce sex-role stereotyping. Since the ecological issue has universal implications, so the argument goes, it should concern men and women alike. Ellen Willis, for instance, wrote recently:

> From a feminist perspective, the only good reasons for women to organize separately from men is to fight sexism. Otherwise women's political organizations simply reinforce female segregation and further the idea that certain activities and interests are inherently feminine. All-female groups that work against consumer fraud, or for the improvement of schools, implicitly acqui-

From Ynestra King, "Feminism and the Revolt of Nature," *Heresies,* no. 13 (1981): 12–16.

> esce in the notion that women have special responsibilities as housewives and mothers, that it is not men's job to worry about what goes on at the supermarket, or the conditions of their children's education. Similarly, groups like Women Strike for Peace, Women's International League for Peace and Freedom, and Another Mother for Peace perpetuate the idea that women have a specifically female interest in preventing war. . . . If feminism means anything, it's that women are capable of the full range of human emotions and behavior; politics based on received definitions of women's nature and role are oppressive, whether promoted by men or by my alleged sisters.[1]

Other radical feminists—most notably Mary Daly and Susan Griffin—have taken the opposite position. Daly believes that women should identify with nature against men, and that *whatever* we do, we should do it separately from men. For her, the oppression of women under patriarchy and the pillage of the natural environment are basically the same phenomenon.[2] Griffin's book is a long prose poem (actually the form defies precise description; it is truly original).[3] It is not intended to spell out a political philosophy, but to let us know and feel how the woman/nature connection has been played out historically in the victimization of women and nature. It suggests a powerful potential for a movement linking feminism and ecology.

So how do women who call themselves radical feminists come to such divergent positions? Radical feminism roots the oppression of women in biological difference. It sees patriarchy (the systematic dominance of men) preceding and laying the foundation for other forms of oppression and exploitation; it sees men hating and fearing women (misogyny) and identifying us with nature; it sees men seeking to enlist both women and nature in the service of male projects designed to protect men from feared nature and mortality. The notion of women being closer to nature is essential to such projects. If patriarchy is the archetypal form of human oppression, then radical feminists argue that getting rid of it will also cause other forms of oppression to crumble. But the essential difference between the two or more types of radical feminists is whether the woman/nature connection is potentially liberating or simply a rationale for the continued subordination of women.

Other questions follow from this theoretical disagreement: (1) Is there a separate female life experience in this society? If so, is there a separate female culture? (2) If there is, is a female culture merely a male-contrived ghetto constructed long ago by forcibly taking advantage of our physical vulnerability born of our child-bearing function and smaller stature? Or does it suggest a way of life providing a critical vantage point on male society? (3) What are the implications of gender difference? Do we want to do away with gender difference? (4) Can we recognize "difference" without shoring up dominance based on difference?

Rationalist radical feminists (Wills' position) and radical cultural feminists (Daly's and Griffin's position) offer opposite answers, just as they come to opposite conclusions on connecting feminism to ecology—and for the same reasons. The problem with both analyses, however, is that gender identity is neither fully natural nor fully cultural. And it is neither inherently oppressive nor inherently liberating. It depends on other historical factors, and how we consciously understand woman-identification and feminism.

Socialist Feminism and Ecology[4]

Socialist feminists have for the most part yet to enter feminist debates on "the ecology question." They tend to be uneasy with ecological feminism, fearing that it is based on an ahistorical, anti-rational woman/nature identification; or they see the cultural emphasis in ecological feminism as "idealist" rather than "materialist." The Marxist side of their politics implies a primacy of material transformation (economic/structural transformation precedes changes in ideas/culture/consciousness). Cultural and material changes are not completely separate. There is a dialectical interaction between the two, but in the last instance the cultural is part of the superstructure and the material is the base.

Historically socialism and feminism have had a curious courtship[5] and a rather unhappy marriage,[6] characterized by a tug of war over which is the primary contradiction—sex or class. In an uneasy truce, socialist feminists try to overcome the contradictions, to show how the economic structure and the sex-gender system[7] are mutually reinforced in historically specific ways depending on material conditions, and to show their interdependence. They suggest the need for an "autonomous" (as opposed to a "separatist") women's movement, to maintain vigilance over women's concerns within the production and politics of a mixed society. They see patriarchy as different under feudalism, capitalism and even under socialism without feminism.[8] And they hold that nobody is free until everybody is free.

Socialist feminists see themselves as integrating the best of Marxism and radical feminism. They have been weak on radical cultural critique and strong on helping us to understand how people's material situations condition their consciousnesses and their possibilities for social transformation. But adherence to Marxism with its economic orientation means opting for the rationalist severance of the woman/nature connection and advocating the integration of women into production. It does not challenge the culture-versus-nature formulation itself. Even where the issue of woman's oppression and its identification with that of nature has been taken up, the socialist feminist solution has been to align women with culture in culture's ongoing struggle with nature.[9]

Here We Go Again, This Argument Is at Least 100 Years Old!

The radical feminist/socialist feminist debate does sometimes seem to be the romantic feminist/rationalist feminist debate of the late nineteenth century revisited.[10] We can imagine nineteenth-century women watching the development of robber-baron capitalism, "the demise of morality" and the rise of the liberal state which furthered capitalist interests while touting liberty, equality and fraternity. Small wonder that they saw in the domestic sphere vestiges of a more ethical way of life, and thought its values could be carried into the public sphere. This perspective romanticized women, although it is easy to sympathize with it and share the abhorrence of the pillage and plunder imposed by the masculinist mentality in modern industrial society. But what nineteenth-century women proclaiming the virtues of womanhood did not understand was that they were a repository of organic social values in an increasingly inorganic world. Women placed in male-identified power positions can be as warlike as men. The assimilation or neutralization of enfranchised women into the American political structure has a sad history.

Rationalist feminists in the nineteenth century, on the other hand, were concerned with acquiring power and representing women's interests. They opposed anything that reinforced the idea that women were "different" and wanted male prerogatives extended to women. They were contemptuous of romantic feminists and were themselves imbued with the modern ethic of Progress. They opposed political activity by women over issues not seen as exclusively feminist for the same reasons rationalist radical feminists today opposed the feminism/ecology connection.

The Dialectic of Modern Feminism

According to the false dichotomy between subjective and objective—one legacy of male Western philosophy to feminist thought—we must root our movement *either* in a rationalist-materialist humanism *or* in a metaphysical-feminist naturalism. This supposed choice is crucial as we approach the ecology issue. *Either* we take the anthropocentric position that nature exists solely to serve the needs of the male bourgeois who has crawled out of the slime to be lord and master of everything, *or* we take the naturalist position that nature has a purpose of its own apart from serving "man." We are *either* concerned with the "environment" because we are dependent on it, *or* we understand ourselves to be *of* it, with human oppression part and parcel of the domination of nature. For some radical feminists, only women are capable of full consciousness.[11] Socialist feminists tend to consider the naturalist position as historically regressive, antirational and probably fascistic. This is the crux of the anthropocentric/naturalist debate, which is emotionally loaded for both sides, but especially for those who equate progress and rationality.

However, we do not have to make such choices. Feminism is both the product and potentially the negation of the modern rationalist world view and capitalism. There was one benefit for women in the "disenchantment of the world,"[12] the process by which all magical and spiritual beliefs were denigrated as superstitious nonsense and the death of nature was accomplished in the minds of men.[13] This process tore asunder women's traditional sphere of influence, but it also undermined the ideology of "natural" social roles, opening a space for women to question what was "natural" for them to be and to do. In traditional Western societies, social and economic relationships were connected to a land-based way of life. One was assigned a special role based on one's sex, race, class and place of birth. In the domestic sphere children were socialized, food prepared and men sheltered from their public cares. But the nineteenth-century "home" also encompassed the production of what people ate, used and wore. It included much more of human life and filled many more human needs than its modern corollary—the nuclear family—which purchases commodities to meet its needs. The importance of the domestic sphere, and hence women's influence, declined with the advent of market society.

Feminism also negates capitalist social relations by challenging the lopsided male-biased values of our culture. When coupled with an ecological perspective, it insists that we remember our origins in nature, our connections to one another as daughters, sisters and mothers. It refuses any longer to be the unwitting powerless symbol of all the things men wish to deny in themselves and project onto us—the refusal to be the "other."[14] It can heal the splits in a world divided against itself and built on a fundamental lie: the defining of culture in opposition to nature.

The dialectic moves on. Now it is possible that a conscious visionary feminism could place our technology and productive apparatus in the service of a society based on ecological principles and values, with roots in traditional women's ways of being in the world. This in turn might make possible a total cultural critique. Women can remember what men have denied in themselves (nature), and women can know what men know (culture). Now we must develop a transformative feminism that sparks our utopian imaginations and embodies our deepest knowledge—a feminism that is an affirmation of our vision at the same time it is a negation of patriarchy. The skewed reasoning that opposes matter and spirit and refuses to concern itself with the objects and ends of life, which views internal nature and external nature as one big hunting ground to be quantified and conquered is, in the end, not only irrational but deadly. To fulfill its liberatory potential, feminism needs to pose a *rational reenchantment* that brings together spiritual and material, being and knowing. This is the promise of ecological feminism.

Notes

1. Ellen Willis, *The Village Voice* (June 23, 1980). In the *Voice* (July 16–22, 1980), Willis began with the question: "Is ecology a feminist issue?" and was more ambiguous than in her earlier column, although her theoretical position was the same.

2. Mary Daly, *Gyn/Ecology: The Meta-Ethics of Radical Feminism* (Boston: Beacon Press, 1978).

3. Susan Griffin, *Woman and Nature: The Roaring Inside Her* (New York: Harper & Row, 1979).

4. For an overview of socialist feminist theory, see Zillah Eisenstein, Ed., *Capitalist Patriarchy and the Case for Socialist Feminism* (New York: Monthly Review Press, 1979).

5. See Batya Weinbaum, *The Curious Courtship of Women's Liberation and Socialism* (Boston: South End Press, 1978).

6. See Heidi Hartman, "The Unhappy Marriage of Marxism and Feminism: Towards a More Progressive Union," *Capital and Class,* no. 8 (Summer 1979).

7. The notion of a "sex-gender system" was first developed by Gayle Rubin in "The Traffic in Women," *Toward an Anthropology of Women*, ed. R.R. Reiter (New York: Monthly Review Press, 1975).

8. See Hilda Scott, *Does Socialism Liberate Women?* (Boston: Beacon Press, 1976).

9. See Sherry B. Ortner, "Is Woman to Nature as Man Is to Culture?," *Woman, Culture, and Society*, ed. M.Z. Rosaldo & L. Lamphere (Stanford: Stanford University Press, 1974).

10. For a social history of the 19th-century romanticist/rationalist debate, see Barbara Ehrenreich and Dierdre English, *For Her Own Good* (New York: Doubleday/Anchor, 1979).

11. Mary Daly comes very close to this position. Other naturalist feminists have a less clear stance on *essential* differences between women and men.

12. The "disenchantment of the world" is another way of talking about the process of rationalization discussed above. The term was coined by Max Weber.

13. See Carolyn Merchant, *The Death of Nature: Women, Ecology and the Scientific Revolution* (San Francisco: Harper & Row, 1980).

14. For a full development of the idea of "woman as other," see Simone de Beauvoir, *The Second Sex* (New York: Modern Library, 1968).

25

MURRAY BOOKCHIN

The Concept of Social Ecology

The legends of the Norsemen tell of a time when all beings were apportioned their worldly domains: the gods occupied a celestial domain, Asgard, and men lived on the earth, Midgard, below which lay Niffleheim, the dark, icy domain of the giants, dwarfs, and the dead. These domains were linked together by an enormous ash, the World Tree. Its lofty branches reached into the sky, and its roots into the furthermost depths of the earth. Although the World Tree was constantly being gnawed by animals, it remained ever green, renewed by a magic fountain that infused it continually with life.

The gods, who had fashioned this world, presided over a precarious state of tranquility. They had banished their enemies, the giants, to the land of ice. Fenris the wolf was enchained, and the great serpent of the Midgard was held at bay. Despite the lurking dangers, a general peace prevailed, and plenty existed for the gods, men, and all living things. Odin, the god of wisdom, reigned over all the deities; the wisest and strongest, he watched over the battles of men and selected the most heroic of the fallen to feast with him in his great fortress, Valhalla. Thor, the son of Odin, was not only a powerful warrior, the defender of Asgard against the restive giants, but also a deity of order, who saw to the keeping of faith between men and obedience to the treaties. There were gods and goddesses of plenty, of fertility, of love, of law, of the sea and ships, and a multitude of animistic spirits who inhabited all things and beings of the earth.

But the world order began to break down when the gods, greedy for riches, tortured the witch Gullveig, the maker of gold, to compel her to reveal her secrets. Discord now became rampant among the gods and men. The gods began to break their oaths; corruption, treachery, rivalry, and

---

From Murray Bookchin, *The Ecology of Freedom* (Palo Alto, CA: Cheshire Books, 1982).

greed began to dominate the world. With the breakdown of the primal unity, the days of the gods and men, of Asgard and Midgard, were numbered. Inexorably, the violation of the world order would lead to Ragnarok—the death of the gods in a great conflict before Valhalla. The gods would go down in a terrible battle with the giants, Fenris the wolf, and the serpent of the Midgard. With the mutual destruction of all the combatants, humanity too would perish, and nothing would remain but bare rock and overflowing oceans in a void of cold and darkness. Having thus disintegrated into its beginnings, however, the world would be renewed, purged of its earlier evils and the corruption that destroyed it. Nor would the new world emerging from the void suffer another catastrophic end, for the second generation of gods and goddesses would learn from the mistakes of their antecedents. The prophetess who recounts the story tells us that humanity thenceforth will "live in joy for as long as one can foresee."

In this Norse cosmography, there seems to be more than the old theme of "eternal recurrence," of a time-sense that spins around perpetual cycles of birth, maturation, death, and rebirth. Rather, one is aware of prophecy infused with historical trauma; the legend belongs to a little-explored area of mythology that might be called "myths of disintegration." Although the Ragnarok legend is known to be quite old, we know very little about when it appeared in the evolution of the Norse sagas. We do know that Christianity, with its bargain of eternal reward, came later to the Norsemen than to any other large ethnic group in western Europe, and its roots were shallow for generations afterward. The heathenism of the north had long made contact with the commerce of the south. During the Viking raids on Europe, the sacred places of the north had become polluted by gold, and the pursuit of riches was dividing kinsman from kinsman. Hierarchies erected by valor were being eroded by systems of privilege based on wealth. The clans and tribes were breaking down; the oaths between men, from which stemmed the unity of their primordial world, were being dishonored, and the magic fountain that kept the World Tree alive was being clogged by the debris of commerce. "Brothers fight and slay one another," laments the prophetess, "children deny their own ancestry . . . this is the age of wind, of wolf, until the very day when the world shall be no more."

What haunts us in such myths of disintegration are not their histories, but their prophecies. Like the Norsemen, and perhaps even more, like the people at the close of the Middle Ages, we sense that our world, too, is breaking down—institutionally, culturally, and physically. Whether we are faced with a new, paradisiacal era or a catastrophe like the Norse Ragnarok is still unclear, but there can be no lengthy period of compromise between past and future in an ambiguous present. The reconstructive and destructive tendencies in our time are too much at odds with each other to admit of reconciliation. The social horizon presents the starkly conflicting prospects of a harmonized world with an ecological sensibility based on a rich commitment to community, mutual aid, and new technologies, on the one hand, and the terrifying prospect of some sort of thermonuclear disaster on the other. Our world, it would appear, will either undergo revolutionary changes, so far-reaching in character that humanity will totally transform its social relations and its very conception of life, or it will suffer an apocalypse that may well end humanity's tenure on the planet.

The tension between these two prospects has already subverted the morale of the traditional social order. We have entered an era that consists no longer of institutional stabilization but of institutional decay. A widespread alienation is developing toward the forms, the aspirations, the demands, and above all, the institutions of the established order. The most exuberant, theatrical evidence of this alienation occurred in the 1960s, when the "youth revolt" in the early half of the decade exploded into what seemed to be a counterculture. Considerably more than protest and adolescent nihilism marked the period. Almost intuitively, new values of sensuousness, new forms of communal lifestyle, changes in dress, language, music, all borne on the wave of a deep sense of impending social change, infused a sizable section of an entire generation. We still do not know in what sense this wave began to ebb: whether as a historic retreat or as a transformation into a serious project for inner and social development. That the symbols of this movement eventually became the artifacts for a new culture industry does not alter its far-reaching effects. Western society will never be the same again—all the sneers of its academics and its critics of "narcissism" notwithstanding.

What makes this ceaseless movement of deinstitutionalization and delegitimation so significant is that it has found its bedrock in a vast stratum of western society. Alienation permeates not only the poor but also the relatively affluent, not only the young but also their elders, not only the visibly denied but also the seemingly privileged. The prevailing order is beginning to lose the loyalty of social strata that traditionally rallied to its support and in which its roots were firmly planted in past periods.

Crucial as this decay of institutions and values may be, it by no means exhausts the problems that confront the existing society. Intertwined with the social crisis is a crisis that has emerged directly from man's exploitation of the planet.[1] Established society is faced with a breakdown not only of its values and institutions, but also of its natural environment. This problem is not unique to our times. The desiccated wastelands of the Near East, where the arts of agriculture and urbanism had their beginnings, are evidence of ancient human despoliation, but this example pales before the massive destruction of the environment that has occurred since the days of the Industrial Revolution, and especially since the end of the Second World War. The damage inflicted on the environment by contemporary society encompasses the entire earth. Volumes have been written on the immense losses of productive soil that occur annually in almost every continent of the earth; on the extensive destruction of tree cover in areas vulnerable to erosion; on lethal air-pollution episodes in major urban areas; on the worldwide diffusion of toxic agents from agriculture, industry, and power-producing installations; on the chemicalization of humanity's immediate environment with industrial wastes, pesticide residues, and food additives. The exploitation and pollution of the earth has damaged not only the integrity of the atmosphere, climate, water resources, soil, flora and fauna of specific regions, but also the basic natural cycles on which all living things depend.

Yet modern man's capacity for destruction is quixotic evidence of humanity's capacity for reconstruction. The powerful technological agents we have unleashed against the environment include many of the very agents we require for its reconstruction. The knowledge and physical instruments for promoting a harmonization of humanity with nature and of human with human are largely at hand or could easily be devised. Many of physical principles used to construct such patently harmful facilities as conventional power plants, energy-consuming vehicles, surface-mining equipment and the like could be directed to the construction of small-scale solar and wind energy devices, efficient means of transportation, and energy-saving shelters. What we crucially lack is the consciousness and sensibility that will help us achieve such eminently desirable goals—a consciousness and sensibility far broader than customarily meant by these terms. Our definitions must include not only the ability to reason logically and respond emotionally in a humanistic fashion; they must also include a fresh awareness of the relatedness between things and an imaginative insight into the possible. On this score, Marx was entirely correct to emphasize that the revolution required by our time must draw its poetry not from the past but from the future, from the humanistic potentialities that lie on the horizons of social life.

The new consciousness and sensibility cannot be poetic alone; they must also be scientific. Indeed, there is a level at which our consciousness must be neither poetry nor science, but a transcendence of both into a new realm of theory and practice, an artfulness that combines fancy with reason, imagination with logic, vision with technique. We cannot shed our scientific heritage without returning to a rudimentary technology with its shackles of material insecurity, toil, and renunciation. And we cannot allow ourselves to be imprisoned within a mechanistic outlook and a dehumanizing technology—with its shackles of alienation, competition, and a brute denial of humanity's potentialities. Poetry and imagination must be integrated with science and technology, for we have evolved beyond an innocence that can be nourished exclusively by myths and dreams.

Is there a scientific discipline that allows for the indiscipline of fancy, imagination, and artfulness? Can it encompass problems created by the social and environmental crises of our time? Can it integrate critique with reconstruction, theory with practice, vision with technique?

In almost every period since the Renaissance, a very close link has existed between radical advances in the natural sciences and upheavals in social thought. In the sixteenth and seventeenth centuries, the emerging sciences of astronomy and mechanics, with their liberating visions of a heliocentric world and the unity of local and cosmic motion, found their social counterparts in equally critical and rational social ideologies that challenged religious bigotry and political absolutism. The Enlightenment brought a new appreciation of sensory perception and the claims of human reason to divine a world that had been the ideological monopoly of the clergy. Later, anthropology and evolutionary biology demolished traditional static notions of the human enterprise along with its myths of original creation and history as a theological calling. By enlarging the map and revealing the earthly dynamics of social history, these sciences reinforced the new doctrines of socialism, with its ideal of human progress, that followed the French Revolution.

In view of the enormous dislocations that now confront us, our own era needs a more sweeping and insightful body of knowledge—scientific as well as social—to deal with our problems. Without renouncing the gains of earlier scientific and social theories, we must develop a more rounded critical analysis of our relationship with the natural world. We must seek the foundations for a more reconstructive approach to the grave problems posed by the apparent "contradictions" between nature and society. We can no longer afford to remain captives to the tendency of the more traditional sciences to dissect phenomena and examine their fragments. We must combine them, relate them, and see them in their totality as well as their specificity.

In response to these needs, we have formulated a discipline unique to our age: *social ecology*. The more well-known term "ecology" was coined by Ernst Haeckel a century ago to denote the investigation of the interrelationships between animals, plants, and their inorganic environment. Since Haeckel's day, the term has been expanded to include ecologies of cities, of health, and of the mind. This proliferation of a word into widely disparate areas may seem particularly desirable to an age that fervently seeks some kind of intellectual coherence and unity of perception. But it can also prove to be extremely treacherous. Like such newly arrived words as holism, decentralization, and dialectics, the term ecology runs the peril of merely hanging in the air without any roots, context, or texture. Often it is used as a metaphor, an alluring catchword, that loses the potentially compelling internal logic of its premises.

Accordingly, the radical thrust of these words is easily neutralized. "Holism" evaporates into a mystical sigh, a rhetorical expression for ecological fellowship and community that ends with such in-group greetings and salutations as "holistically yours." What was once a serious philosophical stance has been reduced to environmentalist kitsch. Decentralization commonly means logistical alternatives to gigantism, not the human scale that would make an intimate and direct democracy possible. Ecology fares even worse. All too often it becomes a metaphor, like the word dialectics, for any kind of integration and development.

Perhaps even more troubling, the word in recent years has been identified with a very crude form of natural engineering that might well be called *environmentalism.*

I am mindful that many ecologically oriented individuals use "ecology" and "environmentalism" interchangeably. Here, I would like to draw a semantically convenient distinction. By "environmentalism" I propose to designate a mechanistic, instrumental outlook that sees nature as a passive habitat composed of "objects" such as animals, plants, minerals, and the like that must merely be rendered more serviceable for human use. Given my use of the term, environmentalism tends to reduce nature to a storage bin of "natural resources" or "raw materials." Within the context, very little of a social nature is spared form the environmentalist's vocabulary: cities become "urban resources" and their inhabitants "human resources." If the word *resources* leaps out so frequently from environmentalistic discussions of nature, cities, and people, an issue more important than mere word play is at stake. Environmentalism, as I use this term, tends to view the ecological project for attaining a harmonious relationship between humanity and nature as a truce rather than a lasting equilibrium. The "harmony" of the environmentalist centers around the development of new techniques for plundering the natural world with minimal disruption of the human "habitat." Environmentalism does not question the most basic premise of the present society, notably, that humanity must dominate nature; rather, it seeks to *facilitate* that notion by developing techniques for diminishing the hazards caused by the reckless despoliation of the environment.

To distinguish ecology from environmentalism and from abstract, often obfuscatory definitions of the term, I must return to its original usage and explore its direct relevance to society. Put quite simply, ecology deals with the dynamic balance of nature, with the interdependence of living and non-living things. Since nature also includes human beings, the science must include humanity's role in the natural world—specifically, the character, form, and structure of humanity's relationship with other species and with the inorganic substrate of the biotic environment. From a critical viewpoint, ecology opens to wide purview the vast disequilibrium that has emerged from humanity's split with the natural world. One of nature's very unique species, *homo sapiens,* has slowly and painstakingly developed from the natural world into a unique social world of its own. As both worlds interact with each other through highly complex phases of evolution, it has become as important to speak of a social ecology as to speak of a natural ecology.

Let me emphasize that the failure to explore these phases of human evolution—which have yielded a succession of hierarchies, classes, cities, and finally states—is to make a mockery of the term social ecology. Unfortunately, the discipline has been beleaguered by self-professed adherents who continually try to collapse all the phases of natural and human development into a universal "oneness" (not wholeness), a yawning "night in which all cows are black," to borrow one of Hegel's caustic phrases. If nothing else, our common use of the word *species* to denote the wealth of life around us should alert us to the fact of *specificity,* of *particularity*—the rich abundance of *differentiated* beings and things that enter into the very subject-matter of natural ecology. To explore these differentia, to examine the phases and interfaces that enter into their making and into humanity's long development from animality to society—a development latent with problems and possibilities—is to make social ecology one of the most powerful disciplines from which to draw our critique of the present social order.

But social ecology provides more than a critique of the split between humanity and nature; it also poses the need to heal them. Indeed, it poses the need to radically transcend them. As E.A. Gutkind pointed out, "the goal of Social Ecology is wholeness, and not mere adding together of innumerable details collected at random and interpreted subjectively and insufficiently." The science deals with social and natural relationships in communities or "ecosystems."[2] In conceiving them holistically, that is to say, in terms of their mutual interdependence, social ecology seeks to unravel the forms and patterns of interrelationships that give intelligibility to a community, be it natural or social. Holism, here, is the result of a conscious effort to discern how the particulars of a community are arranged, how its "geometry" (as the Greeks might have put it) makes the "whole more than the sum of its parts." Hence, the "wholeness" to which Gutkind refers is not to be mistaken for a spectral "oneness" that yields cosmic dissolution in a structureless nirvana; it is a richly articulated structure with a history and internal logic of its own.

History, in fact, is as important as form or structure. To a large extent, the history of a phenomenon *is* the phenomenon itself. We are, in a real sense, everything that existed before us and, in turn, we can eventually become vastly more than we are. Surprisingly, very little in the evolution of life-forms has been lost in natural and social evolution, indeed in our very bodies as our embryonic development attests. Evolution lies within us (as well as around us) as parts of the very nature of our beings.

For the present, it suffices to say that wholeness is not a bleak undifferentiated "universality" that involves the reduction of a phenomenon to what it has in common with everything else. Nor is it a celestial, omnipresent "energy" that replaces the vast material differentia of which the natural and social realms are composed. To the contrary, wholeness comprises the variegated structures, the articulations, and the mediations that impart to the whole a rich variety of forms and thereby add unique qualitative properties to what a strictly analytic mind often reduces to "innumerable" and "random" details.

Notes

1. I use the word "man," here, advisedly. The split between humanity and nature has been precisely the work of the male, who, in the memorable lines of Theodor Adorno and Max Horkheimer, "dreamed of acquiring absolute mastery over nature, of converting the cosmos into one immense hunting-ground." *(Dialectic of Enlightenment,* New York: Seabury Press, 1972, p. 248). For the words "one immense hunting-ground," I would be disposed to substitute "one immense killing-ground" to describe the male-oriented "civilization" of our era.

2. The term ecosystem—or ecological system—is often used loosely in many ecological works. Here, I employ it, as in natural ecology, to mean a fairly demarcatable animal-plant community and the abiotic, or nonliving, factors needed to sustain it. I also use it in social ecology to mean a distinct human and natural community, the social as well as organic factors that interrelate to provide the basis for an ecologically rounded and balanced community.

26

Edward O. Wilson

The Diversity of Life

For the green prehuman earth is the mystery we were chosen to solve, a guide to the birthplace of our spirit, but it is slipping away. The way back seems harder every year. If there is danger in the human trajectory, it is not so much in the survival of our own species as in the fulfillment of the ultimate irony of organic evolution: that in the instant of achieving self-understanding through the mind of man, life has doomed its most beautiful creations. And thus humanity closes the door to its past.

The creation of that diversity came slow and hard: 3 billion years of evolution to start the profusion of animals that occupy the seas, another 350 million years to assemble the rain forests in which half or more of the species on earth now live. There was a succession of dynasties. Some species split into two or several daughter species, and their daughters split yet again to create swarms of descendants that deploy as plant feeders, carnivores, free swimmers, gliders, sprinters, and burrowers, in countless motley combinations. These ensembles then gave way by partial or total extinction to newer dynasties, and so on to form a gentle upward swell that carried biodiversity to a peak—just before the arrival of humans. Life had stalled on plateaus along the way, and on five occasions it suffered extinction spasms that took 10 million years to repair. But the thrust was upward. Today the diversity of life is greater than it was 100 million years ago—and far greater than 500 million years before that.

Most dynasties contained a few species that expanded disproportionately to create satrapies of lesser rank. Each species and its descendants, a sliver of the whole, lived an average of hundreds of thousands to millions of years. Longevity varied according to taxonomic group. Echinoderm lineages, for

From Edward O. Wilson, *The Diversity of Life* (New York: W.W. Norton and Company, 1993), pp. 344–347.

example, persisted longer than those of flowering plants, and both endured longer than those of mammals.

Ninety-nine percent of all the species that ever lived are now extinct. The modern fauna and flora are composed of survivors that somehow managed to dodge and weave through all the radiations and extinctions of geological history. Many contemporary world dominant groups, such as rats, ranid frogs, nymphalid butterflies, and plants of the aster family Compositae, attained their status not long before the Age of Man. Young or old, all living species are direct descendants of the organisms that lived 3.8 billion years ago. They are living genetic libraries, composed of nucleotide sequences, the equivalent of words and sentences, which record evolutionary events all across that immense span of time. Organisms more complex than bacteria—protists, fungi, plants, animals—contain between one and ten billion nucleotide letters, more than enough in pure information to compose an equivalent of the *Encyclopaedia Britannica.* Each species is the product of mutations and recombinations too complex to be grasped by unaided intuition. It was sculpted and burnished by an astronomical number of events in natural selection, which killed off or otherwise blocked from reproduction the vast majority of its member organisms before they completed their lifespan. Viewed from the perspective of evolutionary time, all other species are a distant kin because we share a remote ancestry. We still use a common vocabulary, the nucleic-acid code, even though it has been sorted into radically different hereditary languages. . . .

Enchanted by the continuous emergence of new technologies and supported by generous funding for medical research, biologists have probed deeply along a narrow sector of the front. Now it is time to expand laterally, to get on with the great Linnean enterprise and finish mapping the biosphere. The most compelling reason for the broadening of goals is that, unlike the rest of science, the study of biodiversity has a time limit. Species are disappearing at an accelerated rate through human action, primarily habitat destruction but also pollution and the introduction of exotic species into residual natural environments. I have said that a fifth or more of the species of plants and animals could vanish or be doomed to early extinction by the year 2020 unless better efforts are made to save them. This estimate comes from the known quantitative relation between the area of habitats and the diversity that habitats can sustain. These area-biodiversity curves are supported by the general but not universal principal that when certain groups of organisms are studied closely, such as snails and fishes and flowering plants, extinction is determined to be widespread. And the corollary: among plant and animal remains in archaeological deposits, we usually find extinct species and races. As the last forests are felled in forest strongholds like the Philippines and Ecuador, the decline of species will accelerate even more. In the world as a whole, extinction rates are already hundreds or thousands of times higher than before the coming of man. They cannot be balanced by new evolution in any period of time that has meaning for the human race.

Why should we care? What difference does it make if some species are extinguished, if even half of all the species on earth disappear? Let me count the ways. New sources of information will be lost. Vast potential biological wealth will be destroyed. Still undeveloped medicines, crops, pharmaceuticals, timber, fibers, pulp, soil-restoring vegetation, petroleum substitutes, and other products and amenities will never come to light. It is fashionable in some quarters to wave aside the small and obscure, the bugs and weeds, forgetting that an obscure moth from Latin America saved Australia's pasture-land from overgrowth by cactus, that the rosy periwinkle provided the cure for Hodgkin's disease and childhood lymphocytic leukemia, that the bark of the Pacific yew offers hope for victims of ovarian and breast cancer, that a chemical from the saliva of leeches dissolves blood clots during surgery, and so on down a roster already grown long and illustrious despite the limited research addressed to it.

In amnesiac revery it is also easy to overlook the services that ecosystems provide humanity. They enrich the soil and create the very air we breathe. Without these amenities, the remaining tenure of the human race would be nasty and brief. The life-sustaining matrix is built of green plants with legions of microorganisms and mostly small, obscure animals—in other words, weeds and bugs. Such organisms support the world with efficiency because they are so diverse, allowing them to divide labor and swarm over every square meter of the earth's surface. They run the world precisely as we would wish it to be run, because humanity evolved within living communities and our body functions are finely adjusted to the idiosyncratic environment already created. Mother Earth, lately called Gaia, is no more than the commonality of organisms and the physical environment they maintain with each passing moment, an environment that will destabilize and turn lethal if the organisms are disturbed too much. A near infinity of other mother planets can be envisioned, each with its own fauna and flora, all producing physical environments uncongenial to human life. To disregard diversity of life is to risk catapulting ourselves into an alien environment. We will have become like the pilot whales that inexplicably beach themselves on New England's shores.

27

Robert D. Bullard

Environmental Racism and the Environmental Justice Movement

Communities are not all created equal. In the United States, for example, some communities are routinely poisoned while the government looks the other way. Environmental regulations have not uniformly benefited all segments of society. People of color (African Americans, Latinos, Asians, Pacific Islanders, and Native Americans) are disproportionately harmed by industrial toxins on their jobs and in their neighborhoods. These groups must contend with dirty air and drinking water—the byproducts of municipal landfills, incinerators, polluting industries, and hazardous waste treatment, storage, and disposal facilities.

Why do some communities get "dumped on" while others escape? Why are environmental regulations vigorously enforced in some communities and not in others? Why are some workers protected from environmental threats to their health while others (such as migrant farmworkers) are still being poisoned? How can environmental justice be incorporated into the campaign for environmental protection? What institutional changes would enable the United States to become a just and sustainable society? What community organizing strategies are effective against environmental racism? These are some of the many questions addressed in this book.

This chapter sketches out the basic environmental problems communities of color face, discusses how the mainstream environmental movement does not provide an adequate organizational base, analysis, vision, or strategy to address these problems, and finally, provides a glimpse of several represen-

---

Reprinted from *Confronting Environmental Racism: Voices from the Grassroots* by Robert D. Bullard (Boston: South End Press, 1993), with permission from the publisher, South End Press, 116 Saint Botolph Street, Boston, MA 02115.

tative struggles within the grassroots environmental justice movement. For these purposes, the pervasive reality of racism is placed at the very center of the analysis.

Internal Colonialism and White Racism

The history of the United States has long been grounded in white racism. The nation was founded on the principles of "free land" (stolen from Native Americans and Mexicans), "free labor" (cruelly extracted from African slaves), and "free men" (white men with property). From the outset, institutional racism shaped the economic, political, and ecological landscape, and buttressed the exploitation of both land and people. Indeed, it has allowed communities of color to exist as internal colonies characterized by dependent (and unequal) relationships with the dominant white society or "Mother Country." In their 1967 book, *Black Power,* Carmichael and Hamilton were among the first to explore the "internal" colonial model as a way to explain the racial inequality, political exploitation, and social isolation of African Americans. As Carmichael and Hamilton write:

> The economic relationship of America's black communities [to white society] . . . reflects their colonial status. The political power exercised over those communities goes hand in glove with the economic deprivation experienced by the black citizens.
>
> Historically, colonies have existed for the sole purpose of enriching, in one form or another, the "colonizer"; the consequence is to maintain the economic dependency of the "colonized." (pp. 16–17)

Generally, people of color in the United States—like their counterparts in formerly colonized lands of Africa, Asia, and Latin America—have not had the same opportunities as whites. The social forces that have organized oppressed colonies internationally still operate in the "heart of the colonizer's mother country" (Blauner 1972, p. 26). For Blauner, people of color are subjected to five principal colonizing processes: they enter the "host" society and economy involuntarily; their native culture is destroyed; white-dominated bureaucracies impose restrictions from which whites are exempt; the dominant group uses institutionalized racism to justify its actions; and a dual or "split labor market" emerges based on ethnicity and race. Such domination is also buttressed by state institutions. Social scientists Omi and Winant (1986, pp. 76–78) go so far as to insist that "every state institution is a racial institution." Clearly, whites receive benefits from racism, while people of color bear most of the cost.

Environmental Racism

Racism plays a key factor in environmental planning and decisionmaking. Indeed, environmental racism is reinforced by government, legal, economic, political, and military institutions. It is a fact of life in the United States that the mainstream environmental movement is only beginning to wake up to. Yet, without a doubt, racism influences the likelihood of exposure to environmental and health risks and the accessibility to health care. Racism provides whites of all class levels with an "edge" in gaining access to a healthy physical environment. This has been documented again and again.

Whether by conscious design or institutional neglect, communities of color in urban ghettos, in rural "poverty pockets," or on economically impoverished Native-American reservations face some of the worst environmental devastation in the nation. Clearly, racial discrimination was not legislated out of existence in the 1960s. While some significant progress was made during this decade, people of color continue to struggle for equal treatment in many areas, including environmental justice. Agencies at all levels of government, including the federal EPA, have done a poor job protecting people of color from the ravages of pollution and industrial encroachment. It has thus been an up-hill battle convincing white judges, juries, government officials, and policymakers that racism exists in environmental protection, enforcement, and policy formulation.

The most polluted urban communities are those with crumbling infrastructure, ongoing economic disinvestment, deteriorating housing, inadequate schools, chronic unemployment, a high poverty rate, and an overloaded health-care system. Riot-torn South Central Los Angeles typifies this urban neglect. It is not surprising that the "dirtiest" zip code in California belongs to the mostly African-American and Latino neighborhood in that part of the city (Kay 1991). In the Los Angeles basin, over 71 percent of the African Americans and 50 percent of the Latinos live in areas with the most polluted air, while only 34 percent of the white population does (Ong and Blumenberg 1990; Mann 1991). This pattern exists nationally as well. As researchers Wernette and Nieves note:

> In the 1990s, 437 of the 3,109 counties and independent cities failed to meet at least one of the EPA ambient air quality standards. . . . 57 percent of whites, 65 percent of African Americans, and 80 percent of Hispanics live in 437 counties with substandard air quality. Out of the whole population, a total of 33 percent of whites, 50 percent of African Americans, and 60 percent of Hispanics live in the 136 counties in which two or more air pollutants exceed standards. The percentage living in the 29 counties designated

> as nonattainment areas for three or more pollutants are 12 percent of whites, 20 percent of African Americans, and 31 percent of Hispanics. (pp. 16–17)

Income alone does not account for these above-average percentages. Housing segregation and development patterns play a key role in determining where people live. Moreover, urban development and the "spatial configuration" of communities flow from the forces and relationships of industrial production which, in turn, are influenced and subsidized by government policy (Feagin 1988; Gottdiener 1988). There is widespread agreement that vestiges of race-based decisionmaking still influence housing, education, employment, and criminal justice. The same is true for municipal services such as garbage pickup and disposal, neighborhood sanitation, fire and police protection, and library services. Institutional racism influences decisions on local land use, enforcement of environmental regulations, industrial facility siting, management of economic vulnerability, and the paths of freeways and highways.

People skeptical of the assertion that poor people and people of color are targeted for waste-disposal sites should consider the report the Cerrell Associates provided the California Waste Management Board. In their 1984 report, *Political Difficulties Facing Waste-to-Energy Conversion Plant Siting,* they offered a detailed profile of those neighborhoods most likely to organize effective resistance against incinerators. The policy conclusion based on this analysis is clear. As the report states:

> All socioeconomic groupings tend to resent the nearby siting of major facilities, but middle and upper socioeconomic strata possess better resources to effectuate their opposition. Middle and higher socioeconomic strata neighborhoods should not fall within the one-mile and five-mile radius of the proposed site. (p. 43)

Where then will incinerators or other polluting facilities be sited? For Cerrell Associates, the answer is low-income, disempowered neighborhoods with a high concentration of nonvoters. The ideal site, according their report, has nothing to do with environmental soundness but everything to do with lack of social power. Communities of color in California are far more likely to fit this profile than are their white counterparts.

Those still skeptical of the existence of environmental racism should also consider the fact that zoning boards and planning commissions are typically stacked with white developers. Generally, the decisions of these bodies reflect the special interests of the individuals who sit on these boards. People of color have been systematically excluded from these decisionmaking boards, commissions, and governmental agencies (or allowed only token representation). Grassroots leaders are now demanding a shared role in all the decisions that shape their communities. They are challenging the intended or unintended racist assumptions underlying environmental and industrial policies.

Toxic Colonialism Abroad

To understand the global ecological crisis, it is important to understand that the poisoning of African Americans in South Central Los Angeles and of Mexicans in border *maquiladoras* have their roots in the same system of economic exploitation, racial oppression, and devaluation of human life. The quest for solutions to environmental problems and for ways to achieve sustainable development in the United States has considerable implications for the global environmental movement.

Today, more than 1,900 *maquiladoras,* assembly plants operated by American, Japanese, and other foreign countries, are located along the 2,000-mile U.S.-Mexico border (Center for Investigative Reporting 1990; Sanchez 1990; Zuniga 1992, p. 22A). These plants use cheap Mexican labor to assemble products from imported components and raw materials, and then ship them back to the United States (Witt 1991). Nearly half a million Mexicans work in the *maquiladoras.* They earn an average of $3.75 a day. While these plants bring jobs, albeit low-paying ones, they exacerbate local pollution by overcrowding the border towns, straining sewage and water systems, and reducing air quality. All this compromises the health of workers and nearby community residents. The Mexican environmental regulatory agency is understaffed and ill-equipped to adequately enforce the country's laws (Working Group on Canada-Mexico Free Trade 1991).

The practice of targeting poor communities of color in the Third World for waste disposal and the introduction of risky technologies from industrialized countries are forms of "toxic colonialism," what some activists have dubbed the "subjugation of people to an ecologically-destructive economic order by entities over which the people have no control" (Greenpeace 1992, p. 3). The industrialized world's controversial Third World dumping policy was made public by the release of an internal, December 12, 1991, memorandum authored by Lawrence Summers, chief economist of the World Bank. It shocked the world and touched off a global scandal. Here are the highlights: "Dirty" Industries: Just between you and me, shouldn't the World Bank be encouraging MORE migration of the dirty industries to the LDCs [Less Developed Countries]? I can think of three reasons:

1) The measurement of the costs of health impairing pollution depends on the foregone earnings from increased morbidity and mortality. From this

point of view a given amount of health impairing pollution should be done in the country with the lowest cost, which will be the country with the lowest wages. I think the economic logic behind dumping a load of toxic waste in the lowest wage country is impeccable and we should face up to that.

2) The costs of pollution are likely to be non-linear as the initial increments of pollution probably have very low cost. I've always thought that under-polluted areas in Africa are vastly UNDER-polluted; their air quality is probably vastly inefficiently low compared to Los Angeles or Mexico City. Only the lamentable facts that so much pollution is generated by non-tradable industries (transport, electrical generation) and that the unit transport costs of solid waste are so high prevent world welfare-enhancing trade in air pollution and waste.

3) The demand for a clean environment for aesthetic and health reasons is likely to have very high income elasticity. The concern over an agent that causes a one in a million change in the odds of prostate cancer is obviously going to be much higher in a country where people survive to get prostate cancer than in a country where under 5 [year-old] mortality is 200 per thousand. Also, much of the concern over industrial atmosphere discharge is about visibility impairing particulates. These discharges may have very little direct health impact. Clearly trade in goods that embody aesthetic pollution concerns could be welfare enhancing. While production is mobile the consumption of pretty air is a nontradable.

The problem with the arguments against all of these proposals for more pollution in LDCs (intrinsic rights to certain goods, moral reasons, social concerns, lack of adequate markets, etc.) could be turned around and used more or less effectively against every Bank proposal. . . .

Beyond the Race vs. Class Trap

Whether at home or abroad, the question of who *pays* and who *benefits* from current industrial and development policies is central to any analysis of environmental racism. In the United States, race interacts with class to create special environmental and health vulnerabilities. People of color, however, face elevated toxic exposure levels even when social class variables (income, education, and occupational status) are held constant (Bryant and Mohai 1992). Race has been found to be an independent factor, not reducible to class, in predicting the distribution of 1) air pollution in our society (Freeman 1971; Gianessi, Peskin, and Wolff 1979; Gelobter 1988; Wernette and Nieves 1992); 2) contaminated fish consumption (West, Fly, and Marans 1990); 3) the location of municipal landfills and incinerators

(Bullard 1983, 1987, 1990, 1991); 4) the location of abandoned toxic waste dumps (United Church of Christ Commission for Racial Justice 1987); and 5) lead poisoning in children (Agency for Toxic Substances and Disease Registry 1988).

Lead poisoning is a classic case in which race, not just class, determines exposure. It affects between three and four million children in the United States—most of whom are African Americans and Latinos living in urban areas. Among children five years old and younger, the percentage of African Americans who have excessive levels of lead in their blood far exceeds the percentage of whites at all income levels (Agency for Toxic Substances and Disease Registry 1988, pp. 1–12).

The federal Agency for Toxic Substances and Disease Registry found that for families earning less than $6,000 annually an estimated 68 percent of African-American children had lead poisoning, compared with 36 percent for white children. For families with incomes exceeding $15,000, more than 38 percent of African-American children have been poisoned, compared with 12 percent of white children. African-American children are two to three times more likely than their white counterparts to suffer from lead poisoning independent of class factors.

One reason for this is that African Americans and whites do not have the same opportunities to "vote with their feet" by leaving unhealthy physical environments. The ability of an individual to escape a health-threatening environment is usually correlated with income. However, racial barriers make it even harder for millions of African-Americans, Latinos, Asians, Pacific Islanders, and Native Americans to relocate. Housing discrimination, redlining, and other market forces, make it difficult for millions of households to buy their way out of polluted environments. For example, an affluent African-American family (with an income of $50,000 or more) is as segregated as an African-American family with an annual income of $5,000 (Denton and Massey 1988; Jaynes and Williams 1989). Thus, lead poisoning of African-American children is not just a "poverty thing."

White racism helped create our current separate and unequal communities. It defines the boundaries of the urban ghetto, *barrio,* and reservation, and influences the provision of environmental protection and other public services. Apartheid-type housing and development policies reduce neighborhood options, limit mobility, diminish job opportunities, and decrease environmental choices for millions of Americans. It is unlikely that this nation will ever achieve lasting solutions to its environmental problems unless it also addresses the system of racial injustice that helps sustain the existence of powerless communities forced to bear disproportionate environmental costs.

References

Agency for Toxic Substances and Disease Registry. 1988. *The Nature and Extent of Lead Poisoning in Children in the United States: A Reprint to Congress.* Atlanta: U.S. Department of Health and Human Services.

Blauner, Robert. 1972. *Racial Oppression in America.* New York: Harper and Row.

Bullard, Robert D. 1983. "Solid Waste Sites and the Black Houston Community." *Sociological Inquiry,* 53 (Spring).

———. 1987. *Invisible Houston: The Black Experience in Boom and Bust.* College Station, TX: Texas A & M University Press.

———. 1990. *Dumping in Dixie: Race, Class, and Environmental Quality.* Boulder, CO: Westview Press.

———. 1991. "Environmental Justice for All." *EnviroAction, Environmental News Digest for the National Wildlife Federation* (November).

Bryant, Bunyan and Paul Mohai. 1992. *Race and the Incidence of Environmental Hazards.* Boulder: Westview Press.

Carmichael, S. and C.V. Hamilton. 1967. *Black Power.* New York: Vintage.

Center for Investigative Reporting and Bill Moyers. 1990. *Global Dumping Grounds: The International Trade in Hazardous Waste.* Washington, DC: Seven Locks Press.

Cerrell Associates, Inc. 1984. *Political Difficulties Facing Waste-to-Energy Conversion Plant Siting.* California Waste Management Board, Technical Information Series.

Denton, Nancy A. and Douglas S. Massey. 1988. "Residential Segregation of Blacks, Hispanics, and Asians by Socioeconomic Class and Generation." *Social Science Quarterly,* 69.

Feagin, Joe R. 1988. *Free Enterprise City: Houston in Political and Economic Perspective.* Englewood Cliffs, NJ: Prentice Hall.

Freeman, Myrick A. 1971. "The Distribution of Environmental Quality." In Allen V. Kneese and Blair T. Bower (eds.) *Environmental Quality Analysis.* Baltimore, MD: Johns Hopkins University Press for Resources for the Future.

Gelobter, Michel. 1988. "The Distribution of Air Pollution by Income and Race." Paper presented at the Second Symposium on Social Science in Resource Management, Urbana, Illinois, June.

Gianessi, Leonard, H.M. Peskin, and E. Wolff. 1979. "The Distributional Effects of Uniform Air Pollution Policy in the U.S." *Quarterly Journal of Economics* (May).

Gottdiener, Mark. 1988. *The Social Production of Space.* Austin: University of Texas Press.

Greenpeace. 1992. "The 'Logic' Behind Hazardous Waste Export." *Greenpeace Waste Trade Update* (First Quarter: 1–2).

Jaynes, Gerald D. and Robin M. Williams, Jr. 1989. *A Common Destiny: Blacks and American Society.* Washington, DC: National Academy Press.

Kay, Jane. 1991. "Fighting Toxic Racism: L.A.'s Minority Neighborhood is the 'Dirtiest' in the State." *San Francisco Examiner,* 7 April.

Mann, Eric. 1991. *L.A.'s Lethal Air: New Perspectives for Policy, Organizing, and Action.* Los Angeles: Labor/Community Strategy Center.

Omi, Michael and Howard Winant. 1986. *Racial Formation in the United States: From the 1960s to the 1980s.* New York: Routledge, Kegan and Paul.

Ong, Paul and Evelyn Blumenberg. 1990. "Race and Environmentalism." Paper read at UCLA Graduate School of Architecture and Urban Planning, 14 March.

Sanchez, Roberto. 1990. "Health and Environmental Risks of the Maquiladora in Mexicali." *Natural Resources Journal,* 30 (Winter).

United Church of Christ Commission for Racial Justice. 1987. *Toxic Wastes and Race in the United States, A National Report on the Racial and Socio-Economic Characteristics of Communities with Hazardous Waste Sites.* New York: United Church of Christ.

Wernette, D.R. and L.A. Nieves. 1992. "Breathing Polluted Air." *EPA Journal.* 18 (March/April).

West, Pat, F. Fly, and R. Marans. 1990. "Minority Anglers and Toxic Fish Consumption: Evidence from a State-Wide Survey of Michigan." In B. Bryant and P. Mohai (eds.) *The Proceedings of the Michigan Conference on Race and the Incidence of Environmental Hazards.* Ann Arbor: University of Michigan School of Natural Resources.

Witt, Matthew. 1991. "An Injury to One Is a Gravio a Todo: The Need for a Mexico-U.S. Health and Safety Movement." *New Solutions, A Journal of Environmental and Occupational Health Policy,* 1 (March: 28–33).

Working Group on Canada-Mexico Free Trade. 1991. "Que Pasa? A Canada-Mexico 'Free' Trade Deal." *New Solutions, A Journal of Environmental and Occupational Health Policy,* 2 (January).

Zuniga, Jo Ann. 1992. "Watchdog Keeps Tabs on Politics of Environment Along Border." *Houston Chronicle,* 24 May, p. 22A.

Part IV

Accommodating the Future

28

MATTHEW CAHN

Accommodating the Future: Strategies for Resolving the Environmental Quagmire

Clearly, the existing environmental infrastructure has been inadequate to resolve the environmental problematic. Traditional efforts to improve environmental quality have approached different types of environmental degradation as independent problems requiring independent solutions. But, as we have seen, environmental problems are interdependent. There is a growing discourse on building more effective policy tools for confronting the growing challenges. This section of the book explores where the discourse on nature and the physical world is headed.

Where We've Come From, Where We're Going

The evolution of thought and action on nature and the environment illustrates the convergence of several factors making the environmental problematic extremely vexing. Changing behavior patterns, complex international market-based economies, differing assessments on how nature and development should be balanced, and conflicting assessments of the risks posed by toxins in the environment all come together to make environmental challenges extremely difficult to solve.

Pre-industrial societies tended to observe a system of riparian rights. Anyone who shared a stream or river was thought to have an equal right to that resource. And, since downstream users had the same right as upstream users, there was an obligation to maintain an adequate flow. Upstream users could not divert or destroy the riparian environment. The concept of a communal right, however, was lost during the eighteenth century with the rise of property rights. Emerging liberalism created a system of first-in-time users. That is to say, if one were to "discover" a stream or well, that individual could assert a property right to that resource. This established the intellectual foundation for a commodity-based system of resource allocation and use. If one could "own" natural resources, those materials could be used in whatever way the owner thought appropriate. There was no longer a compulsion to think about later users (Cahn 1995).

The abandonment of riparian rights was the first step in abandoning the notion of maintaining natural resources for all generations. As the physical world came to be seen as a collection of potential commodities, natural resources, including animals, plants, waterways, timber, soil, even air, came to be managed by a market ethic. Short-term economic gain for "owners" came to outweigh the long-term value of maintaining environmental quality. Emerging industrial technologies only exacerbated this trend. Technology is not the cause of degradation; it simply allows for a quicker, and more brutal, destruction of habitats.

By the late nineteenth century there was increasing recognition that natural resources are not infinite, and that environmental damage may be irreversible. This led to the initial conservation era in the 1890s. In the United States, for example, the preservationist movement—the precursor of the contemporary environmental movement—fought to set aside pristine wilderness areas as national parks. Yosemite Valley was established as a state park in 1860, and designated as a national park in 1890. Yellowstone National Park was designated in 1872.

It wasn't until the postwar era (1945–1960) that environmental protection in its current manifestation was considered—perhaps as a consequence of the new wealth that industrial democracies were experiencing. Early environmental policies focused on research to identify the extent of environmental dangers. By 1961 the "New Politics" era gave focus to the emerging environmental constituency. Kennedy's "Special Message" to Congress articulated what came to be the core environmental agenda for the next thirty years: an expansion of public lands, new clean air and clean water legislation, and endangered species protection.

By 1970 environmental issues were highly salient. An environmental ethic had permeated the political culture. It wasn't that pollution was new, it was just that a public politicized by a growing environmental discourse began paying attention to the increasing severity of environmental degradation. Earth Day came to symbolize a widely politicized public with a clear environmental agenda. The 1970 Clean Air Act, the 1972 Clean Water Act, the 1973 Endangered Species Act, the 1974 Safe Drinking Water Act, and the 1976 Toxic Substances Control Act were emblematic of the emerging controls on environmental degradation, creating the foundation of the contemporary environmental infrastructure. All were designed to satisfy a palpable public demand, and all turned out to be overly optimistic. Since 1970, the environmental discourse has focused on how we might improve the models that have been in place for the past three decades.

Approaches for Resolving the Environmental Problematic

The evolving environmental quagmire has proven extremely difficult to resolve. The traditional command-and-control approaches have not produced the anticipated results, leaving many scholars to conclude that something much deeper is necessary. The readings in this section of the book explore several different approaches to resolving the environmental problematic. They have been included because they provide the reader with unique, and complementary, conceptual tools for thinking about these issues.

Wenz (1988) integrates the ethic of justice into the environmental problematic. Because environmental regulation provides significant burdens as well as benefits, it is necessary to assure citizens that they are making fair sacrifices and receiving a fair share of benefits. Policy decision processes, therefore, must be widely seen as just. The current debate on U.S. environmental policy, for example, rotates around the "fairness" issue. If it were possible to create consensus on the *process* of deciding policy directions, support of the outcome would be much higher.

Christopher Stone suggests that the dilemma is a structural result of our rights-based legal system. In the classical discourse, only humans enjoy natural rights. The environmental consequence is that natural objects—or their advocates—have no ability to seek redress on their own behalf. In *Should Trees Have Standing?* Stone suggests that if natural objects had standing, resource management would look very different. Since anthropocentrism creates a problem for resource management, it may be efficacious to extend liberal rights to nonhuman entities. This would allow nonhuman resources to compete, through the agency of trustees, in their own self-interest. The result: humans would be forced to consider the rights not only of other humans, but also of plants and animals.

Orr suggests that it may be possible to achieve environmentally friendly behavior change through a systematic reordering of priorities. This will come about only through ecological literacy—educating people on what they "need to know to live responsibly and well in a finite world" (Orr 1992, 133):

> The historic upheavals in the Soviet Union and Eastern Europe in 1989–1990 are ample evidence that communism, or at least a particular version of

> it, has failed. We have to admit that Western capitalism has failed as well. Our failures are still concealed by bad book-keeping (both fiscal and ecological), dishonest rhetoric, and wishful thinking. . . . Communism has all but collapsed because it could not produce enough; capitalism is failing because it produces too much and shares too little. . . . Neither system is sustainable in either human or ecological terms. We now face the task of rebuilding something different, a postmodern world that protects individual rights while protecting the larger interests of the planet and our children who live on it. (Orr 1992, ix)

Orr argues that as people come to realize the failure of capitalism—through the process of environmental consciousness-raising—the ideals of the "postmodern world" will gain salience. Thus, for Orr, like Paehlke, ecocentric education becomes a dynamic for social evolution.

Similarly, Milbrath argues that environmental degradation can only be resolved through a change of social paradigms. To this end, he envisions a New Environmental Paradigm (NEP) replacing the Dominant Social Paradigm (DSP), perhaps through an Orr-like ecoliteracy approach. The NEP differs from the dominant social paradigm in several significant ways: the NEP values nature, the DSP exploits nature; NEP is ecocentric, the DSP is anthropocentric; the NEP favors limited growth, the DSP favors unlimited growth. This may sound like a radical change but, as Milbrath points out, human civilization has already changed radically to accommodate the current degradation. For example, one could look to traffic congestion or living with urban pollution to see just a few changes that society has come to accommodate over the past century. In short, Milbrath reminds us that change is occurring whether we face it or not: "avoiding change will make us victims of change" (1989, 341).

Free market environmentalists argue that it is efficacious to utilize market incentives in the fight against pollution. It is useful to encourage property rights, they argue, because property owners can be held responsible for environmental degradation caused by the use of their property. Anderson and Leal (1991) describe a property-rights approach to address mobile-source air emissions. If highways were privatized, and strict liability were enforced, highway owners would have an incentive to reduce emissions. They might achieve this by charging higher tolls for vehicles that lack appropriate pollution-control equipment. The key is in making the polluter pay, whether the polluter be defined as the vehicle owner or as the highway owner. Preventing polluters from externalizing pollution costs creates an incentive to minimize emissions.

Herman Daly disagrees, arguing that free market ethics are at the heart of our environmental problem. He describes the environmental problem with free market economics this way:

> Consider a boat. Suppose we want to maximize the load that the boat carries. If we place all the weight in one corner of the boat it will quickly sink or capsize. Therefore, we spread the weight out evenly. To do this we may create a pricing system. The heavier the load in one part of the boat the higher the price of adding another pound in that place. We allocate the weight so as to equalize the cost per additional capacity used in all parts of the boat. . . . This pricing rule is an allocative mechanism only, a useful but dumb computer algorithm that sees no reason not to keep adding weight and allocating it optimally until the optimally loaded boat sinks, optimally of course, to the bottom of the sea. What is lacking is an absolute limit on scale. . . . Pricing is only a tool for finding optimal allocation. . . . The market by itself has no criterion by which to limit its scale relative to its environment. (Daly 1991, 190)

If capitalism is inconsistent with environmental quality, environmental improvement may only be possible through an economic system that brings consumption and waste into equilibrium with the resource capacity of the ecosystem. The move to a sustainable society requires a shift in existing belief systems. Limiting consumption and economic expansion is antithetical to dominant ideals and values. Consequently, moving toward the sustainable society requires a fundamental shift in the way most people think.

Paehlke agrees. In *Environmentalism and the Future of Progressive Politics*, he suggests that environmentalism will compete with liberal capitalism in defining future options. In order to compete with liberalism, environmentalism, as an ideology—"a set of political ideals, a worldview both value laden and comprehensive"—must develop clear positions on the entire range of social and political issues (Paehlke 1989, 3–5). In this way, an ecocentric worldview may offer an alternative to liberal assumptions on a range of issues, including unemployment, social programs, national defense, and the economy. The environmental ideology, as Paehlke defines it, replaces the liberal self-interest model with a common-interest model centered around maximizing environmental quality:

> The first principle of environmentalism is that the earth-as-a-whole, for all time, must be seen as a "commons." Environmentalism grants both other species and future human generations consideration in economic and resource decisions. (Paehlke 1989, 8)

Such a shift will require more than traditional policy models offer. O'Brien points out that scarce-resource management requires complex ethical models that have traditionally been missing from policy debates. Like Wenz, O'Brien sees a value in revisiting ethical argumentation in normative political philosophy.

It has become increasingly obvious that the development of efficacious environmental policies requires sophisticated knowledge. There is a growing need, therefore, to rely on environmental experts—biologists, chemists, physicists, and so forth. The growing reliance on environmental experts has many scholars concerned about the growing tension between developing complex environmental regulations and maintaining an open political process. In *Democratic Dilemmas in the Age of Ecology,* Daniel Press argues that a more participatory democracy is necessary to alleviate this tension. As community members participate in environmental decision making, they will acquire the greater knowledge necessary for substantive input. On the other hand, if citizens remain passive, participating in policy decisions only through periodic elections, the tension will only increase.

Accommodating the Future

How we approach environmental problems today will carry critical implications for environmental quality in the future. James Hudson explains that the difficult task may be in assessing *how* current actions will affect both environmental quality and individual rights in the future. Should we choose to continue living as we have, relying on continually expanding industrial production to provide a stable economy, the environmental crisis will intensify until life on earth becomes unbearable. Heilbroner (1980) suggests that human civilization lacks the empathetic ability to foresee our tragic fate:

> Will mankind survive? Who knows? . . . How many of us would be willing to give up some minor convenience—say the use of aerosols—in the hope that this might extend the life of man on earth by a hundred years? Suppose we knew with a high degree of certainty that humankind could not survive a thousand years unless we gave up our wasteful diet of meat, abandoned all pleasure driving, cut back on every use of energy that was not essential to that maintenance of a bare minimum. Would we care enough for posterity to pay the price of its survival? (Robert Heilbroner 1980, 179)

Ultimately, our future will depend on finding that empathy—on caring about posterity. The selections below begin that process.

References

Anderson, Terry L., and Donald R. Leal. 1991. *Free Market Environmentalism.* San Francisco: Pacific Research Institute for Public Policy.

Cahn, Matthew. 1995. *Environmental Deceptions.* Albany: State University of New York Press.

Daly, Herman E. 1991. *Steady-State Economics.* 2d ed. Washington, DC: Island Press.

Heilbroner, Robert L. 1980. *An Inquiry into the Human Prospect.* New York: W.W. Norton and Company.
Hudson, James L. 1989. "Rights and the Further Future." In *Right Conduct: Theories and Applications,* ed. Bayles and Henley. New York: Random House.
Milbrath, Lester W. 1989. *Envisioning a Sustainable Society: Learning Our Way Out.* Albany: State University of New York Press.
O'Brien, Rory. Forthcoming. *Just Enough Water: Distributive Justice and Scarce Resource Management.*
Orr, David. 1992. *Ecological Literacy.* Albany: State University of New York Press.
Paehlke, Robert. 1989. *Environmentalism and the Future of Progressive Politics.* New Haven: Yale University Press.
Press, Daniel. 1994. *Democratic Dilemmas in the Age of Ecology.* Durham, NC: Duke University Press.
Stone, Christopher. 1974. *Should Trees Have Standing?* Los Altos, CA: William Kaufman Inc.
Wenz, Peter. 1988. *Environmental Justice.* Albany: State University of New York Press.

29

PETER WENZ

Environmental Justice

The Context of Justice

When I was eleven years old, my friend Billy Rohmann often came over to my house on Saturdays. We usually made a pizza for lunch. I remember very little of who bought the pizza mix or how we made the pizza. But I do remember how we divided it between us. We flipped a coin to determine who would cut the pizza in half. After it was cut, the one who had not done the cutting would pick the half that he wanted. We both had seemingly insatiable appetites for pizza, and each would have been glad to eat the whole thing. Yet we never fought about the shares that we assigned to ourselves in this way.

This story illustrates several things about justice. Justice usually becomes an issue in contexts like this one, in which people's wants or needs exceed the means of their satisfaction. For example, if Billy and I had been given money by our parents to go to a restaurant where people could have all the pizza they could eat for a flat fee, the situation would have been entirely different. We would have developed no rules for dividing the first pizza brought to us, because neither would have been concerned about getting his fair share of that pizza. We would simply have gotten another pizza when that one was finished, and another after that, if need be. We might have been interested in how much pizza we ate, and we probably would have competed with one another to see who could eat the most. But because the supply would have exceeded our wants and needs, our relative pizza consumption would have raised no issue between us. We would have taken no measures to ensure that each received his fair share.

From Peter Wenz, *Environmental Justice* (Albany: State University of New York Press, 1988), pp. 6–13; 19–21. Reprinted by permission of the State University of New York Press.

The difference that an ample supply can make is illustrated well in the case of water. People need water wherever they live; but water is scarce in some places, ample in others. Where it is scarce, societies have devised elaborate methods of apportioning the water among those who need and desire it. Infringing upon the water rights of another is considered a serious injustice. In societies with advanced legal systems, such as in the United States, the apportionment of water in areas of scarcity is governed by intricate legal rules. But where water is plentiful, the situation is entirely different. In some parts of England, residents are charged a quarterly fee for the maintenance of the water works and sewage installation. The fee does not vary according to the amount of water used. In fact, there is no water meter to determine the amount used. Because there is enough water to serve everyone's wants and needs, people do not care how much they or their neighbors consume.

In sum, questions about justice arise concerning those things that are, or are perceived to be, in short supply relative to the demand for them. In these situations, people are concerned about getting their fair share, and arrangements are made, or institutions are generated, to allocate the scarce things among those who want or need them.

These generalizations are subject to two qualifications. First, the people sharing the scarce good must care enough about what they receive to desire their fair share. When I am sharing a pizza with one of my daughters, I (sometimes) care more about her enjoyment of the meal than about receiving my fair share. (I can always eat some leftovers if I'm still hungry.) Even if there is less pizza than we would like to eat (scarcity), arrangements are not made under these circumstances to ensure that each gets a fair share, nor do I feel cheated if she eats more than I do. However, when those with whom I must share something are not as personally important to me, and when the thing shared is more important, I am more likely to be concerned about getting my fair share. In a drought, I am likely to want my house to be allocated its fair share of water by those at our local utility. Water is very important to me. I am not personally acquainted with most people in my town. I am not so benevolent as to want those among them who are no worse off than I to be given more water than I am given. So limited benevolence is, along with scarcity, an element of situations in which issues of justice arise.

The second qualification is this: Arrangements or institutions designed to allocate scarce things make sense only for those things that people are able to distribute. Billy and I were able to distribute pizza, and the people at City Water, Light and Power are able to distribute water from the reservoir. But the ability people have to distribute rain, good fortune, and perfect pitch is very limited. These things may be scarce, and people may want their fair shares, but there are no arrangements or institutions designed to allocate them, because people lack the power of distribution. . . .

The Need for Coordinated Environmental Restraint

Allowing people to make, take, or receive whatever they can get—so long as they do not directly attack, brutalize, or steal from others—will sometimes make scarcity worse, hurting everyone in the long run. Garrett Hardin calls this "The Tragedy of the Commons." Imagine a pasture that can be used in common by many herdsmen. It is a limited resource, but one capable of supplying enough food for the animals that the herdsmen depend upon for their livelihood. Suppose that one of the herdsmen wants to increase his income. He can do this by doubling his herd. He will have to work harder to care for the larger herd, but he feels that the increased income is worth the effort. He is not directly attacking, brutalizing, or stealing from anyone else, so his extra income is earned within the rules that prohibit these things. The pasture is not appreciably damaged by the grazing of these extra animals because, though they double the individual's herd, they do not significantly increase the total number of animals grazing on the common pasture.

Since it is a common pasture, other herdsmen who wish to increase their income are also free to double or triple their flocks. However, as more and more animals graze in common pasture, the flora is ruined owing to overgrazing. The result is the destruction of the common resource, the pasture, on which all had depended for a livelihood. No one committed barbarous acts against anyone else; yet, while literally minding their own business, they ruined the basis of that business. Their efforts to increase their incomes were self-defeating. In situations like this one, allowing people to take whatever they want of a scarce resource results in its destruction. The appropriation made by each person must be coordinate with those of others to ensure that the collective appropriation is not excessive and ruinous. So in these situations it is practical to determine each person's fair share of the collective good in order to avoid the tragedy of the commons. Such a determination can be made only by reference to an agreed standard of justice. Philosophical investigations into the nature and principles of justice are required.

Many environmental resources are like the pasture in Hardin's story. The oceans, the air, and the ozone layer are as important to our lives as was the pasture to the herdsmen. Yet no one owns them. If, in the pursuit of her own pleasure, gain, or preferred lifestyle, each person is free to use or despoil these natural resources in any way that does not directly brutalize other human beings, everyone will suffer in the long run. The ozone layer, for example, protects us all from solar radiation that can cause cancer. Suppose that the use of aerosol sprays diminishes the ozone layer. No single individual's use of aerosol sprays has an appreciable effect on the layer, so anyone can use such sprays without harming anyone else. But if millions use these sprays over long periods of time, the protection provided by the layer against harmful solar radiation could be significantly diminished. This could harm everyone, including those who make and use aerosol sprays. So if millions of people would like to use these sprays, some restraint must be exercised. One way of effecting such restraint would be to devise and enforce a system that permits people to use only limited amounts of aerosol spray. But what should the limit be? As in the case of the common pasture, it makes sense for each to be given her fair share, whatever that may be. Practicality again suggests that mutually agreeable principles of justice be discovered and employed in order to determine everyone's fair share.

This reasoning applies to pollution, generally. Whether it is a banana peel tossed from a car window on the highway or a gram of carbon monoxide emitted from the car's exhaust, every little bit does *not* hurt. It is the concentration of litter bits that hurts, and this concentration usually hurts those who do the polluting as well as others. Our waste products are integral to our life processes. In limited concentrations, they aid the life process as a whole. But our preferred lifestyles and activities tend to generate kinds and levels of waste that pollute our environment and can eventually make it uninhabitable. So restraint is necessary in a great many matters, ranging from our use of the National Parks to our consumption of fossil fuels. And again, when restraint is necessary to preserve the environment, it seems that everyone should receive a fair share, and be restrained to a fair degree, in accordance with reasonable principles of justice. This is environmental justice.

. . . A shared vision of environmental justice may not yet be considered absolutely essential, however. The preservation of the environment requires restraint. If the restraint is sufficient, the environment will be preserved regardless of who makes the required sacrifices. From the environmental perspective, the sacrifice could be distributed very unfairly or unjustly. Philosophical investigations into the nature and principles of justice may be useful, because they facilitate an acceptable distribution of the benefits and burdens associated with the interaction between human beings and their environment. But is an equitable distribution, and the philosophical discussion that facilitates it, really a practical necessity? The environment requires only restraint, not justice. . . .

The Need for Environmental Justice

The conditions of justice recur frequently with respect to the environment. Arrangements must often be made to allocate access to activities and commodities so as to insure that the uses people make of the environment are compatible with one another, and with the environment's continued habitability. For example, it is now widely believed that burning large amounts of coal that contain significant quantities of sulfur results in acid rain. This rain is blamed for the defoliation of forests in the northeastern United States, southeastern Canada, and southern Germany. Many people use these forests as sources of recreation. They are also used by the lumber industry, and serve to retard soil erosion. So there is pressure to decrease significantly the amount of high sulfur coal that is burned, or to require that smokestacks of furnaces using this coal be fitted with scrubbers that prevent a very high percentage of the sulfur from escaping into the atmosphere. The coal is burned hundreds of miles away from the affected forests. It is used to power factories and to provide people with electricity. Significant reductions in the use of this coal would adversely affect the owners of the mines from which the coal is extracted, as well as the workers in those mines. The factories that currently use this coal would have either to use alternate, usually more expensive fuels, or else install expensive scrubbers. Either course would make their products more expensive. Products that become too expensive will no longer be marketable, and the factories that produce them will have to shut down, putting many people out of work. Electricity that is produced for household consumption would have to become more expensive for the same reasons.

Because the areas where the mines are located and where the coal is used are so far from the areas where the forests are damaged, the people who benefit from the current use of high sulfur coal, and who would be adversely affected by proposed changes, are for the most part different from the direct beneficiaries of forest preservation. Their interests are opposed. The more that one group gets of what it wants, the less the other group can get. The two groups are in this respect situated as Billy Rohmann and I were with respect to the pizza. The more he got, the less I would get, and the more I got, the less he would get. Each wants to get his fair share. Decisions of public policy are required concerning the use of high-sulfur coal. People will not feel well-served by their government if this policy, which could put them out of work, or result in a mud slide covering their houses, is not clearly defensible. People will want to know why they should have to make the sacrifices that are required of them, and how these sacrifices compare to those that are required of others. The government will have to employ defensible principles of justice in fashioning its environmental policy if those affected by it are to believe that the sacrifices required of them are justified.

The same is true of most other environmental policies. They require people to make important sacrifices. Many policies are designed to deal with situations resembling the tragedy of the commons. Uncontrolled automobile emissions of carbon monoxide will jeopardize the health of many people, especially children, the aged, and those with emphysema. Emissions could be reduced by improving mass transit systems at public expense, on the assumption that the use of mass transit would then replace some automobile use. The improvement in air quality would in this case be paid for by the taxpaying public. This may seem equitable, since clean air is a public good. But members of the public would not benefit equally from this policy. Those living in urban areas would benefit most for two reasons: The air quality would be improved most in those areas, and urban residents would have available inexpensive public transportation. Should all taxpayers have to pay for benefits that accrue disproportionately to urban residents?

Alternatively, automobile emissions could be reduced by placing heavy taxes on gasoline, thereby discouraging its use. The improvement in air quality would be more widespread, because automobile use would be reduced generally, not just in urban areas. But do rural areas require such improvement? And are the burdens allocated equitably? On this plan, the user pays. This would hit hardest lower-income people and those in rural areas who must use their cars to get to work. Rich people would be virtually unaffected.

Many other plans could be devised to reduce air pollution caused by automobile emissions, and various plans can be combined with one another. Although all are aimed at reducing air pollution, each plan, and each combination of plans, benefits different people and/or places different burdens on different groups. Because these benefits and burdens can be significant, it will be necessary to assure people that they are receiving their fair share of benefits and are not being required unfairly to shoulder great burdens. The social fabric will not be destroyed by any one environmental policy that is perceived to be unjust. But the number and extent of environmental policies have increased and will continue to increase considerably. The perception that these policies are consistently biased in favor of some groups and against others could undermine the voluntary cooperation that is necessary for the maintenance of social order. Voluntary cooperation is especially necessary if the social order is to be maintained in a relatively open society where authoritarian measures are the exception rather than the rule. Thus, because social solidarity and the maintenance of order in a relatively free society require that people consider their sacrifices to be justified in relation to the sacrifices of others, environmental public policies will have to embody principles of environmental justice that the vast majority of people consider reasonable.

30

CHRISTOPHER STONE

Should Trees Have Standing?

It is not inevitable, nor is it wise, that natural objects should have no rights to seek redress in their own behalf. It is no answer to say that streams and forests cannot have standing because streams and forests cannot speak. Corporations cannot speak either; nor can states, estates, infants, incompetents, municipalities or universities. Lawyers speak for them, as they customarily do for the ordinary citizen with legal problems. One ought, I think, to handle the legal problems of natural objects as one does the problems of legal incompetents—human beings who have become vegetable. If a human being shows signs of becoming senile and has affairs that he is de jure incompetent to manage, those concerned with his well being make such a showing to the court, and someone is designated by the court with the authority to manage the incompetent's affairs. The guardian (or "conservator" or "committee"—the terminology varies) then represents the incompetent in his legal affairs. Courts make similar appointments when a corporation has become "incompetent"—they appoint a trustee in bankruptcy or reorganization to oversee its affairs and speak for it in court when that becomes necessary.

On a parity of reasoning, we should have a system in which, when a friend to a natural object perceives it to be endangered, he can apply to a court for the creation of a guardianship. Perhaps we already have the machinery to do so. California law, for example, defines an incompetent as "any person, whether insane or not, who by reason of old age, disease, weakness of mind, or other cause, is unable, unassisted, properly to manage and take care of himself or his property, and by reason thereof is likely to be deceived or imposed upon by artful or designing persons." Of course, to

---

From Christopher Stone, *Should Trees Have Standing* (Los Altos, CA: William Kaufmann Inc., 1974), pp. 27–26. Reprinted by permission.

urge a court that an endangered river is "a person" under this provision will call for lawyers as bold and imaginative as those who convinced the Supreme Court that a railroad corporation was a "person" under the fourteenth amendment, a constitutional provision theretofore generally thought of as designed to secure the rights of freedmen. (As this article was going to press, Professor Byrn of Fordham petitioned the New York Supreme Court to appoint him legal guardian for an unrelated fetuses scheduled for abortion so as to enable him to bring a class action on behalf of all fetuses similarly situated in New York City's 18 municipal hospitals. Judge Holtzman granted the petition of guardianship.) If such an argument based on present statutes should fail, special environmental legislation could be enacted along traditional guardianship lines. Such provisions could provide for guardianship both in the instance of public natural objects and also, perhaps with slightly different standards, in the instance of natural objects on "private" land.

The potential "friends" that such a statutory scheme would require will hardly be lacking. The Sierra Club, Environmental Defense Fund, Friends of the Earth, Natural Resources Defense Counsel, and the Izaak Walton League are just some of the many groups which have manifested unflagging dedication to the environment and which are becoming increasingly capable of marshalling the requisite technical experts and lawyers. If, for example, the Environmental Defense Fund should have reason to believe that some company's strip mining operations might be irreparably destroying the ecological balance of large tracts of land, it could, under this procedure, apply to the court in which the lands were situated to be appointed guardian. As guardian it might be given rights of inspection (or visitation) to determine and bring to the court's attention a fuller finding on the land's condition. If there were indications that under the substantive law some redress might be available on the land's behalf, then the guardian would be entitled to raise the land's rights in the land's name, *i.e.*, without having to make the roundabout and often unavailing demonstration, discussed below, that the "rights" of the club's members were being invaded. Guardians would also be looked to for a host of other protective tasks, *e.g.*, monitoring effluents (and/or monitoring the monitors), and representing their "wards" at legislative and administrative hearings on such matters as the setting of state water quality standards. Procedures exist, and can be strengthened, to move a court for the removal and substitution of guardians, for conflicts of interest or for other reasons, as well as for the termination of the guardianship.

In point of fact, there is a movement in the law toward giving the environment the benefits of standing, although not in a manner as satisfactory as the guardianship approach. What I am referring to is the marked liberalization of traditional standing requirements in recent cases in which environmental action groups have challenged federal government action. *Scenic Hudson Preservation Conference v. FPC* is a good example of this development. There, the Federal Power Commission had granted New York's Consolidated Edison a license to construct a hydroelectric project on the Hudson River at Storm King Mountain. The grant of license had been opposed by conservation interests on the grounds that the transmission lines would be unsightly, fish would be destroyed, and nature trails would be inundated. Two of these conservation groups, united under the name Scenic Hudson Preservation Conference, petitioned the Second Circuit to set aside the grant. Despite the claim that Scenic Hudson had no standing because it had not made the traditional claim "of any personal economic injury resulting from the Commission's actions," the petitions were heard, and the case sent back to the Commission. On the standing point, the court noted that Section 313(b) of the Federal Power Act gave a right of instituting review to any party "aggrieved by an order issued by the Commission"; it thereupon read "aggrieved by" as not limited to those alleging the traditional personal economic injury, but as broad enough to include "those who by their activities and conduct have exhibited a special interest" in "the aesthetic, conservational, and recreational aspects of power development." A similar reasoning has swayed other circuits to allow proposed actions by the Federal Power Commission, the Department of Interior, and the Department of Health, Education and Welfare to be challenged by environmental action groups on the basis of, *e.g.*, recreational and esthetic interests of members, in lieu of direct economic injury. Only the Ninth Circuit has balked, and one of these cases, involving the Sierra Club's attempt to challenge a Walt Disney development in the Sequoia National Forest, is at the time of this writing awaiting decision by the United States Supreme Court.

Even if the Supreme Court should reverse the Ninth Circuit in the Walt Disney–Sequoia National Forest matter, thereby encouraging the circuits to continue their trend toward liberalized standing in this area, there are significant reasons to press for the guardianship approach notwithstanding. For one thing, the cases of this sort have extended standing on the basis of interpretations of specific federal statutes—the Federal Power Commission Act, the Administrative Procedure Act, the Federal Insecticide, Fungicide and Rodenticide Act, and others. Such a basis supports environmental suits only where acts of federal agencies are involved; and even there, perhaps, only when there is some special statutory language, such as "aggrieved by" in the Federal Power Act, on which the action groups can rely. Witness, for example, *Bass Angler Sportsman Society v. United States Steel Corp.* There, plaintiffs sued 175 corporate defendants located throughout Alabama, relying on 33 U.S.C. Section 407 (1970), which provides:

> It shall not be lawful to throw, discharge, or deposit . . . any refuse matter . . . into any navigable water of the United States, or into any tributary of any navigable water from which the same shall float or be washed into such navigable water. . . .

Another section of the Act provides that one-half the fines shall be paid to the person or persons giving information which shall lead to a conviction. Relying on this latter provision, the plaintiff designated his action a *qui tam* action and sought to enforce the Act by injunction and fine. The District Court ruled that, in the absence of express language to the contrary, no one outside the Department of Justice had standing to sue under a criminal act and refused to research the question of whether violations were occurring.

Unlike the liberalized standing approach, the guardianship approach would secure an effective voice for the environment even where federal administrative action and public lands and waters were not involved. It would also allay one of the fears courts—such as the Ninth Circuit—have about the extended standing concept: if any ad hoc group can spring up overnight, invoke some "right" as universally claimable as the esthetic and recreational interests of its members and thereby get into court, how can a flood of litigation be prevented? If an ad hoc committee loses a suit brought *sub nom.* Committee to Preserve our Trees, what happens when its very same members reorganize two years later and sue *sub nom.* The Massapequa Sylvan Protection League? Is the new group bound by *res judicata?* Class action law may be capable of ameliorating some of the more obvious problems. But even so, court economy might be better served by simply designating the guardian de jure representative of the natural object, with rights of discretionary intervention by others, but with the understanding that the natural object is "bound" by an adverse judgment. The guardian concept, too, would provide the endangered natural object with what the trustee in bankruptcy provides the endangered corporation: a continuous supervision over a period of time, with a consequent deeper understanding of a broad range of the ward's problems, not just the problems present in one particular piece of litigation. It would thus assure the courts that the plaintiff has the expertise and genuine adversity in pressing a claim which are the prerequisites of a true "case or controversy."

The guardianship approach, however, is apt to raise two objections, neither of which seems to me to have much force. The first is that a committee or guardian could not judge the needs of the river or forest in its charge; indeed, the very concept of "needs," it might be said, could be used here only in the most metaphorical way. The second objection is that such a system would not be much different from what we now have: is not the Department of Interior already such a guardian for public lands, and do not most states have legislation empowering their attorneys-general to seek relief—in a sort of *parens patriae* way—for such injuries as a guardian might concern himself with?

As for the first objection, natural objects can communicate their wants (needs) to us, and in ways that are not terribly ambiguous. I am sure I can judge with more certainty and meaningfulness whether and when my lawn wants (needs) water, than the Attorney General can judge whether and when the United States wants (needs) to take an appeal from an adverse judgment by a lower court. The lawn tells me that it wants water by a certain dryness of the blades and soil—immediately obvious to the touch—the appearance of bald spots, yellowing, and a lack of springiness after being walked on; how does "the United States" communicate to the Attorney General? For similar reasons, the guardian-attorney for a smog-endangered stand of pines could venture with more confidence that his client wants the smog stopped, than the directors of a corporation can assert that "the corporation" wants dividends declared. We make decisions on behalf of, and in the purported interests of, others every day; these "others" are often creatures whose wants are far less verifiable, and even far more metaphysical in conception, than the wants of rivers, trees, and lands.

As for the second objection, one can indeed find evidence that the Department of Interior was conceived as a sort of guardian of the public lands. But there are two points to keep in mind. First, insofar as the Department already is an adequate guardian it is only with respect to the federal public lands as per Article IV, section 3 of the Constitution. Its guardianship includes neither local public lands nor private lands. Second, to judge from the environmentalist literature and from the cases environmental action groups have been bringing, the Department is itself one of the bogeys of the environmental movement. (One thinks of the uneasy peace between the Indians and the Bureau of Indian Affairs.) Whether the various charges be right or wrong, one cannot help but observe that the Department has been charged with several institutional goals (never an easy burden), and is currently looked to for action by quite a variety of interest groups, only one of which is the environmentalists. In this context, a guardian outside the institution becomes especially valuable. Besides, what a person wants, fully to secure his rights, is the ability to retain independent counsel even when, and perhaps especially when, the government is acting "for him" in a beneficent way. I have no reason to doubt, for example, that the Social Security System is being managed "for me"; but I would not want to abdicate my right to challenge its actions as they affect me, should the need arise. I would not ask more trust of national forests, vis-à-vis the Department of Interior. The same considerations apply in the instance of local agencies, such as regional water pollution boards, whose members' expertise in pollution matters is often all too credible.

The objection regarding the availability of attorneys-general as protectors of the environment within the existing structure is somewhat the same. Their statutory powers are limited and sometimes unclear. As political creatures, they must exercise the discretion they have with an eye toward advancing and reconciling a broad variety of important social goals, from preserving morality to increasing their jurisdiction's tax base. The present state of our environment, and the history of cautious application and development of environmental protection laws long on the books, testifies that the burdens of an attorney-general's broad responsibility have apparently not left much manpower for the protection of nature. (Cf. *Bass Anglers,* above.) No doubt, strengthening interest in the environment will increase the zest of public attorneys even where, as will often be the case, well-represented corporate polluters are the quarry. Indeed, the United States Attorney General has stepped up anti-pollution activity, and ought to be further encouraged in this direction. The statutory powers of the attorneys-general should be enlarged, and they should be armed with criminal penalties made at least commensurate with the likely economic benefits of violating the law. On the other hand, one cannot ignore the fact that there is increased pressure on public law-enforcement offices to give more attention to a host of other problems, from crime "on the streets" (why don't we say "in the rivers"?) to consumerism and school busing. If the environment is not to get lost in the shuffle, we would do well, I think, to adopt the guardianship approach as an additional safeguard, conceptualizing major natural objects as holders of their own rights, raisable by the court-appointed guardian.

31

David W. Orr

Ecological Literacy

Literacy is the ability to read. Numeracy is the ability to count. Ecological literacy, according to Garrett Hardin, is the ability to ask "What then?" Considerable attention is properly being given to our shortcomings in teaching the young to read, count, and compute, but not nearly enough to ecological literacy. Reading, after all, is an ancient skill. And for most of the twentieth century we have been busy adding, subtracting, multiplying, dividing, and now computing. But "What then?" Questions have not come easy for us despite all of our formidable advances in other areas. Napoleon did not ask the question, I gather, until he had reached the outskirts of Moscow, by which time no one could give a good answer except "Let's go back home." If Custer asked the question, we have no record of it. His last known words at Little Big Horn were, "Hurrah, boys, now we have them," a stirring if dubious pronouncement. And economists, who are certainly both numerate and numerous, have not asked the question often enough. Asking "What then?" on the west side of the Niemen River, or at Fort Laramie, would have saved a lot of trouble. For the same reason, "What then?" is also an appropriate question to ask before the last rain forests disappear, before the growth economy consumes itself into oblivion, and before we have warmed the planet intolerably.

The failure to develop ecological literacy is a sign of omission and of commission. Not only are we failing to teach the basics about the earth and how it works, but we are in fact teaching a large amount of stuff that is simply wrong. By failing to include ecological perspectives in any number of subjects, students are taught that ecology is unimportant for history, politics, economics, society, and so forth. And through television they learn

---

From David W. Orr, *Ecological Literacy* (Albany: State University of New York Press, 1992), pp. 85–92.

that the earth is theirs for the taking. The result is a generation of ecological yahoos without a clue why the color of water in their rivers is related to their food supply, or why storms are becoming more severe as the planet warms. The same persons as adults will create businesses, vote, have families, and above all, consume. If they come to reflect on the discrepancy between the splendor of their private lives in a hotter, more toxic and violent world, as ecological illiterates they will have roughly the same success as one trying to balance a checkbook without knowing arithmetic.

Formation of Attitudes

To become ecologically literate one must certainly be able to read and, I think, even like to read. Ecological literacy also presumes an ability to use numbers, and the ability to know what is countable and what is not, which is to say the limits of numbers. But these are indoor skills. Ecological literacy also requires the more demanding capacity to observe nature with insight, a merger of landscape and mindscape. "The interior landscape," in Barry Lopez's words, "responds to the character and subtlety of an exterior landscape; the shape of the individual mind is affected by land as it is by genes."[1] The quality of thought is related to the ability to relate to "where on this earth one goes, what one touches, the patterns one observes in nature—the intricate history of one's life in the land, even a life in the city, where wind, the chirp of birds, the line of a falling leaf, are known." The fact that this kind of intimate knowledge of our landscapes is rapidly disappearing can only impoverish our mental landscapes as well. People who do not know the ground on which they stand miss one of the elements of good thinking which is the capacity to distinguish between health and disease in natural systems and their relation to health and disease in human ones.

If literacy is driven by the search for knowledge, ecological literacy is driven by the sense of wonder, the sheer delight in being alive in a beautiful, mysterious, bountiful world. The darkness and disorder that we have brought to that world give ecological literacy an urgency it lacked a century ago. We can now look over the abyss and see the end of it all. Ecological literacy begins in childhood. "To keep alive his inborn sense of wonder," a child, in Rachel Carson's words, "needs the companionship of at least one adult who can share it, rediscovering with him the joy, excitement and mystery of the world we live in."[2] The sense of wonder is rooted in the emotions or what E.O. Wilson has called "biophilia," which is simply the affinity for the living world.[3] The nourishment of that affinity is the beginning point for the sense of kinship with life, without which literacy of any sort will not help much. This is to say that even a thorough knowledge of the facts of life and of the threats to it will not save us in the absence of the feeling of kinship with life of the sort that cannot entirely be put into words.

There are, I think, several reasons why ecological literacy has been so difficult for Western culture. First, it implies the ability to think broadly, to know something of what is hitched to what. This ability is being lost in an age of specialization. Scientists of the quality of Rachel Carson or Aldo Leopold are rarities who must buck the pressures toward narrowness and also endure a great deal of professional rejection and hostility. By inquiring into the relationship between chlorinated hydrocarbon pesticides and bird populations, Rachel Carson was asking an ecolate question. Many others failed to ask, not because they did not like birds, but because they had not, for whatever reasons, thought beyond the conventional categories. To do so would have required that they relate their food system to the decline in the number of birds in their neighborhood. This means that they would have had some direct knowledge of farms and farming practices, as well as a comprehension of ornithology. To think in ecolate fashion presumes a breadth of experience with healthy natural systems, both of which are increasingly rare. It also presumes that the persons be willing and able to "think at right angles" to their particular specializations, as Leopold put it.

Ecological literacy is difficult, second, because we have come to believe that education is solely an indoor activity. A good part of it, of necessity, must be, but there is a price. William Morton Wheeler once compared the naturalist with the professional biologist in these words: "[The naturalist] is primarily an observer and fond of outdoor life, a collector, a classifier, a describer, deeply impressed by the overwhelming intricacy of natural phenomena and revelling in their very complexity." The biologist, on the other hand, "is oriented toward and dominated by ideas, and rather terrified or oppressed by the intricate hurly-burly of concrete, sensuous reality. . . . He is a denizen of the laboratory. His besetting sin is oversimplification and the tendency to undue isolation of the organisms he studies from their natural environment."[4] Since Wheeler wrote, ecology has become increasingly specialized and, one suspects, remote from its subject matter. Ecology, like most learning worthy of the effort, is an applied subject. Its goal is not just a comprehension of how the world works, but, in the light of that knowledge, a life lived accordingly. The same is true of theology, sociology, political science, and most other subjects that grace the conventional curriculum.

The decline in the capacity for aesthetic appreciation is a third factor working against ecological literacy. We have become comfortable with all kinds of ugliness and seem incapable of effective protest against its purveyors: urban developers, businessmen, government officials, television executives, timber and mining companies, utilities, and advertisers. Rene Dubos once stated that our greatest disservice to our children was to give them the belief that ugliness was somehow normal. But disordered landscapes are not just an aesthetic problem. Ugliness signifies a more fundamental disharmony between people and between people and the land. Ugliness is, I think, the surest sign of disease, or what is now being called "unsustainability." Show me the hamburger stands, neon tick-tacky strips leading toward every city in America, and the shopping malls, and I'll show you devastated rain forests, a decaying countryside, a politically dependent population, and toxic waste dumps. It is all of a fabric.

And this is the heart of the matter. To see things in their wholeness is politically threatening. To understand that our manner of living, so comfortable for some, is linked to cancer rates in migrant laborers in California, the disappearance of tropical rain forests, fifty thousand toxic dumps across the U.S.A., and the depletion of the ozone layer is to see the need for a change in our way of life. To see things whole is to see both the wounds we have inflicted on the natural world in the name of mastery and those we have inflicted on ourselves and on our children for no good reason, whatever our stated intentions. Real ecological literacy is radicalizing in that it forces us to reckon with the roots of our ailments, not just with their symptoms. For this reason, I think it leads to a revitalization and broadening of the concept of citizenship to include membership in a planetwide community of humans and living things.

And how does this striving for community come into being? I doubt that there is a single path, but there are certain common elements. First, in the lives of most if not all people who define themselves as environmentalists, there is experience in the natural world at an early age. Leopold came to know birds and wildlife in the marshes and fields around his home in Burlington, Iowa before his teens. David Brower, as a young boy on long walks over the Berkeley hills, learned to describe the flora to his nearly blind mother. Second, and not surprisingly, there is often an older teacher or mentor as a role model: a grandfather, a neighbor, an older brother, a parent, or teacher. Third, there are seminal books that explain, heighten, and say what we have felt deeply, but not said so well. In my own life, Rene Dubos and Loren Eiseley served this function of helping to bring feelings to articulate consciousness.

Ecological literacy is becoming more difficult, I believe, not because there are fewer books about nature, but because there is less opportunity for the direct experience of it. Fewer people grow up on farms or in rural areas where access is easy and where it is easy to learn a degree of competence and self-confidence toward the natural world. Where the ratio between the human-created environment to the purely natural world exceeds some point, the sense of place can only be a sense of habitat. One finds the habitat familiar and/or likeable but without any real sense of belonging in the natural world. A sense of place requires more direct contact with the natural aspects of a place, with soils, landscape, and wildlife. This sense is lost as we move down the continuum toward the totalized urban environment where nature exists in tiny, isolated fragments by permission only. Said differently, this is an argument for more urban parks, summer camps, green belts, wilderness areas, public seashores. If we must live in an increasingly urban world, let's make it one of well-designed compact green cities that include trees, river parks, meandering greenbelts, and urban farms where people can see, touch, and experience nature in a variety of ways. In fact, no other cities will be sustainable in a greenhouse world.

Ecological Literacy and Formal Education

The goal of ecological literacy as I have described it has striking implications for that part of education that must occur in classrooms, libraries, and laboratories. To the extent that most educators have noticed the environment, they have regarded it as a set of problems which are: (1) solvable (unlike dilemmas, which are not) by (2) the analytic tools and methods of reductionist science which (3) create value-neutral, technological remedies that will not create even worse side effects. Solutions, therefore, originate at the top of society, from governments and corporations, and are passed down to a passive citizenry in the form of laws, policies, and technologies. The results, it is assumed, will be socially, ethically, politically, and humanly desirable, and the will to live and to sustain a humane culture can be preserved in a technocratic society. In other words, business can go on as usual. Since there is no particular need for an ecologically literate and ecologically competent public, environmental education is most often regarded as an extra in the curriculum, not as a core requirement or as an aspect pervading the entire educational process.

Clearly, some parts of the crisis can be accurately described as problems. Some of these can be solved by technology, particularly those that require increased resource efficiency. It is a mistake, however, to think that all we need is better technology, not an ecologically literate and caring public willing to help reduce the scale of problems by reducing its demands on the environment and to accept (even demand) public policies that require sacrifices. It all comes down to whether the public understands the relation between its well-being and the health of the natural systems.

For this to occur, we must rethink both the substance and the process of education at all levels. What does it mean to educate people to live sustainably, going, in Aldo Leopold's words, from "conqueror of the land community to plain member and citizen of it"?[5] However it is applied in practice, the answer will rest on six foundations.

The first is the recognition that *all education is environmental education.* By what is included or excluded, emphasized or ignored students learn that they are a part of or apart from the natural world. Through all education we inculcate the ideas of careful stewardship or carelessness. Conventional education, by and large, has been a celebration of all that is human to the exclusion of our dependence on nature. As a result, students frequently resemble what Wendell Berry has called "itinerant professional vandals," persons devoid of any sense of place or stewardship, or inkling of why these are important.[6]

Second, *environmental issues are complex and cannot be understood through a single discipline or department.* Despite a decade or more of discussion and experimentation, interdisciplinary education remains an unfulfilled promise. The failure occurred, I submit, because it was tried within discipline-centric institutions. A more promising approach is to reshape institutions to function as transdisciplinary laboratories that include components such as agriculture, solar technologies, forestry, land management, wildlife, waste cycling, architectural design, and economics.[7] Part of the task, then, of Earth-centered education is the study of interactions across the boundaries of conventional knowledge and experience.

Third, *for inhabitants, education occurs in part as a dialogue with a place and has the characteristics of good conversation.* Formal education happens mostly as a monologue of human interest, desires, and accomplishments that drowns out all other sounds. It is the logical outcome of the belief that we are alone in a dead world of inanimate matter, energy flows, and biogeochemical cycles. But true conversation can occur only if we acknowledge the existence and interests of the other. In conversation, we define ourselves, but in relation to another. The quality of conversation does not rest on the brilliance of one or the other person. It is more like a dance in which the artistry is mutual.

In good conversation, words represent reality faithfully. And words have power. They can enliven or deaden, elevate or degrade, but they are never neutral, because they affect our perception and ultimately our behavior. The use of words such as "resources," "manage," "channelize," "engineer," and "produce" makes our relation to nature a monologue rather than a conversation. The language of nature includes the sounds of animals, whales, birds, insects, wind, and water—a language more ancient and basic than human speech. Its books are the etchings of life on the face of the land. To hear this language requires patient, disciplined study of the natural world. But it is a language for which we have an affinity.

Good conversation is unhurried. It has its own rhythm and pace. Dialogue with nature cannot be rushed. It will be governed by cycles of day and night, the seasons, the pace of procreation, and by the larger rhythm of evolutionary and geologic time. Human sense of time is increasingly frenetic, driven by clocks, computers, and revolutions in transportation and communication.

Good conversation has form, structure, and purpose. Conversation with nature has the purpose of establishing, in Wendell Berry's words: "What is here? What will nature permit here? What will nature help us do here?"[8] The form and structure of any conversation with the natural world is that of the discipline of ecology as a restorative process and healing art.

Fourth, it follows that *the way education occurs is as important as its content.* Students taught environmental awareness in a setting that does not alter their relationship to basic life-support systems learn that it is sufficient to intellectualize, emote, or posture about such things without having to live differently. Environmental education ought to change the way people live, not just how they talk. This understanding of education is drawn from the writings of John Dewey, Alfred North Whitehead, J. Glenn Gray, Paulo Friere, Ivan Illich, and Eliot Wigginton. Learning in this view best occurs in response to real needs and the life situation of the learner. The radical distinctions typically drawn between teacher and student, between the school and the community, and those between areas of knowledge, are dissolved. Real learning is participatory and experiential, not just didactic. The flow can be two ways between teachers, who best function as facilitators, and students who are expected to be active agents in defining what is learned and how.

Fifth, *experience in the natural world is both an essential part of understanding the environment, and conducive to good thinking.* Experience, properly conceived, trains the intellect to observe the land carefully and to distinguish between health and its opposite. Direct experience is an antidote to indoor, abstract learning. It is also a wellspring of good thinking. Understanding nature demands a disciplined and observant intellect. But nature, in Emerson's words, is also "the vehicle of thought" as a source of language, metaphor, and symbol. Natural diversity may well be the source of much of human creativity and intelligence. If so, the simplification and homogenization of ecosystems can only result in a lowering of human intelligence.

Sixth, *education relevant to the challenge of building a sustainable society will enhance the learner's competence with natural systems.* For reasons once explained by Whitehead and Dewey, practical competence is an indispensable source of good thinking. Good thinking proceeds from the friction between reflective thought and real problems. Aside from its effects on thinking, practical competence will be essential if sustainability requires, as I think it does, that people must take an active part in rebuilding their homes, businesses, neighborhoods, communities, and towns. Shortening supply lines for food, energy, water, and materials—while recycling waste locally—implies a high degree of competence not necessary in a society dependent on central vendors and experts. . . .

If these can be taken as the foundations of Earth-centered education, what can be said of its larger purpose? In a phrase, it is that quality of mind that seeks out connections. It is the opposite of the specialization and narrowness characteristic of most education. The ecologically literate person has the knowledge necessary to comprehend interrelatedness, and an attitude of care or stewardship. Such a person would also have the practical competence required to act on the basis of knowledge and feeling. Competence can only be derived from the experience of doing and the mastery of what Alasdair MacIntyre describes as a "practice."[9] Knowing, caring, and practical competence constitute the basis of ecological literacy.

Notes

1. Barry Lopez, *Crossing Open Ground* (New York: Vintage, 1989), 65.
2. Rachel Carson, *The Sense of Wonder* (New York: Harper and Row, 1984), 45.
3. E. O. Wilson, *Biophilia* (Cambridge: Harvard University Press, 1984).
4. In Charles P. Curtis, Jr. and Ferris Greenslet, eds., *The Practical Cogitator,* 3rd ed. (Boston: Houghton Mifflin Co., 1962), 226–29.
5. Aldo Leopold, *A Sand County Almanac* (New York: Ballantine, 1966), 240.
6. Wendell Berry, *Home Economics* (San Francisco: North Point Press, 1987), 50.
7. On the structure of environmental education, see Lyndon K. Caldwell, "Environmental Studies: Discipline or Metadiscipline," *The Environmental Professional* (1983): 247–59.
8. Wendell Berry, *Home Economics* (San Francisco: North Point Press, 1987), 146.
9. Alasdair MacIntyre, *After Virtue* (South Bend, IN: Notre Dame University Press, 1981), 168–89.

32

LESTER MILBRATH

Envisioning a Sustainable Society: Learning Our Way Out

Growth is an honorific word in modern society. We are told constantly that we should be growing in economic output, in population, in prestige, in strength, in stature, in complexity. Growth is associated with development, health, and progress. Nongrowth is associated with decline, illness, and lack of progress. Progress, defined as growth, is believed to be inevitable and good. Some people even believe that if we do not grow we will die. . . .

This perspective on growth applies to Third World countries as well as to developed countries. Third World countries have adopted a "development ideology" that equates development with growth (Woodhouse, 1972; Orr, 1979). This developmental growth is expected to lift people from poverty and provide them with the good life that they see in the developed part of the globe.

In the early 1970s, a great debate got underway about whether growth has limits. A study of growth was initiated by The Club of Rome (a prestigious group of approximately 100 scientists, businessmen, and national leaders). The club commissioned a work group at The Massachusetts Institute of Technology (MIT) to estimate with a new computer model how long it would be before modern society would run out of critical resources. The MIT group published *The Limits to Growth* (Meadows, et al., 1972) that was eventually translated into about 30 languages. It sold millions of copies. This analysis so strongly challenged the conventional wisdom about growth that it ignited a storm of controversy. Some research teams challenged the validity of the computer model. Some analysts using new models

---

From Lester Milbrath, *Envisioning a Sustainable Society: Learning Our Way Out* (Albany: State University of New York Press, 1989), pp. 9–17. Reprinted by permission of the State University of New York Press.

confirmed the original analysis that growth has limits (Mesarovic and Pestel, 1974). Other analysts claimed that growth has no serious limits (Simon, 1981). The debate has raged ever since and is far from concluded. National survey studies in the early 1980s showed that within the U.S. public, about as many people believe there are limits to growth as deny there are limits, whereas in West Germany, nearly everyone believes there are limits to growth (Milbrath, 1984).

We can usefully distinguish organismal growth, which naturally limits itself, from growth in numbers that must be limited externally. Organisms experience phased growth, much as a child growing into adulthood and eventually dying. Growth in early stages is good but is no longer desirable when adulthood is reached. Growth also cannot forestall death; in fact, death from cancer results from growth. This kind of growth was not discussed in the debate over limits to growth although it might have been usefully considered.

Growth in numbers of a species is different. The offspring of adults soon become adults who, in turn, have more offspring. When growth is exponential, it can accelerate very rapidly. Two doubles to 4 doubles to 8, 16, 32, 64, 128, 256, 512, 1,024, 2,048; ten doublings increase 2 to 2,048. Analysts of exponential growth speak of doubling times; if the doubling time is long, growth is slow; if it is short, growth can be very swift. This principle is illustrated by a classic riddle: "Imagine a pond with a water lily growing in it. The lily doubles in size every day. At thirty days it covers the entire pond. On which day did it cover half the pond?" The first response of most people is the fifteenth day; only after closer reflection do they recognize that the lily does not become large enough to cover one-half of the pond until the twenty-ninth day. It takes only one additional day to cover the remainder of the pond.

The speed of doublings can be roughly calculated by the "law of sevens": The percentage rate of growth per year is divided into seventy to give the doubling time. For example, a species increasing in numbers at the rate of 1 percent per year will double in seventy years. If it is increasing at the rate of 2 percent per year, it will double in thirty-five years. At the rate of 3 percent per year, it will double in less than twenty-four years. At the rate of 7 percent per year, it will double in ten years. At 10 percent per year, it will double in seven years. At the rate of 10 percent per year, ten doublings would take only seventy years; that would mean more than a thousandfold increase in only seventy years. Money invested at 10 percent interest, where the interest is also invested, would show such an increase. During the 1960s, energy consumption in the United States increased at the rate of 7 percent per year. This increase led a utility executive to exuberantly claim in the early 1970s that the United States would consume as much energy in that decade as in all its previous history. This did not happen because of energy shortages and changes in consumption patterns. The executive's projection illustrates the foolhardiness of predicting the future from simple trend lines.

All species have the potential for exponential growth if the resources and other conditions needed for speedy reproduction are present. Biologists speak of fast exponential growth of a species as an *irruption.* Algae, bacteria, and other small organisms may "bloom" to many millions in a few hours if conditions for reproduction are favorable. For example, an algae bloom devastated near-shore marine life in the North Sea in late May 1988; some people called it a *red tide;* in Norway, they called it the *death algae.* I was in Norway at the time; most observers were ascribing the bloom to nutrients washed down from overfertilized farmlands and carried into the North Sea by rivers. The algae so densely concentrated in near-shore waters (many billions in a cubic meter) that they choked off all other forms of marine life. Ocean fisheries, a veritable lifeline in the Norwegian economy, were wiped out for a time.

Nature has several mechanisms for keeping the number of members of a species within acceptable bounds. Once the available food supply is exhausted, the species must die back. It is not uncommon in the natural world for a given species to reproduce so rapidly that it goes into "overshoot"; its consumption exceeds the resources it needs to sustain life. The faster the rate of reproduction, the greater the overshoot and the more swift the dieback. (The red tide in the North Sea in 1988 disappeared about as swiftly as it bloomed.)

Disease also reduces numbers rather quickly. Natural predators are another check on species growth. For example, rabbits reproduce rapidly; as they do so, they provide more food to their predators (foxes) who also reproduce more rapidly. As the number of foxes increases, the number of rabbits declines, and eventually the number of foxes also declines.

With these natural checks working, nature's systemic processes eventually work out a balance in which the reproduction and survival rates of a diversity of species are maintained at a sustainable level. An ecosystem with many species living in balance will have a certain "carrying capacity." If a certain species reproduces so quickly as to exceed its carrying capacity, the ecosystem probably will be sufficiently damaged so that its overall carrying capacity will be reduced; this is what happened in the North Sea in 1988. When the offending species is as powerful as *Homo sapiens,* the reduction in carrying capacity can be devastating to all creatures.

Garrett Hardin wrote a classic essay in 1968 titled, "The Tragedy of the

Commons." In it he illustrates how humans who act freely in their own interest can exceed the carrying capacity of an ecosystem. He invites us to imagine a pasture (such as the Commons in an English village) that is open to all villagers. It is worthwhile for each villager to graze as many cattle on the commons as possible. Even though adding an additional cow might lead to overgrazing, it is in the interest of each villager to add it because he receives all the benefits from its feeding while the losses in grazing capacity are shared by all. Therein is the tragedy. The system encourages each villager to increase his herd without limit—but the limited commons is destroyed. Under conditions of overpopulation, freedom in an unmanaged commons brings ruin to all.

With these concepts in mind, we can evaluate the meaning of what has happened to the population of humans in the last few centuries. . . . Clearly, *Homo sapiens* have experienced an irruption in population in the last two centuries. Population, worldwide, grew at a rate exceeding 2 percent per year in the 1960s. Recently, it has declined to about 1.7 percent. Remember, at the 2 percent rate, world population doubles in about thirty-five years. . . . Most of the recent and projected growth is occurring in the less developed countries where they have the least capability to provide a decent life for people. If we allow two more doublings to occur, our current population, which exceeds 5 billion, will become 20 billion before the next century has run its course. In my judgment, the human population growth rate must be brought to zero within the next fifty years. . . . Growth beyond one more doubling would seriously diminish quality of life and also would be likely to destroy some of the carrying capacity of ecosystems. If we do not learn how to plan for and voluntarily limit human population in the next fifty years, nature's own limits will force decline through human deaths.

When this century began, scarcely one lifespan ago, world population numbered 1.6 billion. Assuming an average per capita income of $400 per year (1986 dollars), the gross world product was $640 billion, just slightly more than France's 1986 national product of $550 billion. Over the next half-century, world population grew by nearly a billion, bringing the total to 2.5 billion. Modest progress in raising per capita income brought the gross world product to roughly $3 trillion in 1950.

Though impressive by historical standards, this growth was dwarfed by what followed. Between 1950 and 1986 human numbers doubled to five billion, expanding as much during these 36 years as during the preceding few million. Per capita income also roughly doubled, pushing the gross world product over $13 trillion. Within a generation, the global output of goods and services quadrupled. . . . Between 1950 and 1986 world fossil fuel consumption also increased fourfold. . . . Stanford University biologist

Peter M. Vitousek, and his colleagues, estimate that nearly 40 percent of the potential net primary productivity on land is now used directly or indirectly by human populations. . . . The portion remaining to sustain all other species, and to maintain the integrity of natural systems, gets smaller and smaller as the size and demands of the human population mount (Brown, et al., 1987, pp. 5, 9). . . .

How did it come about the humans were able to reproduce so swiftly? Two developments in recent history enabled humans to increase their numbers dramatically. About 400 years ago, Europeans discovered and began colonizing North and South America; later they colonized other large land masses like Australia and Africa. These continents, sparsely populated by humans who made their living mainly by hunting and gathering, provided a bountiful habitat that Europeans could expropriate as their own niche. The new methods of warfare, agriculture, and industry they brought to the new lands enabled them not only to displace the indigenous humans but also to so modify the habitats as to encourage growth in human numbers. Humans spurted in population growth.

The second major development was the flowering of the Industrial Revolution which was accelerated by the swift development of science and technology. New tools and techniques enabled humans to do many things that formerly were impossible when they possessed only simple hand tools and beasts of burden. Now swamps can be filled, mountains leveled, and roads constructed into remote places. Humans can now live in very diverse habitats, tolerating a wider range of climate and terrains than any other species. As our habitat range has expanded, we have been reducing the carrying capacity of these habitats for other species, and may soon reduce it for ourselves.

The development of medical science and technology was even more important for population growth. Modern medicine was carried to the far corners of the globe by colonizers, missionaries, and international agencies. Infant mortality has dropped dramatically throughout the world and human life expectancy has doubled. Our ability to keep people alive has temporarily upset one of nature's methods for keeping human population in check. Either we will learn to voluntarily adopt our own checks or nature will eventually provide the checks, perhaps in a fashion we will regret.

The tools and techniques of modern industrial man may be thought of as prosthetic devices that have so extended human capabilities that our species has been transformed from being *Homo sapiens* to being *Homo colossus* (Catton, 1980). We have shown that we can conquer any other species; we have not yet learned that, in so doing, we may destroy ourselves. Herein lie the similarities and dissimilarities between humans and other animals; both are bound by ecological carrying capacity, but mankind alone is able to *temporarily* transcend the bondage.

Now, we should think about a third kind of growth—the speed with which we consume resources. We normally recognize that science and technology have provided us with new prosthetic devices such as tools, tractors, trucks, computers, trains, airplanes, automobiles, and boats. We sometimes forget that their development and use has been subsidized by fossil fuels. We use fossil fuels to extract materials from the earth's crust, manufacture them into goods, and process them into wastes. Many of these devices also are powered by fossil fuels. These same fossil fuels are used as a raw material to make many consumer goods (plastics) and also to make fertilizer.

Fossil energy has made such a contribution to the capacity of the planet to support humans that it may be thought of as "ghost acreage." Catton (1980, p. 276) defines it as, "the additional farmland a given nation would need in order to supply that net portion of the food or fuel it uses but does not obtain from contemporary growth of organisms within its borders." American agriculture, much heralded for its productivity, requires approximately ten calories of fossil energy input for each calorie of food delivered to a dinner table. How long can this continue? This ghost acreage, on which we are so dependent, was built up through billions of years of plant and animal growth and cannot be thought of as renewable within the few generations that are the primary concern of people living now. The rate extraction (misleadingly called *production*) is 10,000 times the rate of renewal (Catton, 1980, p. 49).

We humans have become so adept at extracting resources from the earth to serve not only our vital needs but our pleasures that we have become exuberant and wasteful, multiplying prodigiously in numbers and even more expansively in resource consumption. . . . Gross world product and fossil fuel consumption have increased much faster than population. Metallic resource reserves are being depleted almost as swiftly as fossil energy reserves. The average modern American consumes approximately sixty times as many resources as the average citizen of India (Catton, 1980, p. 205). The resource consumption ratio is even more expansive when we compare ourselves to prehistoric humans. I invite readers to pay attention for just one day to the number of prosthetic devices we command and the energy we consume. If we reflect on our growth in numbers and our growth in resource consumption, we can readily see why we humans are facing overshoot. "We are living on four parts of phantom carrying capacity for every one part of permanent (real) carrying capacity" (Catton, 1980, p. 46).

How long can this last? No definite answer can be given because it depends on what new resource reserves are discovered, on our cleverness in conserving, on developing new technologies that are less resource consumptive or that turn new materials into resources, on our ability to limit births, and on our lifestyles. If we continue in our present ways, most analysts doubt that this bounty can last for another 100 years. Many think we already are feeling shortages and that they will become severe in about twenty years. Will we be foresighted, compassionate, and conserving as we adjust to these shortages? Probably not. Historical experience suggests that *Homo colossus* will continue to draw down the ghost acreage in the earth's crust. The earth's carrying capacity will be reduced considerably below the level that we might have made sustainable had we used more foresight.

All growth in population and in resource consumption is exponential. The swifter the growth of a population in a finite environment, the greater the likelihood of overshoot and dieback. Overshoot is likely to reduce the carrying capacity of the ecosphere. The physical limits to growth in human uses of a finite planet indicate that we cannot sustain our present trajectory. In order to change our trajectory, it is imperative that we change our society. If we do not plan ahead and change thoughtfully, nature will force change upon us through pain and death.

References

Brown, Lester R. et al., 1987. *State of the World: A Worldwatch Institute Report on Progress Toward a Sustainable Society.* New York: Norton.

Catton, William R. 1980. *Overshoot: The Ecological Basis of Revolutionary Change.* Urbana: University of Illinois Press.

Hardin, Garrett. 1968. "The Tragedy of the Commons," *Science,* vol. 162 (December 13), pp. 1243–48.

Meadows, Donella, Dennis Meadows, Jorgen Randers, and William Behrens III. 1972. *The Limits of Growth.* New York: Universe Books.

Mesarovic, Mihaljo and Eduard Pestel. 1974. *Mankind at the Turning Point.* New York: Dutton.

Milbrath, Lester W. 1984. *Environmentalists: Vanguard for a New Society.* Albany: State University of New York Press.

Orr, David. 1979. "In the Tracks of the Dinosaur: Modernization and the Ecological Perspective," *Polity,* vol. 11 (Summer), pp. 562–87.

Simon, Julian. 1981. *The Ultimate Resource.* Princeton: Princeton University Press.

Woodhouse, Edward J. 1972. "Re-Visioning the Future of the Third World: An Ecological Perspective on Development," *World Politics,* vol. 25 (October), pp. 1–33.

33

Terry L. Anderson and Donald R. Leal

Free Market Environmentalism

Many people see free markets and the environment as incompatible; for them, the very notion of free market environmentalism is an oxymoron. Even many "free marketeers" find themselves on opposite sides of the fence when it comes to governmental regulation of the environment. Some will hold fast to the conviction that markets work best to allocate most of the goods and services we enjoy, but they will also argue that the environment is different and is too precious to be allocated on the basis of profits.

The view that markets and the environment do not mix is buttressed by the perception that resource exploitation and environmental degradation are inextricably linked to economic growth. This view, which first emerged with industrialization, builds on fears that we are running out of resources because economic growth based on materialistic values is tempting us to squander our natural endowment. During the Industrial Revolution in England, the Reverend Thomas Malthus articulated this view by hypothesizing that exponential population growth would eventually result in famine and pestilence; productivity simply would not be able to keep up with population. The human propensity to reproduce, according to Malthus, would eventually surpass our ability to feed ourselves.

Modern-day Malthusians have given such dire predictions an aura of credibility by using complex computer models to predict precisely when Malthusian calamities will occur. In early 1974, a group of scientists from the Massachusetts Institute of Technology predicted:

> If the present growth trends in world population, industrialization, pollution, food production, and resource depletion continue unchanged, the limits to growth on this planet will be reached sometime within the next one hun-

---

Pages 1–8 from *Free Market Environmentalism* by Terry L. Anderson and Donald R. Leal.

> dred years. The most probable result will be a rather sudden and uncontrollable decline in both population and industrial capacity.[1]

In a graph generated by its computer model, the scientific team showed that the "uncontrollable decline" would begin shortly after the turn of the century—in 2005, to be exact—with a precipitous decline in industrial output, food supplies and population.[2]

The Global 2000 Report commissioned by President Jimmy Carter arrived at similar conclusions in its prediction of what the state of the world's population and natural resources would be at the turn of the next century. "If present trends continue," the report claimed, "the world in 2000 will be more crowded, more polluted, less stable ecologically, and more vulnerable to disruption than the world we live in now. Serious stresses involving population, resources, and environment are clearly visible ahead." In every resource category, Global 2000 predicted overuse and declines in quantity and quality.

But there is no indication that these predictions will come to pass, and many of them have already been proven wrong.[3] The problem rests in the acceptance of Malthus's initial premise that demands on resources will be exponential while the supply is finite. All of these forecasts fail to take account of the ability of humans to react to problems of scarcity by reducing consumption, finding substitutes, and improving productivity. As economist Julian Simon observed, the "ultimate resource" is the human mind, which has allowed us to avoid Malthusian cycles.[4]

Neo-Malthusians might agree with Simon about the value of the human mind, but they generally see political controls of resource use as the only way to implement this human ingenuity. If markets that promote resource consumption are the cause of the problem, then government must be the solution. When nineteenth-century timber harvests denuded portions of the upper Midwest, there was a call to nationalize the forests to ensure against predicted timber famines. Although there has been no timber famine and private forests continue to be more productive than public forests, the political response has endured. From land to water to air, governmental control—which means political control—is seen as a necessary check on the environmental ravages of free markets.

This book will challenge this common perception and offer an alternative way of thinking about environmental issues, markets, and political choice. This way of thinking does not always provide solutions; instead, it concentrates on how alternative processes link information about the environment with individual incentives to interact with it. Here, the environment and the market are inextricably connected in a positive rather than a negative way.

At the heart of free market environmentalism is a system of well-specified property rights to natural resources. Whether these rights are held by individuals, corporations, non-profit environmental groups, or communal groups, a discipline is imposed on resource users because the wealth of the owner of the property right is at stake if bad decisions are made. Of course, the further a decision maker is removed from this discipline—as he is when there is political control—the less likely it is that good resource stewardship will result. Moreover, if well-specified property rights are transferable, owners must not only consider their own values, they must also consider what others are willing to pay.

The Nature Conservancy's private land management program offers an excellent example of how free market environmentalism works.[5] When the Conservancy obtains title to a parcel of land, the group's wealth, defined in terms of preserving habitat for a rare or endangered species, depends on good stewardship. When The Wisconsin Nature Conservancy was given title to forty acres of beachfront property on St. Croix, Virgin Islands, some may have thought that the group would protect that pristine beach at all costs. But the Conservancy traded the property (with covenants) for a larger parcel of rocky hillside in northern Wisconsin. The trade allowed the Conservancy to protect an entire watershed containing many endangered plant species. To be sure, tradeoffs were made, but through the exchange of well-defined and enforced property rights—that is, markets—The Nature Conservancy's wealth in the form of environmental amenities was enhanced.

Free market environmentalism emphasizes an important role for government in the enforcement of property rights. With clearly specified titles—obtained from land recording systems, strict liability rules, and adjudication of disputed property rights in courts—market processes can encourage good resource stewardship. It is when rights are unclear and not well enforced that over-exploitation occurs.

This way of thinking will be alien to some and acceptable to others largely because of the different "visions" each person brings to the issue. In *A Conflict of Visions*, Thomas Sowell described a vision as

> what we sense or feel *before* we have constructed any systematic reasoning that could be called a theory, much less deduced any specific consequences as hypotheses to be tested against evidence. . . . Visions are the foundations on which theories are built.[6]

The theory of free market environmentalism is founded on certain visions regarding human nature, knowledge, and processes. A consideration of these visions helps explain why some people accept this way of thinking as the only alternative to bureaucratic control and why others reject it as a contradiction in terms.

Human nature: Free market environmentalism views man as self-interested. This self-interest may be enlightened to the extent that people are capable of setting aside their own well-being for close relatives and friends or that they may be conditioned by moral principles. But beyond this, good intentions will not suffice to produce good results. Developing an environmental ethic may be desirable, but it is unlikely to change basic human nature. Instead of intentions, good resource stewardship depends on how well social institutions harness self-interest through individual incentives.

Knowledge: In addition to incentives, good resource stewardship depends on the information available to self-interested individuals. Free market environmentalism views this information or knowledge as diffuse rather than concentrated. Because ecosystems depend on the interaction of many different natural forces, they cannot be "managed" from afar. The information necessary for good management varies significantly from time to time and from place to place, and resource management requires knowledge that can only be obtained "on the ground." Therefore, knowledge cannot be gathered into a single mind or group of minds that can then capably manage all of society's natural resources.

The difference between perceptions of knowledge under centralized, political resource management and free market environmentalism centers on the distribution of knowledge among individuals. In visions of centralized, political control, the distribution has a low mean with a high variance. That is, the common man is not perceived as knowing much about the environment, and what he does know (including knowledge of his own values) is incorrect; the high variance means that experts can manage for the good of the masses. Free market environmentalism sees a much smaller knowledge gap between the experts and the average individual. In this view, individual property owners, who are in a position and have an incentive to obtain time- and place-specific information about their resource endowments, are better suited than centralized bureaucracies to manage resources.

Processes or solutions: These visions of human nature and knowledge combine to make free market environmentalism a study of process rather than a prescription for solutions. If man can rise above self-interest and if knowledge can be concentrated, then the possibility for solutions through political control is more likely. But if there are self-interested individuals with diffuse knowledge, then processes must generate a multitude of solutions conditioned by the checks and balances implicit in the process. By linking wealth to good stewardship through private ownership, the market process generates many individual experiments; and those that are successful will be copied. The question is not whether the right solution has been achieved but whether the relevant trade-offs are being considered in the process.

These three elements of free market environmentalism also characterize the interaction of organisms in ecosystems. Since Charles Darwin's revolutionary study of evolution, most scientific approaches have implicitly assumed that self-interest dominates behavior for higher as well as lower forms of life. Individual members of a species may act in "altruistic" ways and may cooperate with other species, but species survival depends on adjustments to changing parameters in ways that enhance the probability of survival. To assume that man is not self-interested or that he can rise above self-interest because he is part of a political process requires heroic assumptions about homo sapiens vis-à-vis other species.

Ecology also emphasizes the importance of time-and place-specific information in nature. Because the parameters to which species respond vary considerably within ecosystems, each member of a species must respond to time- and place-specific characteristics with the knowledge that each possesses. These parameters can vary widely, so it is imperative for survival that responses utilize the diffuse knowledge. Of course, the higher the level of communication among members of a species, the easier it is to accumulate and concentrate time- and place-specific knowledge. Again, however, it requires a giant leap of faith to assume that man's ability to accumulate and assimilate knowledge is so refined that he can centrally manage the economy or the environment for himself and for all other species. Recent evidence from Eastern Europe underscores the environmental problems that can arise with centralized management.

Ecology is also the study of processes and interaction among species; it is not a scientific prescription for solutions to environmental changes. Like free market environmentalism, ecology focuses on the information and incentives that reach the members of a species. When a niche in an ecosystem is left open, a species can "profit" from filling that niche and other species can benefit as well. If an elk herd grows, there is additional food for bears and wolves and the number of predators will expand as they take advantage of this "profit" opportunity. Individual elk will suffer at the expense of predators, but elk numbers will be controlled. In the process, plant species will survive and other vertebrates will retain their place in the ecosystem. No central planner knows the best solution for filling niches; it is the individualistic process that rewards the efficient use of time- and place-specific information.

Comparing free market environmentalism with ecosystems serves to emphasize how market processes can be compatible with good resource stewardship and environmental quality. As survival rewards species that successfully fill a niche, increased wealth rewards owners who efficiently manage their resources. Profits link self-interest with good resource management by attracting entrepreneurs to open niches. If bad decisions are being made, then a niche will be open. Whether an entrepreneur sees the opportunity and acts on it will depend on his ability to assess time- and place-specific information and act on his assessment. As with an ecosystem, however, the diffuse nature of this information makes it impossible for a central planner to determine which niches are open and how they should be filled. If the link between self-interest and good resource stewardship is broken because good stewards cannot reap the benefits, do not bear the costs of their decisions, or receive distorted information through political intervention, then the efficacy of free market environmentalism will be impaired in the same way that the efficacy of an ecosystem would be impaired by centralized planning.

Visions of what makes good environmental policy are not easily changed; if they are to change, it will be because we recognize that our visions are not consistent with reality. We must ask ourselves whether well-intentioned individuals armed with sufficient information dominate the political decisions that affect natural resources and the environment. Environmentalist Randal O'Toole answered this question in the context of the U.S. Forest Service:

> While the environmental movement has changed more than the Forest Service, I would modestly guess that I have changed more than most environmental leaders. . . . In 1980, I blamed all the deficiencies in the markets on greed and big business and thought that government should correct these deficiencies with new laws, regulatory agencies, rational planning, and trade and production restrictions. When that didn't work, I continued to blame the failure on greed and big business.
>
> About 1980, someone suggested to me that maybe government didn't solve environmental or other social problems any better than markets. That idea seemed absurd. After all, this is a democracy, a government of the people, and what the people want they should be able to get. Any suggestion that government doesn't work was incomprehensible.
>
> But then I was immersed in the planning processes of one government agency for ten years (sort of like taking a Berlitz course in bureau-speaking). I learned that the decisions made by government officials often ignored the economic and other analyses done by planners. So much for rational planning. Their decisions also often went counter to important laws and regulations. So much for a democratic government.
>
> Yet I came to realize that the decisions were all predictable, based mainly on their effects on forest budget. . . .
>
> I gradually developed a new view of the world that recognized the flaws

> of government as well as the flaws in markets. Reforms should solve problems by creating a system of checks and balances on both processes. . . . The key is to give decision makers the incentives to manage resources properly.[7]

This book provides a "Berlitz course in free market environmentalism." It also challenges entrenched visions. The development of free market environmentalism has progressed from an examination of the relatively easy problems of land and energy development to the tougher problems of water quality and quantity. The evolution of land and water rights on America's frontier illustrates how the creation of property rights responds to scarcity. Massive reservations of land as public domain halter this privatization movement and often subsidize environmental destruction. There is good evidence that political land management has ignored important recreational and amenity values and that there is a potential for providing them through markets in ways that promote harmony between development and ecology. Free market environmentalism has caught on in the area of water policy, and it holds the promise of a more efficient and environmentally acceptable allocation of that scarce resource. If land use constitutes an "easy" problem for free market environmentalism, pollution problems challenge the paradigm. But there is a clear advantage to using the paradigm of free market environmentalism to examine air pollution problems ranging from acid rain to global warming.

By confronting our entrenched visions, we can move beyond the status quo of political control of the environment and unleash environmental entrepreneurs on the tougher problems we face. The popularity of Earth Day 1990 illustrated the heightened environmental consciousness of people around the world. Most of the proposed solutions to perceived environmental problems, however, call for centralized approaches that are not consistent with the science of ecology. Moreover, these solutions pit winners against losers in a zero-sum game that tears at the social fabric. Free market environmentalism depends on a voluntary exchange of property rights between consenting owners and promotes cooperation and compromise. In short, it offers an alternative that channels the heightened environmental consciousness into win-win solutions that can sustain economic growth, enhance environmental quality, and promote harmony.

Notes

1. Donnella H. Meadows, Dennis L. Meadows, Jorgen Randers, William W. Behrens III, *The Limits to Growth: A Report for the Club of Rome's Project on the Predicament of Mankind.* (New York: A Potomac Associates Book, New American Library, 1974), ix-x.

2. For a discussion of additional apocalyptic predictions, see Edith Efron, *The Apocalyptics* (New York: Simon and Schuster, 1984), chap. 1.

3. *Global 2000 Report to the President* (Washington, DC: Government Printing Office, 1980), 1. For a critique of the *Global 2000* findings and for data refuting the predictions, see Julian Simon and Herman Kahn, *The Resourceful Earth: A Response to Global 2000* (Oxford, England: Basil Blackwell, 1984).

4. Julian Simon, *The Ultimate Resource* (Princeton, NJ: Princeton University Press, 1981).

5. The Nature Conservancy controls thousands of acres of private land that fit the free market environmentalism model. But the Conservancy also turns many of its lands over to public agencies, thereby perpetuating political control of resources.

6. Thomas Sowell, *A Conflict of Visions* (New York: William Morrow and Company, 1987), 14.

7. Randal O'Toole, "Learning the Lessons of the 1980s," *Forest Watch 10* (January–February 1990): 6.

34

HERMAN E. DALY

Steady-State Economics

The economy grows in physical scale, but the ecosystem does not. Therefore, as the economy grows it becomes larger in relation to the ecosystem. Standard economics does not ask how large the economy should be relative to the ecosystem. But that is the main question posed by steady-state economics. Standard economics seeks the optimal allocation of resources among alternative uses and is, at best, indifferent to the scale of aggregate resource use. In fact it promotes an ever-expanding scale of resource use by appealing to growth as the cure for all economic and social ills. While not denying the importance of optimal allocation, steady-state economics stresses the importance of another optimum—the optimum scale of total resource use relative to the ecosystem. . . .

What Is a Steady-State Economy?

A steady-state economy (SSE) is an economy with constant stocks of artifacts and people. These two populations (artifacts and people) are constant, but not static. People die, and artifacts depreciate. Births must replace death, and production must replace depreciation. These "input" and "output" rates are to be equal at low levels so that life expectancy of people and durability of artifacts will be high. Since the input flow of matter-energy equals the output flow when both populations are constant, the two flows may be merged into the concept of "throughput." The throughput flow begins with depletion, followed by production, depreciation, and finally pollution as the wastes are returned to the environment. The economy maintains itself by this throughput in the same way that an organism maintains itself by its

---

Granted with permission from Herman E. Daly, *Steady-State Economics* (Washington, DC: Island Press, 1991), pp. 180–186. Copyright © 1991 by Herman E. Daly. Published by Island Press, Washington, DC, & Covelo, California.

metabolic flow. Both economies and organisms must live by sucking low-entropy matter-energy (raw materials) from the environment and expelling high-entropy matter-energy (waste) back to the environment.[1] In the SSE this throughput must be limited in scale so as to be within the regenerative and assimilative capacities of the ecosystem, insofar as possible.

It is important to be clear about what is *not* constant in the SSE. Knowledge and technology are not held constant. Neither is the distribution of income nor the allocation of resources. The SSE can develop qualitatively but does not grow in quantitative scale, just as planet earth, of which the economy is a subsystem, develops without growing. Neoclassical growth models notwithstanding, the surface of the earth does not grow at a rate equal to the rate of interest! Neither can the physical stocks and flows that make up the economy continue for long to grow at compound interest. As Nobel laureate chemist and underground economist Frederick Soddy noted long ago:[2]

> You cannot permanently pit an absurd human convention, such as the spontaneous increment of debt [compound interest], against the natural law of the spontaneous decrement of wealth [entropy].

The concept of the SSE can be clarified by analogy to a steady-state library, an idea that has attracted the attention of some librarians who realize that their stock of books cannot continue to grow exponentially. A steady-state library would have a constant stock of books. Whenever a new book is added, an old one must be gotten rid of. The rule would be to add a book only if it were qualitatively better than some other book whose place it would take. The steady-state library would continue to improve qualitatively, but its quantitative physical scale would remain constant. Likewise for a steady-state economy. The end of physical accretion is not the end of progress. It is more a precondition for future progress, in the sense of qualitative improvement.

One might object to this argument on the grounds that conventional economic growth is not defined in physical units but in terms of GNP, which is in units of value, not tons of steel or barrels of oil. It is quite true that GNP is in value units, because this is necessary to aggregate diverse physical units by means of a common denominator that bears some relation to the degree to which diverse things are wanted. Nevertheless, a dollar's worth of GNP, just like a dollar's worth of gasoline or wheat, is an index of physical quantities. In calculating growth in real GNP, economists correct for price changes in order to capture only changes in quantity. It is also true that GNP includes services, which are not physical things. But a service is always rendered by something physical, either a skilled person or a capital good, over some time period. Growth in the service sector does not escape all physical constraints. In any case the SSE is defined in physical terms, *not* as zero growth in GNP.

What Is Growthmania?

The above definition of a steady-state economy stands in great contrast to the regime of economic growthmania characteristic of the modern world. Economic growth is currently the major goal of both capitalist and socialist countries and, of course, of Third World countries. Population growth is no longer a major goal for most countries, and in fact a slowing of demographic growth is frequently urged in spite of considerable retrogression on this issue by the Reagan administration. But the usual reason for urging slower demographic growth is to make room for faster economic growth. Economic growth is held to be the cure for poverty, unemployment, debt repayment, inflation, balance of payment deficits, pollution, depletion, the population explosion, crime, divorce, and drug addiction. In short, economic growth is both the panacea and the *summum bonum.* This is growthmania. When we add to GNP the costs of defending ourselves against the unwanted consequences of growth and happily count that as further growth, we then have hyper-growthmania. When we deplete geological capital and ecological life-support systems and count that depletion as net current income, then we arrive at our present state of terminal hyper-growthmania.

World leaders seek growth above all else. Therefore to oppose growth, to advocate a SSE, is not something to be done carelessly. One must present good reasons for believing that the growth economy will fail and also offer good reasons for believing that a SSE will work. That is the aim of the remainder of this article.

Origins of the Growth Dogma

How did we come to believe so strongly in the dogma of economic growth? What vision of the world underlies this commitment to continuous expansion, and where does it go wrong?

Open any standard introductory text in economics, and in the first chapter you will find a circular flow diagram. In this diagram, exchange value embodied in goods and services flows from firms to households and is called national product, while an equal flow of exchange value embodied in factors of production returns from households to firms and is called national income. The picture is that of an isolated system. There are no inflows or outflows connecting the circular flow to its "other," the environment.

If we think only in terms of abstract exchange value, the picture is reasonable. If we think in terms of money, the physical token of exchange value, the picture is not unreasonable, but is no longer strictly correct because, although money flows in a circle, on each circuit it wears out a bit. New money must be minted or printed to make up for worn-out money. Thus there is a physical throughput associated with this circulation of currency. Yet we may argue that with money the circular flow is dominant and the throughput is incidental. But when we shift to real goods and services making up national income, the real physical processes of production and consumption, then the throughput is dominant and the circular flow is incidental. Yet we find leading textbooks proclaiming that "The flow of output is circular, self-renewing, and self-feeding" and that "the outputs of the system are returned as fresh inputs."[3] One wonders what "fresh" could possibly mean in this context of an isolated circular flow? The authors were trying to explain how the circular flow is replenished so it can go on for another round. But in an isolated system, replenishment must be internal. A self-replenishing isolated system is a perpetual motion machine! Replenishment requires a throughput. Abstract exchange value may circulate in an isolated system because it has no physical dimension. Money may be thought of as flowing in a circle even though some throughput is required. But real production and consumption are in no way circular. They are based on a linear throughput beginning with depletion and ending with pollution. An economy is an open system, not an isolated system. Connections to the larger environment cannot be abstracted from without losing the most essential fact.

In the circular flow vision, matter is arranged in production, disarranged in consumption, rearranged again in production, etc. Nothing gets used up. The first law of thermodynamics can be appealed to in support of this vision: matter can be neither created nor destroyed, only rearranged. Economic growth is just a question of speeding up the circular flow, and if nothing is used up there are no limits to growth, there is no problem of replenishment from the outside.

Of course this picture flatly contradicts the second law of thermodynamics, which says, in effect, that the capacity to rearrange indestructible building blocks is not itself indestructible. It gets used up irrevocably. As we have seen, the standard vision sees the economy as a perpetual motion machine.

The gravity of such a contradiction for any theory is indicated by Sir Arthur Eddington:[4]

> The law that entropy increases—the Second Law of Thermodynamics—holds, I think, the supreme position among the laws of nature. If someone points out to you that your pet theory of the universe is in disagreement with Maxwell's equations—then so much the worse for Maxwell's equations. If it is found to be contradicted by observation—well, these experimentalists do bungle things sometimes. But if your theory is found to be against the Second Law of Thermodynamics, I can give you no hope; there is nothing for it but to collapse in deepest humiliation.

Economists, however, are not without some excuses for their predicament. They do not really deny that raw materials come from the environment, or that waste returns to the environment. But economic theory developed at a time when the environment was considered an infinite source and sink because it was so large relative to the economy. Since the throughput flow went from an infinite source to an infinite sink it involved no scarcity and could, presumably, be abstracted from for purposes of economic theory. But economic growth means that the scale of the economy gets bigger, and it is now no longer reasonable to treat it as infinitesimal relative to the ecosystem. It is time for the concept of throughput to displace the circular flow from the center stage of economic theory.[5]

If such a restructuring of economic theory is to be avoided, then the assumption of infinite sources and sinks must be in some way maintained, or else a substitute premise that has similar logical consequences must be found. The latter strategy has been more common and consists in discovery of an "ultimate resource," which is both infinite in amount and infinitely substitutable for other resources, and therefore has the same limits-abolishing effect as the original premise of infinite sources and sinks for physical resources. This "unlimited resource" is variously referred to as technology, information, knowledge, or the human mind. Anyone who asserts the existence of limits is soon presented with a whole litany of things that someone once said could never be done but subsequently were done. Certainly it is dangerous business to specify limits to knowledge. But it is equally dangerous to presuppose that the content of new knowledge will abolish old limits faster than it discovers new ones. The discovery of uranium was new knowledge that increased our resource base. The subsequent discovery of the dangers of radioactivity did not further expand the resource base, but contracted it. Before getting carried away with the idea that the human mind is an "ultimate resource" that can generate endless growth, let us remember that, while certainly not reducible to physical or mechanical terms, the mind is not independent of the physical body. "No phosphorous, no thought," as Frederick Soddy put it. Or as Loren Eisley reminds us, "The human mind, so frail, so perishable, so full of inexhaustible dreams and hungers, burns by the power of a leaf." Minds capable of such insight ought to be capable of showing more restraint toward leaves and phosphorous than is usually exhibited by our growth-bound economy. Mere knowledge means little to the economic system unless it is embodied in physical structures. As Boulding reminds us, capital is knowledge imprinted on the physical world in the form of improbable arrangements. But knowledge cannot be imprinted on any kind of matter by any kind of energy. The constricted entry point of knowledge into the physical economy is through the availability of low-entropy resources. No low-entropy resources, no capital—regardless of knowledge, unless the second law of thermodynamics is abolished.

It has been said that the best measure of a scientist's influence is how long he can hold up progress in his own discipline. By this measure, the editors of the major economics journals are probably the most influential scientists of all time! Continuing to study economics only in terms of the circular flow model is like studying an organism only in terms of the circulatory system, without ever mentioning the digestive tract. Yet that is what the mainline professional journals, in their dogmatic commitment to growth, insist on.

Notes

1. For a brilliant analysis of the relevance of entropy law to economics, see Nicholas Georgescu-Roegen, *The Entropy Law and the Economic Process* (Cambridge, MA: Harvard University Press, 1971).
2. *Cartesian Economics* (London, 1922). For an exposition of Soddy's economics and further references, see H.E. Daly, "The Economic Thought of Frederick Soddy," *History of Political Economy,* 12:4, 1980.
3. See Robert Heilbroner and Lester Thurow, *The Economic Problem* (New York: Prentice-Hall, 1981), pp. 127, 135.
4. *The Nature of the Physical World* (New York: Cambridge University Press, 1953), p. 74.
5. H.E. Daly, "The Circular Flow Exchange Value and the Linear Throughput of Matter-Energy: A Case of Misplaced Concreteness," *Review of Social Economy,* December 1985.

35

ROBERT C. PAEHLKE

Environmentalism and the Future of Progressive Politics

Environmentalism as an ideology is now at a stage of development comparable to that of socialism a century ago. Environmentalism may never obtain a mass base similar to that of conservatism, liberalism, or socialism, but it has already transformed the way many people understand the political world. Environmentalists have produced a sociological, political, economic, and philosophical literature of remarkable breadth, depth, and variety that has significantly affected the political and administrative agendas of most nations of the world.

Seeing environmentalism as an ideology may also alter our understanding of the concept of ideology itself. Environmentalism is the first ideology to be deeply rooted in the natural sciences (Marxist claims notwithstanding). Scientific findings do not of themselves lead to a particular set of political conclusions, but they are essential to this ideology in a way that they are not to any other. Furthermore, environmentalism cannot be easily located on a left-right ideological spectrum. Ideology, it now appears, is something more than a matter of the economic self-interest of the poor, the rich, or the middle classes, and ideological categories understood exclusively in distributional terms can no longer account for the whole ideological world. Prior to the rise of environmentalism, this might have been suspected. Now the suspicion is confirmed.

Nevertheless, we cannot ignore distributive issues. Some early environmentalists suffered from the popular perception that those who advocated wilderness protection were elitist. Only the rich could afford the time and

---

From Robert C. Paehlke, *Environmentalism and the Future of Progressive Politics* (New Haven: Yale University Press, 1989), pp. 273–278. Reprinted by permission.

money to "use" the wilderness, the argument went; but less wealthy people enjoy redwood decks and picnic tables, and workers need employment in the woods and sawmills. Although this sort of argument has usually come from those in investment or managerial positions in primary industries, it has also appealed to conservative editorial writers not inclined to the needs of the working class. Once environmentalists began to question the growth ethic and such things as energy megaprojects, they quickly alienated some in construction unions and even at times certain leaders of disadvantaged minorities. Any potential alliance of environmentalism with progressivism is, of course, threatened by such perceptions.

Fortunately these perceptions can be rebutted with the arguments implicit in the jobs/environment literature. They can also be defused through cooperative action and explicit environmental/progressive policy initiatives. For example, energy conservation or recycling programs provide good employment opportunities for the hard-core unemployed. Energy conservation also aids the poor, a disproportionate share of whose income is spent on energy (34 percent for the lowest decile as against 2 percent for the highest). But conservation programs must provide the skills and time the poor often lack and the capital they always lack. In general, environmentalists need to remind themselves that economic growth has never disproportionately aided the poor. Distributive politics are unavoidable, and environmental protection can alter distributional outcomes, either intentionally or unintentionally. Environmentalism is neither left nor right in the sense that environmental policy tools can have a left, right, or centrist character.

Policy analysis is not, as some would have it, simply a matter of evaluating available sets of policy options. Policy analysis must be a more creative process than that; it must be at least as much an art as a science and must incorporate consideration of the evolution of ideas; reflections on the values that are, or might someday be, held by the citizenry at large; and careful consideration of feasibility, prudence, likelihood, and desirability. Most policy analysts reasonably distinguish themselves from those who quickly leap from the "is" to the "ought," or vice versa. But it does not follow that policy analysis should or can avoid normative matters. Both natural and social scientists are frequently overtrained and overcautious on this point. Some researchers should feel an obligation to consider the practical and policy implications of their research. Contrary to the view of many academics this can be done without lapsing into tedious polemics. Thus there is much reason to hope that environmentalism in its various academic guises can open the door to improvements in policy studies generally.

Environmentalists, whether academics or not, who would prefer to develop links to socioeconomic progressives should take care to avoid neither-left-nor-rightism. Political neutrality will leave in place not only the present relative distribution of economic benefits but also the present distribution of political power, assuring a more inequitable economic distribution in whatever difficult economic times lie ahead. The 1980s have shown all too clearly how this can happen. Even the environmentalists' remedial measures might exacerbate distributional inequities—reduced work time, for example, could lead to gender discrimination with regard to work hours. Academic environmentalists clearly have a responsibility to point out such inequitable forms of economic rationalization and environmental activists should actively resist them.

Many corporate decision-makers doubtless find distributionally centrist forms of environmentalism indistinguishable from any other "impractical leftist radicalism." Since this perception is common and likely ineradicable in some circles, environmentalists must also be careful to avoid being perceived by the less advantaged as competitors for scarce governmental resources. Environmentalism is much more than a middle-class luxury, but not enough people perceive all its important dimensions. Again, political action requires either self-deception or conscious adoption of some left, center, or right position. Economically comfortable environmentalists can find an appropriate left/right position on a moral basis (to achieve, if you will, spiritual comfort), an intellectual basis (to achieve consistency), or a tactical basis (to achieve political gains). My view is that the moderate left of center makes sense on all these grounds.

Outside the United States this position might be represented either by democratic socialist parties or by progressive elements within the traditional parties of the center (for example, the Liberal Party in Canada or the Social Democratic Alliance in Britain). In the United States the Democratic Party is the only choice. Crucial to this political conclusion are two inescapable facts. First, neoconservatism has been consistently and deeply hostile to environmental protection in every country in which it has emerged. To the extent that conservative parties have retained any sympathy for environmental protection, they yet carry within them a significant contingent of what in Canada are called "red Tories." In the United States pro-environmental views have long since lost any real influence within the Republican Party (if they ever had any). Second, the less advantaged sectors of society, polls suggest, are concerned about environmental issues, and might become more so if their most pressing economic needs were met, especially the need for an assured source of income. Environmentalism can be creatively associated with the process of achieving social and economic security for such individuals and communities. I make this point prominently here because I do not want the arguments in this book to be taken as part of an easy accommodation of the nonenvironmental status quo.

Let us consider one argument that is open to such an interpretation. Environmentalism as an ideology and as practical politics can adopt an eclectic and pragmatic view of policy tools. Contrary to those firmly wedded to a particular left or right tradition, environmentalists can take advantage of the full range of policy options. They can work within nationalization *and* privatization, entrepreneurship *and* government expenditures to expand education, health protection, social welfare, and the arts; they can seek both economic deregulation (as distinct from health and safety deregulation) *and* significant reductions in military spending. As we have seen, environmental protection does not depend on huge government deficits—some environmentally sound policies might even reduce deficits. But such a policy pattern is one with which neither traditional progressives nor neoconservatives can be fully comfortable.

Environmentalists can distinguish themselves from neoconservatives in at least six ways. Environmentalists would (1) enhance rather than inhibit environmental regulation and enforcement; (2) oppose expansions of military spending; (3) not make rapid economic growth a high policy priority; (4) tend, whenever possible, to increase expenditures on education, social welfare, the arts, and health; (5) systematically increase government revenue in selective ways; and (6) not treat the market economy as an inviolate sacred cow. In addition, environmentalists are much more likely to support enhanced opportunities for women and ethnic minorities than neoconservatives are. Finally, environmentalists might be more comfortable than neoconservatives with *actually* reducing governmental deficits.

One can also list ways in which environmentalists might distinguish themselves from traditional progressives. Environmentalists would (1) promote environmental protection even at the risk of alienating some traditional progressive constituencies; (2) more consistently oppose excessive military spending; (3) promote the technological transformations associated with automation and communications and the demise of smokestack industries; (4) promote reduction of government deficits; (5) be more inclined to political decentralization; (6) promote small and medium-scale entrepreneurship; and (7) flexibly encourage reduced work time as a means of achieving full employment.

Environmentalists' openness to selected parts of the contemporary appeal of neoconservatism could broaden the potential political constituency of an environmentally informed progressivism—at the risk of some losses on the left. But careful policy development or straightforward and open compromise could help to avoid significant losses within traditional progressive constituencies. North Americans, after all, have always been more politically instinctive than politically ideological; and many within traditional progressive constituencies have in recent years voted with the neoconservatives at least temporarily. Whether these losses would be compounded or ameliorated by the addition of a strong environmental sensibility to progressive politics is unknown. But if I were as sure of the hostility of trade unionists as are some environmentalists, I would not have written this book. Similarly, I am one of many environmentalists who think the current public hostility to trade unions is ill founded. All one can say in the end is that opinion polls suggest that environmental issues remain important to large numbers of people and that support for stronger action has an appeal across class, regional, and ethnic lines.

Thus it is important for environmentalists to be receptive to the cross-class appeal of neoconservative ideas. We should not be afraid to look for elements within neoconservatism that might be both compatible with environmental progress and not incompatible with distributive progress. Increased military spending and a too-cautious approach to environmental regulation should be rejected whatever the political risks. But what of a gradual return to fiscal responsibility accompanied by an enthusiasm about creative entrepreneurial initiatives? The latter applies well to recycling, renewable energy, and energy conservation and aids in replacing employment lost through automation and rationalization within the corporate and public sectors. Thus environmentalists need not automatically be hostile to such sociotechnological developments, and enthusiasm about the future is also part of the neoconservative appeal. Of note, too, is neoconservatives' willingness at least temporarily to restrain consumer spending in the interest of long-term economic stability. Environmentalists could give this goal a character very different from that asserted within neoconservative circles, channeling the savings and new capital investment achieved into pollution abatement, urban improvement, education, the arts, energy conservation, and full employment rather than exclusively into such projects as nuclear power plants, corporate jets, office towers, military research, and the array of so-called "paper" manipulations.

36

Rory O'Brien

Normative Theory and Public Policy

Theories, Paradigms, and Models

Decision-makers do not usually consider it necessary to rely heavily on formal theory to guide either policy development or implementation. It is an understatement to say that, in the main, public policy has not been made with reference to notions or concepts drawn from political philosophy. Professionals in the policy-making field (bureaucrats and politicians) are generally opposed, in principle, to making use of ethical or moral arguments when making their decisions. Neither have normative theorists traditionally been concerned with public policy outcomes. Political theorists have, for the most part, found sufficient work in devising explanatory and unifying schemes and structures which might, at best, serve to act as models for future policies.

The issues and domain central to the project of political theory, however, must be oriented towards some sort of outcome. Without the expectation of change in society, the enterprise of normative prescription would never be undertaken in the first place. So it is that public policy decision-making and prescriptive theory need one another: Policies, which are developed in order to have an impact, are based at least on those values or ethical considerations which concern bringing about improvements in society.

Policy Making and Political Thought

Policy-makers often retreat from the use of ethics when coming to a decision because ethical inquiry can threaten their professional and political

From Rory O'Brien, *Just Enough Water: Distributive Justice and Scarce Resource Management*. Forthcoming.

interests. Administrators, legislators, and bureaucrats are all resistant to what one commentator refers to as, "the potential challenges of moral evaluation."[1] Particularly resistant to ethical considerations are policy analysts, who actually develop many of the alternative choices from which decision-makers will choose.

Policy analysts are most often viewed as being purely technical advisers whose work is generally value free and apolitical. Analysts and bureaucrats regularly use a "technocratic" argument to defend their work on the grounds that they (the analysts and bureaucrats) do not make value decisions . . . they just design the most efficient programs. In this way, policy analysts may avoid or ignore moral values, relying instead on a form of utilitarianism better known as cost-benefit analysis.

As long as policies are developed on the basis of greater efficiency, the analyst need look no further than "the bottom line" for answers to questions of morality. But, whether the analyst likes it or not, policy analysis is a normative endeavor, seeking to recommend a "good" policy over a "bad" one, or the "best" policy over other contenders. No matter how value free the analysts attempt to appear, their reliance on this normative dimension will at best be obscured, not eliminated.[2]

Politicians also stay away from ethical or moral debates that might be politically damaging. This group of decision-makers does not wish to alienate either their constituencies or their political allies. Legislators are especially sensitive to the need not to make others uncomfortable with discussions of relevant moral issues. Additionally, politicians are unwilling to challenge the underpinnings of the reigning ideological paradigm. In the U.S. that means not challenging the basic tenets of liberal capitalism, nor trying to make *more* of politics than what most people want from government. In this ideological climate the safest policies reflect the most direct means to solving practical problems while not deliberating on the sophisticated or abstract.

The arguments which seek to bar ethical or moral considerations in the analysis of public policy decisions can be summed up as follows: ethical positions are viewed as either impossible, unnecessary, personally biased, or impractical. . . .

Moral Autonomy and Public Policy

It is through the implementation of just arrangements as the fundamentals of society that future environmental policy can be made more just. Kant's view includes these fundamentals in the form of institutions based on justice.[3] At the same time, Kant's schema interjects the idea of autonomy into the political dialogue. Scarce resources should not be controlled solely by core groups of elite interests who are able to influence policy-makers so as to create policies which work disproportionately to their advantage. Instead, policies regarding resources upon which all depend for life and livelihood must be made with reference to what benefits society at large.

Rawls's interpretation of Kant may also be instructive here in terms of the policy process.[4] In order to function optimally, our policy-making institutions (legislatures, various state and federal government agencies) must be rooted in ideas of just distribution. However, short of restructuring those institutions in which environmental policy is made, it is Kant's notion of justice as a function of moral autonomy which is most easily applied to current policy problems.

One example of the type of restructuring that could take place is in the area of long term contracts which specifically benefit agricultural water users. The Bureau of Reclamation was initially created with the laudable mission of encouraging and helping farmers make a living in arid regions. However, that mission has been perverted as policy-makers have found it more expedient to cater to powerful interests rather than consider more broad ranging concerns. While the numbers reflect what they do—a low percentage of G.S.P. from agriculture in California, and higher levels of usage by agriculture than by any other group throughout the west—the current degree to which the farming industry is subsidized by government is unjust.

To return to Kant, it is by separating or diffusing, as Bluhm puts it, "the weight of sovereign authority as much as possible," that water policy in the west can best be approached.[5] The best critique of restrictive governmental control of water resources throughout the west is that government has proven to be an inefficient and, in many cases, biased manager of this important resource. Through a more liberalized system of transfers, markets and legislation a more equitable distribution of water may be established in the west.

A Kantian set of solutions to resource distribution questions would include the development of policies made with reference to something akin to the Categorical Imperative. Whether this was worked out on the legislative or the administrative level, such an imperative would operate so as to minimize gains by any one group over the foundational notions of the good established for the entire community, or in this case, state. Thus preferential supports for agriculture (the payments for which are shared by all taxpayers) would be permissible only if that sector of the economy consistently provided jobs and revenue or in some other way helped to offset the costs to society.

This is not to say that any particular business interest should be restricted—only that when subsidies are necessary government must be flexible enough to admit changing realities rather than defending entrenched interests. Similarly, continued industrial and population growth would be encouraged only if the long term environmental hazards that such development implies were mitigated in some manner. Beyond policy decisions at the level of government the Kantian view would also hold that individuals, as well as groups, with particularized interests should make their decisions on the basis of justice. Self-interest is well served by being part of a community and thus, community interests must be as important to farmers, water district managers, developers, industrialists and environmentalists as are their own individual gains.

As policy-makers in the west look toward the future, however, they are faced with the reality of a region in which many of the constituent elements are already in place: population, industry, and further growth potential. Development in the western states no longer calls for a frontier mentality. Now it is possible for creative solutions to be drawn from normative prescriptions.

Notes

1. Amy, Douglas J. 1984. "Why Policy Analysis and Ethics Are Incompatible." *Journal of Policy Analysis And Management,* 3, no. 4: 573–91.
2. Ibid.
3. Kant, Immanuel. 1963. *Foundations of the Metaphysics of Morals,* Lewis White Beck, trans. Indianapolis, IN.: The Bobbs-Merrill Co., Inc.
4. Rawls, John. 1971. *A Theory of Justice.* Cambridge, MA: Harvard University Press.
5. Bluhm, William T. 1978. *Theories of the Political System: Classics of Political Thought and Modern Political Analysis.* Englewood Cliffs, NJ: Prentice-Hall Inc.

37

DANIEL PRESS

Democratic Dilemmas in the Age of Ecology

Just as an awareness of environmental problems gathered momentum in the 1960s and 1970s, political theorists, economists, and biologists began to suggest that the pressures of the coming environmental crisis would become so strong that they would destroy democratic political institutions and the economic systems they relied upon. The implication was that no mode of democratic politics currently practiced could possible handle problems of the scope and complexity of global environmental degradation. Democratic politics would be too slow to respond, relying as it did on incrementalism and drawn-out public policy-making. Modern democracies were also faulted for being incapable of protecting interests of future generations.

Environmentalist writers began to claim that if democracies couldn't marshal the consensus and foresight to save the physical environment, maybe centralized power would cut through delays and small-minded policy-making. Enlightened authoritarian regimes could merge ecological awareness with swift, forceful, and comprehensive action to restore ecosystems and restrain human appetites for unsustainable growth. But the alternatives to democracy did not look promising to writers committed to democratic participation. Why should an authoritarian state be a priori better able to cope with environmental problems? After all, centralized bureaucracies are not known for their flexibility, responsiveness, adaptability, for forward-thinking capabilities.

Thus, very early in the 1960s and 1970s debate, modern societies were apparently stuck with a grim choice: either they had to give up the hope of

---

From Daniel Press, *Democratic Dilemmas in the Age of Ecology* (Durham, NC: Duke University Press, 1994), pp. 12–18.

altering their activities fast enough to avert catastrophe, or they had to forgo their cherished democratic ideals in favor of a safer physical environment (albeit an uncertain social future).[1] The writers who articulated this "centralist" analysis have been called "neo-Hobbesians,"[2] "neo-Malthusians,"[3] and "structural reformers"[4]; they include Robert Heilbroner, Garrett Hardin, and to some extent, William Ophuls.

The ecological predicament described by these centralists was destined to set the tone of environmental political theory for the 1970s. In 1968 Garrett Hardin published his influential piece "The Tragedy of the Commons," which presaged environmental crisis unless society agreed to self-restraint through mutual coercion. Hardin's "lifeboat ethics" made the analogy of the earth as an ocean-bound vessel with limited space and limited food to feed its crew. Survival in the lifeboat would require strict discipline and the imposition of rules—for both using resources and giving them away. An ever-increasing number of would-be passengers had to be refused a place on board if the vessel was to avoid sinking. Indeed, Hardin, a biologist, found it to be a greater disservice to prolong the existence of the starving poor than to let them die out, dwindling in number until their populations were sustainable. He also asserted that such an outlook was likely to be considered draconian, perhaps even immoral, and thus only very strong social control could avert the tragedy of the commons.

Economist Robert Heilbroner followed in 1974 with his *Inquiry into the Human Prospect.* Heilbroner agreed with Hardin's analysis, adding that "the pressure of political movements in times of war, civil commotion, or general anxiety pushes in the direction of authority, not away from it."[5] For Heilbroner, such a tendency exists because people have a strong inclination toward obedience, especially of parental figures whose authority is deemed "up to the task" at hand, and also because a sense of social belonging gives people a large capacity for national identification. In turn, such nationalist identification could render society more susceptible to demagoguery. Heilbroner's analysis of political and economic institutions led him to believe that environmental crisis would surely accelerate so fast that societies would be compelled to impose ecologically rational behavior, using authoritarian means if necessary. But Heilbroner was not just projecting what he thought the future of politics would hold in a world saved from environmental disaster; he was willing to curtail democracy if by doing so environmental crisis could be averted: "I not only predict but I prescribe a centralization of power as the only means by which our threatened and dangerous civilization can make way for its successor."[6]

As for decentralized models of environmental governance, Heilbroner argued that "mankind lives in immense urban complexes and these must be sustained and provisioned for a long time . . . pockets of small-scale communities may be established, but they will be parasites to, not genuine alternatives for, the centralized regime that will be struggling to redesign society."[7]

Shortly after Heilbroner's frankly authoritarian statement, William Ophuls published *Ecology and the Politics of Scarcity* (1977). In what is still one of the most widely read treatises on environmental political theory, Ophuls worked his way from a description of the tenets of ecology, through a catalogue of environmental ills, to a critique of laissez-faire economics and status quo politics. His intention was to demonstrate that the logic of healthy, functional ecological systems could only work within limits. Growth beyond such limits would constitute, in effect, living off one's capital (at increasing rates) instead of one's income.

Ophuls then contrasted the ecological limits to a growth model of the world with the wasteful, consumption-driven model of the dominant economic paradigm primarily because it had supplanted politics[8] by "substituting growth for political principle." Economics thus "solves" ecological dilemmas through economic bargains even though they "are not easily compromisable or commensurable, least of all in terms of money."[9]

If political principles were gone, replaced by an economic ideology devoted to infinite growth, Ophuls was convinced that only sharp, coercive actions would allow any kind of survival. He predicted that if society adopted steady-state economics under a crisis regime,[10] the new system might be run by ecological mandarins who would possess the esoteric knowledge needed to run it well.[11] This ecological oligarchy would have to curtail personal freedoms in order to make and implement prudent decisions.

But Ophuls was not a centralist in his recommendations; on the contrary, he concludes his book with a chapter devoted to the importance of participatory democracy, value change, and enlightenment. Thus in his prescriptions Ophuls is very much a decentralist, a point he emphasizes even more strongly in the 1992 second edition of his book. Calling Hardin's solution to the tragedy of the commons "explicitly Hobbesian," Ophuls points out that it was only his *analysis* of the issues that might be termed Hobbesian, not his *prescriptions*.

Most decentralists criticized Ophuls, Hardin, and Heilbroner for both their analyses and prescriptions. Decentralists found their analyses flawed, countering with centralization as the root cause of environmental problems and thus reaching a prescription opposite to that of Hardin and Heilbroner (recommending decentralization and participation as the basis for communicative and ecological rationality).

Through his 1974 book *Man's Responsibility for Nature* Passmore was one of the first to condemn centralized approaches. He stressed that democratic societies are in fact more capable of action than totalitarian states, especially because of their "habits of local action" and their "traditions of public disclosure."[12] Contemporary democracies thus fail "when they are tempted into exactly the same vices as the totalitarian states; spying, soothing utterances from central authorities, face-saving, bureaucratic inertia, censorship, concealment."[13]

David Orr and Stuart Hill (1978) offered a somewhat more precise critique of the centralists and questioned, in particular, their assumptions "(1) that an authoritarian state can cope with its own increased size and complexity; (2) that it can muster sufficient skill to exert control over the external environment; and (3) that these conditions can be maintained in perpetuity" (p. 459).

To these assumptions, they reply that large, highly centralized systems such as bureaucratic organizations tend to be limited in their ability to process complex information with a comprehensive understanding of the universe in which they must act. Orr and Hill also argue that government regulation and bureaucratic fiat have been poor tools for systemic approaches to ecosystem repair, and that truly creative problem solving tends to occur less in authoritarian groups than in their democratic counterparts.

Susan Leeson (1979) agrees that the authoritarian prescription is too simple and doesn't explain how an authoritarian system would operate "ecologically." She also points out the lack of proof we have for the ability—or motivation—of authoritarian systems to manage environmental problems better. Orr and Hill add that since resilience and learning are not characteristics of highly centralized systems, an ecological Leviathan whose legitimacy was predicated on successful environmental management would not have much margin for error. Moreover, successful environmental outcomes are almost always jeopardized by the "megaprojects" many centralized regimes have been so fond of in the past. Such projects would never be attempted if communities were small and self-sufficient (e.g., no larger than 5,000 people).[14]

The decentralists ultimately take issue with the centralists' "model of self-centered man who is incapable of acting in the larger community interest and incapable of deciphering the complexities of ecological problems."[15] On the contrary, "selective decentralization" would permit citizens to retain a high level of involvement in economies that were always "local." Democratic participation would not only be feasible as a political system and effective at safeguarding the environment, it might very well allow *ever increasing* levels of democratization beyond that which current societies had to offer.[16]

In a recent work, Orr (1992) reiterated his belief that decentralized governance is a necessary condition of achieving environmental sustainability. However, like most of the decentralists, Orr does not offer a convincing link between decentralization and sustainability. Why should decentralized governance lead to environmental health and sustainability? Aren't people in small communities just as capable of ransacking their resources and condemning land and water for waste disposal? In response, Orr would say that "the transfer of power, authority, resources, talent, and capital from the countryside, towns, neighborhoods, and communities to the city, corporations, and national government has undermined in varying degrees responsibility, care, thrift, and social cohesion—qualities essential to sustainability" (p. 71).

Orr jumps from civic virtue and participation to sustainability and does not fill the gap with testable propositions. Somehow, sustainability and environmental conservation arise from "good communities . . . and good livelihood."[17] The sentiment is appealing, but the connections between these desirable social traits and environmental action are not clear. Does social cohesion change a community's long-term discount rate, thereby encouraging it to value the future more? Is self-reliance somehow linked to greater participation and consensus building in natural resource management?

Perhaps the decentralists don't elaborate on these connections because they expect that structural (political, institutional) decentralization would have to *simultaneously* be accompanied by self-transformation. John Rodman (1980) stresses that the debate over structural choices reflects a mistaken assumption about how resource limits are imposed. If limits are external, certainly an authoritarian state may be the most direct way to impose them. If resource limits arise from our own dissatisfaction with a pointless life of production and consumption, "then . . ." limits to [industrial] growth" emerge "naturally."[18] The implication for Rodman is that the real locus of change will not be in governments, democratic or authoritarian, but in a "new paradigm . . . [that] is more apt to be discovered than legislated."[19]

Rodman brings the link between decentralization and sustainability into focus, elaborating on Orr and Hill: he associates totalitarianism with ideological monocultural purity ("new Aryan order," "the new Soviet man"), and points out that environmentalists' preoccupation with biodiversity is based on the same ecological reasoning that concludes that totalitarianism is unsustainable; in essence, uniformity breeds instability. This is what Orr means when he says that authoritarian systems are unstable and that "ecosystems are the only systems capable of stability in a world governed by the laws of thermodynamics."[20] Thus, for Rodman, the struggle for preserving biodiversity is "a resistance movement against the imperialism of human monoculture."[21]

Resistance to the inertia of the status quo and the logic of existing economic and political paradigms is the key to the decentralist position. Decentralists reject the authoritarian trade-off between democratic participation and desirable environmental outcomes, thereby simply refusing to rank environmentalism above democracy, or vice versa. In a prescient close to his 1974 book, Passmore summed up this desire to simultaneously maximize good environmental outcomes and preserve just social institutions: "My sole concern is that we should do nothing which will reduce their [future generations'] freedom of thought and action, whether by destroying the natural world which makes that freedom possible or the social traditions which permit and encourage it."[22]

Paradigm Change Through Transformative Politics

Many of the writers discussed above argue that, whatever political path we choose, radical paradigm changes will be necessary to avert environmental crises. Eckersley (1992) points out that much environmental political thought views environmental crisis as an "opportunity for emancipation." She suggests that this emancipatory potential has motivated ecopolitical theorists to direct "considerable attention toward the revitalization of civil society rather than, or in addition to, the state."[23] Can this emancipation or transformation occur under Leviathan rule? Probably not without discarding basic premises of the centralist analysis. The centralist perspective sees a logical contradiction to giving people in the present control over the future. As individually rational actors, people are compelled to destroy collective goods for individual pursuits, and hence they are not even capable of the "metanoia" Ophuls argues. A Leviathan concept—even that of Ophuls's ecological mandarins—implies a regulative approach to mitigating environmental change instead of collective attitudinal transformation.

In contrast, decentralists argue for political decentralization not just for better environmental management but as the best mode for paradigm change. Decentralists might say that you can't "think globally" (with new paradigms) without "acting locally" (through participatory democracy). But they have not suggested *how* democracy and participation can help transform and educate enough people to achieve a paradigm change. . . .

Following the decentralist line of reasoning, intellectual transformation is facilitated by, and requires, a participatory process politics. Why? Because people cannot learn, challenge new information, or deliberate in a closed, nonparticipatory system. And in contrast to environmental political thought, democratic theory has explored innovations, both in social relations and state structures, designed to achieve citizen transformation through political participation. Borrowing from democratic theory, we can ask a series of questions about how different forms of participation might bring about the kinds of attitudinal transformations decentralists predict if their vision becomes reality: How can people learn about complex issues? How can people act (or participate) on these issues? What social goods can people act upon? When people take control of policy, how will they impose limits upon themselves?

Notes

1. As Taylor paraphrases the options, "Is political democracy of greater value than appropriate environmental policy or vice versa?" Taylor, B.P. 1992. *Our Limits Transgressed: Environmental Political Thought in America.* Lawrence, KS: University of Kansas Press, p. 2.

2. Walker, K.J. 1988. "The Environmental Crisis: A Critique of Neo-Hobbesian Responses." *Polity* 21 (1): 67–81.

3. Taylor, 1992.

4. Lester, J.P. and J.S. Dryzek. 1989. "Alternative Views of the Environmental Problematique." In James Lester, ed., *Environmental Politics and Policy: Theories and Evidence.* Durham, NC: Duke University Press.

5. Heilbroner, Robert. 1980. *An Inquiry into the Human Prospect: Updated for the 1980s.* New York: Norton, p. 128.

6. Heilbroner, p. 175.

7. Heilbroner, p. 172.

8. See my discussion of the "economic challenge to democracy" in chapter 3 of Press, Daniel. 1994. *Democratic Dilemmas in the Age of Ecology.* Durham, NC: Duke University Press.

9. Ophuls, W. 1977. *Ecology and the Politics of Scarcity.* San Francisco: W.H. Freeman, pp. 185–86.

10. A steady-state economy would exist, as well as possible, within the physical limits of the earth and would recycle waste with minimum loss. Waste outputs would be recycled into physical systems with high efficiency, while extraction of nonrenewables would be sharply curtailed. For further details see Daly, H., ed. 1980. *Economics, Ecology, Ethics: Essays Toward a Steady-State Economy.* San Francisco: W.H. Freeman.

11. Ophuls, p. 163.

12. Passmore, J. 1974. *Man's Responsibility for Nature.* New York: Scribner's, p. 183.

13. Passmore, p. 183.

14. Orr, D. and S. Hill. 1978. "Leviathan, the Open Society, and the Crisis of Ecology." *Western Political Quarterly* 31 (Dec.), p. 463.

15. Orr and Hill, p. 466.

16. "Bioregionalists" have long argued that decentralization is at the core of the decentralist analysis and prescription. In their view, a sustainable environment and society can *only* be achieved in small, semiautonomous regions delineated by features of "natural" environment (topography, watersheds, ecosystems). For a good introduction to the normative aspects of bioregionalism, see Sale, K. 1991. *Dwellers in the Land: The Bioregional Vision.* Philadelphia: New Society Publishers.

17. Orr, D. 1992. *Ecological Literacy: Education and the Transition to a Postmodern World.* Albany, NY: State University of New York Press, p. 31.

18. Rodman, J. 1980. "Paradigm Change in Political Science: An Ecological Perspective." *American Behavioral Scientist* 24 (1), p. 72.

19. Rodman, p. 74.

20. Orr, p. 34.

21. Rodman, p. 68. Nazarea-Sandoval, 1994, elaborates on this theme by showing how farmers in the Philippines deliberately plant a wide range of sweet potato varieties that are no longer in favor with government extension services. By hiding their old varieties between rows of the government's hybrids, these farmers engage in "everyday forms of resistance" that are as effective as they are undramatic. Nazarea-Sandoval, V. 1994. *Lenses and Latitudes: On the Boundaries and Elasticity of Agricultural Decision Making.* Ithaca, NY: Cornell University Press.

22. Passmore, p. 195.

23. Eckersley, R. 1992. *Environmentalism and Political Theory: Toward an Ecocentric Approach.* Albany, NY: State University of New York Press.

38

James L. Hudson

Rights and the Further Future

In recent years philosophers have devoted a good deal of attention to a new kind of moral problem: the evaluation of actions whose key feature is that they produce bad effects in the distant future. No doubt this interest has been stimulated by the public alarums over pollution, resource depletion, and over-population; but whatever one thinks of these specific policy issues, problems of this type have a theoretical interest which is independent of any immediate applications. In analyzing such problems, moral philosophers have found little use for the notion of a moral right; the problems have seemed to call instead for some form of consequentialist moral theory. The purpose of this note is to suggest that this dismissal of rights theories of morality has been over-hasty, for such theories possess hitherto unused resources for dealing with such problems. It is not clear that these resources are fully adequate, but for now the issue should be regarded as open.

The case against rights theories has been put forward recently by Jefferson McMahan[1] and Derek Parfit.[2] According to them it would be grossly counterintuitive to deny that agents in the present should often act so as to make people in the distant future better off rather than worse off. But this cannot be because of any rights that the future people have to better treatment. For in many cases the people who would exist if we did the favorable action will be numerically different people (though there may be the same number of them) from those who would exist if we did the unfavorable one.[3] Now observance of someone's rights implies better treatment *of that person,* not the suppression of his very coming-to-be and the possible substitution of another person or persons for him. So the kind of procedure we

From James L. Hudson, "Rights and the Further Future," in *Right Conduct: Theories and Applications,* edited by Bayles and Henley (New York: Random House, 1989). Reprinted by permission of the McGraw-Hill Companies.

need in order to evaluate actions with consequences in the distant future will concern itself with *consequences,* but in an *impersonal* way; thus it will not be concerned with *personal rights.*

Further reason for thinking that an appeal to rights could not explain our moral concern for future people comes from the reflection that rights have force only if they are not waived by their possessor. But consider again a recent action with consequences which we could normally consider bad for distantly future people. Would those people, looking back at the action from their later vantage point, object to it? If it had not been done, *they* would not have existed. Perhaps other, happier people would have existed in their place; but who is going to insist, as a matter of right, that he be compensated for having come into the world at all, in place of someone who would have been better off than he? He will, instead, automatically waive his right to object to any action which was a necessary condition of his own existence, provided only that his existence is not utterly miserable. Thus the right which might be thought to protect distantly future people from some of the deleterious consequences of present actions will not actually do so, since they will be automatically waived by their possessors.

Rights theories of morality are thus under serious attack. What response can be made on their behalf?

First, it can simply be denied that the point of a right is to protect certain interests of its possessor. It is closer to the truth to say that rights are for the protection of *possible* interests; that one may have a right to something which is not in fact in his interest (though it might have been). If I have a right to X and yet X is taken from me without my explicit consent, my right has probably been violated even if the taking was in my own best interests, and even if I knew it was so. It is true that implicit or hypothetical consent is sometimes deemed adequate to render this *not* a rights-violation; but it is unclear under what circumstances this is proper. Even though I would have consented to be deprived of X had I been asked, it is still often the case that my being deprived of X *without* being asked *does* violate my right.

A further unclarity is that consent, or the waiver of a right, is normally considered invalid if obtained through coercion; and the concept of coercion is a difficult one. In the case under consideration—in which a person is deemed to have consented to a long-past action which does him present harm, on the grounds that the action was also necessary for his own conception—the individual's position is uncomfortably analogous to that of the traveler confronted with the highwayman's demand: "Your money or your life!" Often when one has a choice between two alternatives, one involving the preservation and the other forfeiture of his own life, he is considered to be choosing under coercion, and his rights-waivers are deemed invalid. And so the validity of any *ex post facto* waiver such as here imagined is at least in doubt.

Still, it is awkward for the rights theorist to be reminded that *at least normally* one observes another's rights by treating him with consideration, not by preventing him from coming into existence in the first place. The rights theorist must deny that this is *always* the case, in order to have a rights-based rationale for our present concern for distantly future people. But then he must deal with the observation that we can always avoid violating the rights of future people by preventing their coming into existence. While present people cannot (for the most part) be killed without violating their rights, it is within our collective power ultimately to *eliminate the violation of rights*—which is the rights-theorist's moral ideal—simply by refraining from procreation.

And can we justify doing any less? Anyone who has a full-blooded conception of rights can be morally certain that his children (if any) will have their rights violated from time to time; they are also likely to violate the rights of others on occasion. These potential rights-violations can be prevented only by having no children. It would seem, then, that the rights-theorist is committed to the collective self-extinction of the class of moral agents.

The best hope for evading this unpalatable conclusion is to draw a distinction between different ways in which a rights-violation can be brought about. Let us say that if I beget or bear a child whose rights are then violated by someone else, I am not responsible, even though my procreative action is a necessary condition for the violation, and even if I foresaw that the violation would occur. Someone else is the rights-violator, for *his* action is the *proximate cause* of the violation. Similarly, if my child violates someone's rights it would not be proper to blame *me* simply because I produced him. On this view the rights-theorist's moral imperative is: Do not *yourself* violate anyone's rights. Only actions which directly result in rights-violations are prohibited, not actions which are mere necessary conditions for the violations. In general, one is not obliged at a given time to prevent others from later acting in violation of rights; and in particular, one is not obliged to remain childless.

This explanation (which requires further spelling-out, of course) addresses most of the problem; but there remains a residue untouched. Consider, for instance, an extreme example of an action with bad consequences in the distant future. Suppose we could now gain some slight advantage by using a nuclear technology that would produce hazardous wastes, which could be stored for a long while but which would inevitably escape eventually, causing deaths and sickness from radiation. Once the wastes exist, their escape is literally inevitable, as is the harm they will do. (Clearly the example is artificial; I am not seriously attempting to evaluate any actual nuclear technology.) This sort of effect, when brought about by human action, is considered by the rights-theorist to be a violation of rights; but by hypothesis none of the affected people have as yet been conceived—perhaps not even their parents have been. Is there any moral objection, from the point of view of a rights theory, to our use of this technology? The moral theory tells us not to violate rights; but is our use of this technology in itself a violation of rights?

It seems rather to be a necessary condition of (certain) violations, which is not *sufficient* without *further* actions—namely, acts of procreation—on the part of others. If the technology is adopted and at the same time procreation ceases, no ill efforts will ever be felt from the radiation; for by the time it escapes, there will be no people. This kind of case differs from the normal one; ordinarily procreation comes first, followed by the action which violates the created person's rights. Then we can regard the procreative act as blameless, the subsequent act as the violation. But in the present case the order is reversed: *first* the nuclear technology is adopted, and *only then* do the acts of procreation take place which result in deaths and sickness. So long as the facts about the nature of this technology are widely known,[4] the people who produce children under the circumstances have no excuse: *their* action is the proximate case of the violation of their children's rights, and so *they* have acted wrongly.

So it seems, if we look only at the rights of the children; but the rights-theorist can also appeal to the rights of the parents. And among them he can discern a new human right—hitherto overlooked, but not implausible—namely, the right to *blameless procreation.* Some writers have upheld a simple right to procreate; i.e., to make one's own decisions as to how many children to have, if any. But none have mentioned that, besides the normal forms of coercion which may not legitimately be applied to determine reproductive behavior, there is a sort of *moral* coercion which is equally illegitimate.

This is illustrated by our example of the nuclear technology. Suppose that before the technology is adopted I could have children without thereby violating their rights; but once the technology is adopted, the radiation will adversely affect any children I might have. Then the adoption of this technology deprives me of an ability which I formerly had—the ability *to have children without thereby violating their rights* (i.e., to procreate blamelessly). Here, then, is the objection to adopting this technology; not that it violates the rights of my (potential) children, but that it violates my right to blameless procreation.

Note that it would not avail the rights theorist to appeal to the simple right to procreate; on this basis alone no clear condemnation of the use of the nuclear technology will be forthcoming. The act of adopting this technology simply creates a conflict between my children's right not to be assaulted by radiation and my simple right to procreate. Creating such a conflict is not violating a right: situations in which rights conflict do not normally involve any rights-violations at all. Instead, the strengths of the competing rights must be weighed against each other; and the weaker must be *overridden* (not violated). In the present case the right not to be assaulted by radiation probably must be adjudged stronger than the right to procreate so the latter must give way before the former. (If, on the contrary, the right to procreate were deemed stronger, then it would remain in full force even after the adoption of the nuclear technology, and would not be *violated* by the latter at all. But the rights-theorist must dismiss this possibility, since he wants to claim that the children's being assaulted by radiation is a *violation,* not merely a *legitimate overriding,* of their rights.)

Perhaps it is preferable to reject the idea of *real* conflicts of rights by conceiving of rights as conditional, each containing the implicit proviso: ". . . provided this does not conflict with the exercise of a stronger right." If so, again, the adoption of the nuclear technology does not violate my (conditional) right to procreate, but (at worst) renders it inoperative by falsifying the proviso. Only the stronger right to *blameless* procreation will give the rights theorist a basis for condemning the adoption of the nuclear technology.

This new right may seem to add to the proliferation of putative rights about which some commentators have complained in recent years. But it actually seems less problematic that many of its fellows. Rights to, e.g., a good diet, a loving and supportive environment, an education, a job, must be conceived as "positive" or "welfare" rights, rights which impose a duty on others not just to refrain from acting upon the rights-possessor in certain ways, but actively to provide him with certain benefits if he lacks them. Such rights are evidently conditional, and not just upon their non-interference with stronger rights: for it might be physically impossible to observe them (there might not be enough food to go around, or enough resources to provide everyone with education). Furthermore, they seem to require some inbuilt qualification to allow for the fact that it may be through one's own reckless or improvident actions that he finds himself without food, universally hated, or otherwise lacking in that to which he allegedly had a right. But the right to blameless procreation can be conceived as a purely negative right—if I am in a position in which I can have children without thereby violating their rights, no one may legitimately force me out of that position. At least for present purposes it need not be added that if I am *not* in that position others are obliged to *put me in it.*

Is this new right a right to *unlimited* blameless procreation, or is it limited to, say, one or two children? In a world choked and suffocating with overpopulation (a hypothetical world, which may or may not be our actual one) would it be plausible to uphold the unlimited version of this right—or even a limited one? I think the unlimited right can be vindicated.

Indeed, in the overpopulated world it may well be that everyone is actually *in a position* to procreate as much as he likes without violating anyone's rights. Since it is hard to see how the rights of bystanders could be violated by the mere production of a new child,[5] let us focus on the rights of the child itself. If there are not welfare rights, or if welfare rights are given a conditional interpretation in which the welfare right to X is just the fact that *if possible* everyone should have, then the child's rights will not be violated by its conception. For example, conceiving a child that inevitably will starve does not violate its rights if it has no right to food, or if it has only a conditional right and the condition is not met (e.g., because there is a food shortage). This is different from the case of conceiving a child after the nuclear technology has been adopted: in the latter the child will be *assaulted,* and so (it is plausible to suppose) a purely negative right of his is violated.

Perhaps, though, there is a stronger sort of welfare right to food, which is violated when parents conceive a child who they know will starve. Still, it is not likely that the parents' procreative act is the proximate cause of the children's starving; for probably there are others who could provide food for the children, even if the parents cannot. If the children nevertheless starve it is these others who have violated the children's welfare right to be fed: the parents are blameless.

But in the absence of such others, and in the presence of strong welfare rights, it is true that people *cannot* procreate blamelessly. They lack the ability or opportunity to do so. However, this is no basis for denying them the right to blameless procreation: the distinction between right and ability or opportunity is fundamental for the understanding of rights. Probably the people came to be unable to procreate blamelessly because their right was violated by someone (e.g., by their parents in conceiving them); although if we introduce "acts of God" or natural disasters as possible proximate causes, we may be able to explain this lack of opportunity without blaming anyone. But in any case let us not confuse right with opportunity. Lack of opportunity may make a right *empty* or *valueless*, but not *non-existent*. . . .

We have discussed the case in which an individual's possible future children would be physically affected by a present action, though he himself would not be; and pointed out that such as action can be viewed as violating one of his rights. Now, because of the nature of this right—the right to blameless procreation—the analysis can be iterated indefinitely, and so applied to cases in which the physical effects are felt only by a more distantly future generation. People in the generation immediately prior to that in which the effects are felt have had one of their rights violated, as has already been explained. But if the action in question occurred before *their* conception, then their parents should not have had *them* (assuming the circumstances were known). For it was already determined beforehand that one of their rights would be violated—namely, the right to blameless procreation. In conceiving them, their parents knowingly caused a violation of their rights, for which the parents must bear the responsibility. But since the parents are thus blameworthy, *their* right to blameless procreation must have been violated. If the action which brought about this situation occurred before *their* conception, their parents ought not to have had *them*; etc. No matter how distant are the consequences, it will still be true that the rights of contemporary people are violated by the same act that would violate the rights of the future people (if there were any). Note that when the physical effects are several generations distant it is even clearer that the right to procreation *simpliciter* does not, while the right to *blameless* procreation does, provide a basis for condemning the action.

In practical cases we would not be sure who would be adversely affected by the radiation, or just when it would escape. This introduces the complicating factor of uncertainty, and raises the question: If I am not sure whether a possible action of mine will violate someone's rights, but believe that the probability is p that it will do so, then how close to unity must p be for the rights theory to forbid my doing the action? This question, though, is beyond the scope of the present note, as are a number of other familiar questions about how a rights theory of morality should be spelled out. Nor have I addressed the difficult general question: which rights are and which are not accompanied by the right to their blameless exercise?

Indeed, my aim has been limited to determining how a rights theory might best cope with the problem of actions affecting the further future. We have seen that, contrary to first appearances, such a theory can forbid certain actions whose negative physical effects occur only in the distant future, on the grounds that they do after all infringe a right of people now living.

There remains of the original problem only this much: that if, contrary to morality, the nuclear technology *is* used and the wastes generated, the rights theory seems to imply that people in the last generation before the radiation escapes should all stop having children, lest they be responsible for the violation of the children's rights. This is not obviously the correct answer, since even if they are condemned to die early from the escaped radiation the children will perhaps have lives that are worth living as a whole. Furthermore, the rights theory might condemn the conception of the children even if the radiation were to produce only sickness, not death: the issue here turns on whether the right not to be sickened by radiation is stronger or weaker than the simple right to procreate. (If stronger, we get an unacceptable conclusion; if weaker, we have no rights-theoretical basis for condemning the adoption of a nuclear technology whose wastes produce only sickness.) Finally, the rights theory seems to condemn the conception of children who would not be affected by the radiation but whose descendants would be. It will do so if the children's right to blameless procreation is considered stronger than the parents' simple right to procreate—as it must be in order to support the rights-theorist's condemnation of the nuclear technology. Clouding these issues is the fact that there are no generally accepted guidelines for weighing rights against each other. But my analysis has at least narrowed the scope of the problem facing the rights-theorist, and indicated the lines along which his defense of his position must proceed.[6]

Notes

1. J. McMahan, "Problems of population theory," *Ethics* 92 (1981), pp. 96–127, Section IX.

2. D. Parfit, *Reasons and Persons* (Oxford, 1984), Part Four, Section 124: "Why an appeal to rights cannot solve the problem."

3. This now-familiar point was first made by Derek Parfit, "On doing the best for our children," in Michael D. Bayles, ed., *Ethics and Population* (Cambridge, MA, 1976), pp. 100–115.

4. I assume full information on the part of every agent in the situation; for my purposes ignorance would present an unprofitable complication.

5. In a fuller analysis the situation of the siblings, if any, would have to be considered explicitly.

6. This paper was read before the Canadian Philosophical Association, May, 1985. For helpful comments I want to thank the CPA referees, especially Trudy Govier, and my commentator, Thomas Hurka.

39

Robert O. Vos

Thinking About Sustainable Development: What's Theory Got to Do With It?

Introduction

The wide scope of classic and contemporary political thought included in this volume challenges readers to link together common themes. Given the expanding magnitude and types of environmental problems as the world approaches the twenty-first century, an additional challenge is to reconsider classic texts in light of new information about the natural world. This concluding chapter responds to these twin challenges by exploring the implications of environmental change for human freedom and thus democracy. A key issue in environmental policy making at the close of the twentieth century is defining the precise terms of "sustainable" development (Vos 1996). Applying Aristotle's theory of freedom and necessity makes for a new and pragmatic way of conceptualizing this issue. Sustainable development may be more precisely defined as: environmental policy choices that, at a minimum, sustain freedom and democracy for future generations.

It is symptomatic of the disciplinary division between scholars of political theory and of environmental policy that the issue has seldom been considered this way. Although environmental scholars have argued extensively about the effect of *liberal democracy upon the environment* (see Press in chapter 37 and Cahn in chapter 15 of this volume), scholars who consider contemporary prospects for democracy have hardly begun to note the effect of *changes in ecology upon freedom and democracy* (Dahl 1989; Held 1993). By bringing important scientific theory and information together with excerpts from classic political texts, this volume provides a solid foundation for making a preliminary inquiry into this issue.

The notion of human freedom is so broad that nearly every chapter in this volume touched on it. At the outset, therefore, it is important to narrow the range of inquiry by specifying the traditional conceptualization of freedom that political philosophers have used since Aristotle first composed the *Politics*. Once Aristotle's theory of the opposing realms of "freedom" and "necessity" is introduced, the chapter will trace the implications of environmental change for this theory through the works of many theorists represented in this volume.

Aristotle's Realms of Freedom and Necessity

At the beginning of part one, a selection from Aristotle provided an effective glimpse of his vision of nature. In essence, Aristotle views nature as a realm of "necessity," a word he uses both in its causal sense (one thing necessitates another) and in the sense of basic "necessities." For Aristotle, nature "comes-to-be" accidentally and is then spontaneously preserved when it fulfills its own needs (or withers and perishes if it fails to do so). In contrast to human endeavors and tools, nature does not do things "by art or after any inquiry or deliberation" (this volume, page 21). It does not choose and is, in this crucial way, "un-free." The realm of necessity (nature) is the opposite (or "antithesis") of the realm of freedom (human potential).

One important implication of this view is that although the realms of necessity and freedom are opposites, they are also very much related to one another. A straightforward way to think about this is to consider one's own life situation: any individual's chance to pursue a lifestyle full of choices (i.e., "free") is predicated upon the satisfaction of a range of basic needs. Thus, the realm of necessity is closely related to the realm of freedom.

Given Aristotle's fundamental observation, it is worthwhile to inquire whether the rapidity and scale of environmental change the world now confronts may, by reshaping the realm of necessity, affect humanity's prospects for freedom and democracy. Continually evolving scientific evidence must be taken into account in order to derive specific answers. But it is already clear that as society grapples with older, "first-generation" environmental problems like basic air and water pollution, newer problems with toxic chemicals and global pollution press for an adequate response (Ringquist 1993).

The seriousness of the global ecological situation indicates that it matters not so much what the precise limit to growth is in terms of human survival (see Daly, chapter 34 in this volume). Rather, freedom for future generations may erode even in the attempt to grow infinitely. As natural capital is irrevocably destroyed and the complexity of ecosystems undermined, the present takes away the capacity of the future to determine its own needs.[1] The future is faced with the extensive costs of cleanup in an ecosystem that is less complex and thus less resilient to human modification. In Aristotelian terms, actions in the present may expand the realm of necessity for the future and thus encroach on its realm of freedom.

Freedom and Necessity Before Environmental Change

For theorists who wrote at the dawn of the modern age, the capacity humans were soon to attain for making large and rapid environmental change was hardly apparent. John Locke, for example, views natural resources as essentially infinite. Sustainability was not an issue. For Locke, the realm of necessity is easily fulfilled by any industrious citizen. His justification for private property in a society where men are "free" and "equal" rests upon this expansive view of natural capital. He writes that the appropriation of any parcel of land, by improving it, is no prejudice to anyone, "since there is still enough, and as good left for others" (chapter 10 this volume).

The essential connection Locke finds between property and freedom derives from Aristotle's argument about freedom and necessity. In short, Locke makes an individual-size version of Aristotle. The ability to hold private property assures the political freedom of an individual who desires to stand apart from his community. Locke's widely practiced theory of individual freedoms, equality, and property rights would need to be different if it were written assuming today's ecological circumstances. The celebrated frontier is a relic of the past (see Cahn, chapter 15).

Locke's claim that "land" would "scarcely be worth any thing" without the application of labor (his "labor theory of value") and that lands that are unused "lie waste" was also a common view at the dawn of modernity. This view clearly reflects an undervaluation of ecological systems, creating a legacy with which we must still grapple today (see Cahn, chapter 15 in this volume).[2]

One solution to this legacy of undervalued ecological systems is proposed in chapter 33 by Anderson and Leal. Founding their argument in a discourse of individual rights and freedom, they advocate removing ecological systems from the common (public) domain of either ownership or regulation by public auction. Theoretically, a free market would then act to price various components of the ecosystem. Eventually, assuming an informed group of consumers, prices might come to reflect the "free" demands of millions of consumers making individual choices about the value of the environment. Such a system, they argue, would be a democratic guide to the level of environmental protection.

There are important questions, however, about whether this hypothetical approach, even if it were technically feasible, would actually provide greater individual freedom. In the short term, their proposal would simply mirror a mass of individual choices, utterly lacking the deliberation of major ethical questions essential to democratic theory. In the long term, their proposal fails to account for freedom and choice for future generations. For example, even with perfect technology, future generations might be forced to accept "ex situ" conservation of a species or a technological re-creation of wilderness if present consumer demand was inadequate to preserve species in their original habitat. The free-market model of "consumer choice" breaks down here and its ethical roots in maximizing individual utility in the present become evident in the rupture. The approach undermines its own claims to provide freedom: future generations must accept "freely" the degradation passed onto them.

Freedom During the Reshaping of Necessity

Although theorists writing at the beginning of modernity could not anticipate the issue of sustainability, several began to question the effect of modernity on human freedom in a different way. These theorists worried about the influence of society and modernity in shifting human perceptions of necessity. In this volume, Rousseau, Emerson, and Thoreau each spoke to this concern about a loss of metaphysical (as opposed to strictly physical/economic) freedom.[3]

In his *Discourse on Inequality,* Rousseau traces his version of the emergence of human society from the state of nature. He writes that enlarging the scope of necessity "was the first yoke they [men] had unwittingly imposed on themselves . . . continuing to soften their bodies and minds, through habit these conveniences lost all their charm and degenerated into real needs, so that the pain of being deprived of them was much greater than the pleasure of having them, and men were unhappy to lose them without being happy to possess them" (this volume, page 67). In short, as man came to live in society he became accustomed to luxuries which increased his estimation of necessity. This in turn undermined his previously free condition as "his multitude of new needs now placed him in subjection to all of nature, so to speak, and especially to his fellow man" (this volume, page 72).

A similar concern with increasing dependence and subjection to society and modern convenience drove Thoreau to experiment with a solitary and independent life on Walden Pond. In *Walden,* he takes note of a set of pure or spiritual needs that he believes were obscured by an increasing emphasis on material and sensual possession. He observes that people who went fishing, "commonly . . . did not think that they were lucky, or well paid for their time, unless they got a long string of fish, though they had the opportunity of seeing the pond the whole time" (see chapter 17). Appetites for certain sensual goods (like money and food) had become so acute, Thoreau argues, that a whole set of social strictures had sprung up around even more basic human needs (like "cohabitation"). Thus he writes, "We are so degraded that we cannot speak simply of the necessary functions of human nature" (this volume, page 145).

In contrast to Thoreau's deep questioning of modernity, Ralph Waldo Emerson provides positive answers as a guide to greater liberty. Emerson surmises that greater freedom can be attained by dropping away one's preconceptions. He reports that, "At the gates of the forest, the surprised man of the world is forced to leave behind his city estimates of great and small, wise and foolish. The knapsack of custom falls off his back with the first step he makes into these precincts" (page 147). Throughout the essay, Emerson writes eloquently of the wonderment and near epiphanies that can be achieved in the natural experience. Needs, he argues, are much more relative and subject to human perception than people normally recognize: "Ah! if the rich were as rich as the poor fancy riches!" (see chapter 18).

Emerson and Thoreau both grapple with the erosion of metaphysical freedom in yet another way, contemplating the result of the technological domination of nature begun as a project of modernity. This question is still relevant, as ultimately such domination is required by theorists (primarily economists) who continue to presume that infinite economic growth is possible (see chapter 34 by Daly for a critical review of these theories). For these theorists, sustainability is about developing the technology to allow ongoing, incremental increases in economic "throughput" ("sustainable growth") (Vos 1996).

Even if such domination were attainable, such a project raises important questions about the impact upon the freedom of the individual human subject. The "other" (realm of necessity, nature) that humans have traditionally defined themselves against would disappear. This idea encompasses the "Hegelian concept of a self that develops by continually reinterpreting the world, enriching and deepening both parties in the process. . . . The individual self recollects and recognizes itself in this, its 'other' (nature), and so comes to know itself" (Hinchman and Hinchman 1989, 207). A wholly dominated or disenchanted nature would interrupt this process of identification by humans with their rational and free natures. Thus, at the very moment that humans achieved technological domination of nature, human nature would become dominated as well. As C. S. Lewis writes, "man surrenders object after object, and finally himself to nature in return for power" (1993, 239).

As the rapid and irreversible changes that humanity can bring upon nature now become more apparent, the scale of the erosion of metaphysical freedom reaches social and not merely individual proportions. Changes to nature such as widespread, human-induced species extinctions take away from future generations the opportunity to choose an ethical path different from that of the present—to choose a different path to a "good life." Stone (1987; 1993) has written about the concept of "moral pluralism," granting varying shades of moral consideration to different beings. He acknowledges that the selection of any one framework cannot be derived from foundational moral postulates. "It is the question with which philosophy began. . . . How ought one to live?" (1993, 280). In the context of debates about sustainability, it is important to recognize that our current path is rapidly depriving future generations of this fundamental choice among ethical frameworks. It may leave them without "liberty" in its most ancient and all-encompassing sense.

Freedom and Necessity in the Modern Age

Following the onset of the modern age, theorists began to deal directly with the implications of modernization (and to some degree environmental change) for the objective, material base that shapes the realm of necessity. Although these thinkers stop short of delineating the implications of modernity for sustainable development, many concepts they develop are key to the understanding of sustainability advanced here. In this volume, Karl Marx and Herbert Marcuse each considered this physical or economic type of freedom in addition to the metaphysical discussed above.

The foundation for much of Marx's political theory is traceable to his fully grasping the implications of Aristotle's realms of freedom and necessity for his own age. One of Marx's major contributions is to advance the case that the market economy (a realm of necessity) is a fundamental force in shaping political life (optimistically a realm of freedom). For Marx, an important and often ignored common denominator across historical epochs is the struggle of the human "species-being" to extract its survival and eventually freedom from the natural world. Thus, Marx criticizes "idealist" thinkers immediately before him for making the historical into something separated from ordinary life.[4] He writes, "With this the relation of man to nature is excluded from history and hence the antithesis of nature and history is created" (Tucker 1978, 165).

Superficial readings of Marx lead many to believe that Marx holds a labor theory of value directly parallel to that of John Locke. Although in the selection from *The Critique of Political Economy* Marx wrote that "as exchange values, all commodities are merely definite quantities of *congealed labour-time,*" this view is supplemented by the important caveat that necessary labor time itself is affected by many conditions, including, "the conditions found in the natural environment" (see chapter 11).

The conceptual leap that Marx makes by understanding the dual relationship between the realms of freedom and necessity thus subtly shifts his labor theory of value. In short, he envisions *some* role for the production of natural systems. When a socialist movement of Marx's own time dutifully regurgitated the idea that "labor is the source of all wealth and culture," Marx complained, "Labour is not the source of all wealth. Nature is just as much a source of use values" (Tucker 1978, 525). To ignore this, Marx writes, is to forget that

> the bourgeois have very good grounds for falsely ascribing supernatural creative power to labour; since precisely from the fact that labour depends on nature it follows that the man who possesses no other property than his labour power must, in all conditions of society and culture, be the slave of other men who have made themselves the owners of the material condition of labour. (Tucker 1978, 526)

To show that this view is not an anomaly in Marx's writings, we need only explore a passage from volume one of *Capital* where he stresses that in the process of transforming nature, man is "constantly helped by natural forces," or, in a vivid metaphor, "labour is the father and earth the mother" (Tucker 1978, 309).

Recent revisions in interpretation of the role of nature in Marx's theory of value increase the usefulness of his theory in conceptualizing sustainability. Scholars are beginning to use Marx to understand the effect of the environmental crisis on the economies of contemporary and future societies. Like much else, the now dead Soviet experiment in "actually-existing socialism" interpreted Marx fundamentally incorrectly on the role of nature in conferring value (Bronner 1990).

Contemporary theorists are now hypothesizing that capitalist accumulation may be threatened by a second crisis as costs can no longer be easily externalized upon (or in Marxist terms "appropriated from") a bountiful ecological system (see O'Connor 1994).[5] This crisis theory roughly parallels the crisis of the centralization of capitals Marx predicts in the second selection from *The Critique of Political Economy.* If the crisis of the centralization of capitals destroys consumer "demand" and thus undermines the process of accumulation, the second ecological crisis, it is hypothesized, results from the destruction of nature's use-values (a crisis of supply) (O'Connor 1994).

The work of Herbert Marcuse (see chapter 14) also continues to be relevant in assessing the impact of modernization on freedom. While Marcuse writes both about human perceptions of need and material conditions, his focus is on the effect of advanced capitalism on material conditions that shape the realm of necessity. Marcuse hopes that, *potentially,* human technological and ethical progress "might release individual energy into a yet uncharted realm of freedom beyond necessity," in which "the individual would be liberated from the work world's imposing upon him alien needs and alien possibilities" (chapter 14, page 112). However, he views the developed modern age as deeply threatening this potential. Developed capitalism is responsible for "the most effective and enduring form of warfare against liberation . . . the implanting of material and intellectual needs that perpetuate obsolete forms of the struggle for existence" (page 113). Such implanting of needs is seen quite directly in environmental terms: increasing appropriation, pollution, and development of ecological systems make it necessary to purchase clean air, clean water, and natural splendor.

In terms of the idea of human freedom, a small-scale example clarifies the concerns these scholars are raising. In Los Angeles's San Gabriel Valley, lingering toxic groundwater pollution is the result of percolation of pollutants from a string of waste sites, many of which are priorities on the federal "Superfund" list. Originally, these dumps represented the externalization of costs (or "appropriation of ecological systems") by various companies growing rapidly in the Los Angeles region's postwar economic boom. However, with drinking water supplies now threatened, the capacity of local governments in the region to budget and plan for water allocations for the future is undermined. The cleanup will be incredibly costly, and in the meantime water must be imported from outside the area. Since clean drinking water is a basic human necessity, the freedom of local citizens and the autonomy of local governments have been directly curtailed. In addition, companies will likely have to take much more costly steps to control such wastes. Mounting costs of this sort on a global scale, it is feared, would cut into profits, undermine accumulation of wealth, and thus induce an economic crisis.

Implications for the Future of Freedom and Democracy

An important theme that emerges from the foregoing discussion of Aristotle's realms of freedom and necessity in contemporary ecological terms is the effect of policy choices made today on freedom for future generations. Rethinking environmental policy choices in Aristotelian terms clarifies what it means to develop sustainably.

The issue of what moral obligation the present holds for posterity is addressed by several authors in this volume. In addition to whatever material wealth the present transmits to posterity, John Rawls reminds us that "capital is not only factories and machines, and so on, but also the knowledge and culture, as well as the techniques and skills, that make possible just institutions and the fair value of liberty" (chapter 13, page 107). In closing, we should briefly consider the implications of our discussion if citizens of the present care to sustain freedom and democracy into the future.

The straightforward way to view this issue is to wonder how extensively various environmental choices might shape the realms of necessity and freedom for posterity. Of course, every generation imposes its choices on other generations to some extent. The question is one of degree: how much ought the present impose? Considered within one generation, this is much the same problem as that behind Kant's Philosophy of Right.[6]

In the *Philosophy of Right,* Kant argues that human subjects must exercise their own rights and freedoms in such a way that, if raised to a universal law, the exercise would not infringe on the rights and freedoms of others. Critics have long pointed out that almost any exercise of rights by one individual will to some extent infringe on the freedom of others. Thus, a fully developed civil society is necessitated in order to deliberate upon and inscribe boundaries for conduct. Similarly, a fully developed democratic discourse about environmental matters will be necessary to inscribe boundaries to protect a range of choices (i.e., freedom) for future generations.

Given the close link between freedom and democracy, the survival of democracy itself may well depend on the accommodations reached regarding rapid and large transformations in the earth's environment. It seems hyperbolic to suggest that we are at such a crucial historical juncture. However, as Rachel Carson reminds us, "In the modern world there is no time" (chapter 19, page 151). The capacity humans have attained to reshape the ecological systems of the earth matches or exceeds nearly every event in the geological history of the planet.

Political scientists have long noted the effect of agenda setting on the opportunity for democratic decision making. Bachrach and Baratz (1962) argue that there are really "two faces" to political power. A polity that chooses between a limited range of alternatives and has no opportunity to shape those alternatives is hardly democratically empowered. Even if no ecological catastrophe occurs in the near term, some choices we are on the verge of making will be substantially irreversible. They will shape the agenda of the future in such a restrictive way as to be incompatible with the "reversibility" principle of rational and democratic decision making procedures (Demirovic 1994, 262).

But the close, nearly tautological association between sustaining democracy and sustaining nature defined here also gives some reason for optimism (see also Press, chapter 37 in this volume). As Achterberg writes, "The insight that the perspective of sustainable development is connected with the normative-political principles which justify liberal democracy may be important in view of the [need for the] legitimation of serious environmental policies" (1993, 91). When the broader public awakes to the close connection between protecting the biosphere and preserving freedom for the future, support may finally emerge to launch the serious transformations required to achieve ecological sustainability into the next century.

Notes

The author wishes to thank Judith Grant, Sheldon Kamieniecki, Matthew Cahn, and Rory O'Brien for helpful comments at various stages in the preparation of this chapter.

1. I use "natural capital" here in the sense of positive entropy. Without violating the second law of thermodynamics, energy used for human gain from reductions in positive entropy can never be recovered (see chapter 34 by Daly in this volume for greater detail).
2. I use the term "ecological systems" here in order to represent a systems or process-oriented approach to natural resources (see Commoner in this volume for greater detail). This approach includes things like the systemic value of viable wetlands in cleaning water resources.
3. Robyn Eckersley labels this the "emancipatory green critique." She particularly includes critical theorists of liberation like Herbert Marcuse (in this volume) in this group. See her 1992 work for details.
4. In this context, "idealism" refers to the preoccupation of German philosophy immediately preceding Marx (i.e., "German Idealism") with ideas as independent from material circumstances (e.g., Kant and Hegel). In this volume, for example, Kant argues that certain postulates could be derived a priori, with no empirical or material basis.
5. Scholars need to exercise caution in interpreting and discussing this "second crisis" of capitalism lest we repeat the same errors of theorizing in an overly determinate and teleological manner as were first made with Marx's theories. O'Connor (1994) comes particularly close to implying a definitive teleology of revolution based upon this theory. However, there are no guarantees: the subjective moment of human identification, thought, and action still must happen.
6. Kant's Philosophy of Right is mainly an extension of his categorical imperative (see chapter 12 in this volume).

References

Achterberg, Wouter. 1993. "Can Liberal Democracy Survive the Environmental Crisis? Sustainability, Liberal Neutrality, and Overlapping Consensus." In *The Politics of Nature,* ed. A. Dobson and P. Lucardie, pp. 81–101. New York: Routledge.

Bachrach, Peter and Morton S. Baratz. 1962. "Two Faces of Power." *American Political Science Review* 56: 947–52.

Bronner, Stephen Eric. 1990. *Socialism Unbound.* New York: Routledge.

Dahl, Robert A. 1989. *Democracy and Its Critics.* New Haven: Yale University Press.

Demirovic, Alex. 1994. "Ecological Crisis and the Future of Democracy." In *Is Capitalism Sustainable? Political Economy and the Politics of Ecology,* ed. M. O'Connor, pp. 253–74. New York: Guilford Press.

Eckersley, Robyn. 1992. *Environmentalism and Political Theory: Toward an Ecocentric Approach.* Albany: State University of New York Press.

Held, David, ed. 1993. *Prospects for Democracy.* Stanford, CA: Stanford University Press.

Hinchman, Lewis P., and Sandra K. Hinchman. 1989. "Deep Ecology and the Revival of Natural Right." *Western Political Quarterly* 42: 201–28.

Lewis, C.S. 1993. "The Abolition of Man." In *Valuing the Earth: Economics, Ecology, Ethics,* ed. H.E. Daly and K. Townsend, pp. 229–41. Cambridge: The Massachusetts Institute of Technology Press.

O'Connor, Martin. 1994. "Introduction: Liberate, Accumulate—and Bust?" In *Is Capitalism Sustainable? Political Economy and the Politics of Ecology,* ed. M. O'Connor, pp. 1–22. New York: Guilford Press.

Ringquist, Evan J. 1993. *Environmental Protection at the State Level: Politics and Progress in Controlling Pollution.* Armonk, NY: M.E. Sharpe, Inc.

Stone, Christopher D. 1987. *Earth and Other Ethics: The Case for Moral Pluralism.* New York: Harper and Row.

———. 1993. *The Gnat Is Older Than Man: Global Environment and Human Agenda.* Princeton, NJ: Princeton University Press.

Tucker, Robert C. 1978. *The Marx-Engels Reader.* New York: W.W. Norton and Company.

Vos, Robert O. 1996 (forthcoming). "Competing Approaches to Sustainability: Dimensions of Controversy." In *Flash Points in Environmental Policymaking: Controversies in Achieving Sustainability,* ed. Sheldon Kamieniecki, George A. Gonzalez, and Robert O. Vos. Albany: State University of New York Press.

Index

Achterberg, Wouter, 290
Acid rain, 218
Air Quality Act, 133
America, John Locke on, 83–85
Anderson, Terry L., 210, 242–248, 283
Anti-class posture, 168–169
Appleby, Joyce, 122
Aristotle, 14, 15, 20–24, 282–283, 286
Art, and nature, 21–22
Augustine, Saint, 15–16, 25–28
Authoritarianism. *See* Government, role of

Bachrach, Peter, 289
Baratz, Morton S., 289
Bass Angler Sportsman Society v. United States Steel Corp., 223–224
Bellah, Robert, 123
Bentham, 174, 175
Berry, Wendell, quoted, 232, 233
Bible, 14, 15, 17, 18–19
Biophilia, 228
Biospherical egalitarianism, 168
Black Power (Carmichael and Hamilton), 197
Blameless procreation, 276–280
Blauner, Robert, 197
Bluhm, William T., quoted, 263
Bookchin, Murray, 136, 185–192
Bourke, John G., 34
Brower, David, 230
Bullard, Robert D., 136, 196–202
Bureau of Reclamation, 263

Cahn, Matthew Alan
  on future strategies, 63, 207–212
  on "Green Critique", 131–137
  on liberalism, 120–126
Cameron, Roderick A., quoted, 164
Capitalism
  and environmental quality, 63, 120, 125, 126, 210–212
  Marx on, 60, 91–95
Capital (Marx), 60, 287
Carmichael, S., 197
Carson, Rachel, 133–134, 150–155, 229
  quoted, 228, 289
Carter, Jimmy, 243
Categorical imperative. *See* Imperatives
Catton, William R., 240
CERCLA (Superfund), 125
Cerrell Associates, 199
Chance, 22
Chemicals, 134, 150, 151–155
"Children of Heaven and Earth, The", 37
Christianity, 13, 14–16, 163
Circular flow, in economics, 252–254
City of God (Augustine), 15–16, 25–28
Civic republicanism, 121
Civil society
  Locke on, 58
  Rousseau on, 60, 64–75
Clean Air Act, 133, 208
Clean Water Act, 208
Closing Circle, The (Commoner), 134, 161–166
Club of Rome, 235
Coal, 218

Colonialism, 239
Commodities, 60, 62–63, 87–91, 115
Commoner, Barry, 134
 on Earth Week, 161–165
 on laws of ecology, 165–166
Commons, the. *See Tragedy of the Commons* (Hardin)
Communal good, 121–122
Community, creating sense of, 230–231
Complexity-not-complication principle, 169–170
Conflict of Visions, A (Sowell), 244
Confronting Environmental Racism (Bullard), 136–137
Conservationism, 132
Control, Marcuse on, 112–119
Creation
 Biblical story of, 14, 18–19
 Native American stories of, 16–17, 29–37, 40–53
 and Saint Augustine, 25–28
Critical theory, 62
Critique of the Political Economy (Marx), 287

Daly, Herman E., 210–211, 250–255
Daly, Mary, 180
David, Rennie, quoted, 164
Davis, Wayne H., quoted, 162
Deep ecology, 135, 167–172
Democratic Dilemmas in the Age of Ecology (Press), 212, 265–271
Democratic Party, 258
Department of the Interior, 224–225
Diegueno creation story, 33–34
Discourse on Inequality (Rousseau), 59, 284
Disintegration, myths of, 185–186
Diversity, principle of, 168–169
Diversity of Life (Wilson), 193–195
Dominant Social Paradigm, 210
Downs, Anthony, 122
DuBois, Constance G., 33, 36, 37
Dubos, Rene, 229–230

Earth Day, 1970, 133
 Barry Commoner on, 161–165
Eckersley, R., 270
Ecological literacy, 227–234
 difficulties of, 229–231
 and education, 231–234
 goal of, 230–231, 234
Ecologism, 172
Ecology
 Bookchin on, 191
 Commoner's law of, 165–166
 definition of, 246
 and democracy, 265–271
 shallow vs. deep, 135, 167–172
 See also Ecological literacy; Environment
Ecology and the Politics of Scarcity (Ophuls), 267
Ecology of Freedom, The (Bookchin), 136
Ecology of Invasions, The (Elton), 154
Economic freedom, 113
Economic growth, 126, 242, 250–255
Ecosophy, 171–172
Eddington, Arthur, on entropy, 253–254
Education, and ecological literacy, 231–234
Ehrlich, Paul, 156–160
 quoted, 162
Eiseley, Loren, 230
 quoted, 254–255
Eisenhower, Dwight D., 132
Elton, Charles, 154
Emerson, Ralph Waldo, 132, 147–149, 285
Endangered Species Act, 133, 208
Entropy, 253–254
Environment
 Commoner on "discovery" of, 161–166
 liberalism and, 120–126
 way of viewing, 11–17
 See also Ecology; Environmentalism
Environmental Defense Fund, 222
Environmental ideology, 211
Environmentalism
 Bookchin on, 190
 free market, 242–248

Environmentalism *(continued)*
history of movement, 131–133, 208–209
and politics, 256–260, 265–271
Environmentalism and the Future of Progressive Politics (Paehlke), 211, 256–260
Environmental justice, 8, 196–202, 214–220
definition of, 217
Envisioning a Sustainable Society: Learning Our Way Out (Milbrath), 235–241
Epicurus, 27
Erlich, Paul, 134
Exchange-value, 88–91
Exponential growth, 236–237
Extinction, 194–195

Families
King on, 183
Rousseau on, 67
Federal Power Commission, 223
Federal Water Pollution Control Administration, 133
Feminism, and the environment, 135–136, 179–184
Fishing, Thoreau on, 141
Food, Thoreau on, 142–143
Fossil energy, 240
Foundations of the Metaphysics of Morals (Kant), 61
Free Market and Environmentalism (Anderson and Leal), 242–248
Fremlin, J.H., 175
on population, 157
Friends of the Earth, 222
Future, rights in, 273–280

Gender
in creation stories, 32–37
See also Feminism
Genesis, 14, 18–19
"Ghost acreage", 240
Global 2000 Report, 243
God. *See City of God*
Government, role of, 58, 242–248, 261–271

Griffin, Susan, 180
Grotius, 71
Growth
economic, 126, 242, 250–255
of population, 13, 156–160, 238–239
sustainable, 235–241
Guardianship, 221–226
Gutkind, E.A., quoted, 191

Haeckel, Ernst, 189
Hamilton, C.V., 197
Handbook of Indians of California (Kroeber), 36, 37
Happiness, Kant on, 98, 99
Hardin, Garrett, 135, 158, 173–178, 216, 266
on ecological literacy, 227
quoted, 162
Hartke, Vance, quoted, 163
Hartz, Louis, 122
Heilbroner, Robert, 212, 266–267
Heizer, Robert, 36, 37
Herzen, 109
Hickel, Walter, 133
Hierarchy
feminists on, 135–136, 179–184
in Luiseño religion, 31–32
Hill, Stuart, 268
Holism, 190, 191
Hopi myth of creation, 16–17, 40–53
Howard, Walter S., quoted, 162
Hudson, James L., 212, 273–280
Hultkrantz, Ake, 36, 37
Hunting, Thoreau on, 140–141
Hypothetical imperatives. *See* Imperatives

Imperatives, 61, 96–102
Industrial Revolution, 239
Inquiry into the Human Prospect (Heilbroner), 266
Insects, 151–155
Introjection, 116
Izaak Walton League, 222

Johnson, Lyndon, 133
Just distribution, 263

Justice, 5, 57
  between generations, 104–111
  environmental, 8, 196–202, 214–220
  Kant on, 61–62, 96–102
  Marcuse on, 62–63
  Rawls on, 62, 104–111
"Just savings principle", 62, 104–111

Kann, Mark E., 121
Kant, Immanuel, 58, 61–62, 96–102, 109, 289
  O'Brien on, 262–264
Kennedy, John F., 132, 208
King, Ynestra, 135–136, 179–184
Knapp, Sherman R., quoted, 162–163
Kroeber, Alfred L., 30, 36, 37

Labor, 169–170
  Locke on, 58–59, 76–86, 283
  Marx on, 60, 87, 89–91
Land and Water Conservation Fund Act, 133
Law, of ecology
  Barry Commoner's, 165–166
Law, rule of, 57
Lead poisoning, 202
Leal, Donald R., 210, 242–248
Leeson, Susan, 268
Leopold, Aldo, 229, 230
  quoted, 232
Lewis, C.S., quoted, 286
Liberal, defined, 137n
Liberalism, 58
  and environment, 120–126
  Lockean, 121–122
Life, diversity of, 193–195
Limits to Growth, The (MIT), 235
Lloyd, William Forster, 176
Local autonomy and decentralization principle, 170
  See also Government, role of
Locke, John, 8, 57–59, 76–86, 283, 287
  quoted, 69
Lopez, Barry, quoted, 228
Luiseño religion, creation story of, 16–17, 29–31

MacIntyre, Alasdair, 234
McMahon, Jefferson, 273
Macpherson, C.B., 122
McWilliams, Wilson, C., 123
Malthus, Thomas, 134, 242
Man's Responsibility for Nature (Passmore), 268
Maquiladoras, 200
Marcuse, Herbert, 62–63, 112–119
Marx, Karl, 57, 60, 87–95, 188, 286, 287
  feminism and, 181–182
Massachusetts Institute of Technology (MIT), 235, 242–243
Mencius, quoted, 144
Mercury, 165–166
Mexico, 200
Milbrath, Lester W., 210, 235–241
Military service, 123
Military spending, 259, 260
Money, Locke on, 81, 85–86
Morality, rights theories of, 273–276
Muir, John, 132
Myths
  of disintegration, 185–186
  See also Creation

Naess, Arne, 135, 167–172
National Park Service, 132, 178
National Trail Systems Act, 133
Native American myths of creation, 16–17, 29–37, 40–53
Natural Resources Defense Council, 222
Nature
  Aristotle on, 15, 20–24
  conversations with, 232–233
  Emerson on, 132, 147–149
  Rousseau on, 75
  state of, 58–59
  Thoreau on, 131–132, 139–146
  value of, 7–8
Nature Conservancy, 244
Needs, true vs. false, 114–115
Neoconservatives, 259–260
New Environmental Paradigm (NEP), 210
New Yorker, 134
Nieves, L.A., 198
Nixon, Richard M., 133
Norse myths, of disintegration, 185–186
North Cascades National Park, 133

O'Brien, Rory, 211, 261–264
on law, property, and environment, 57–63
on physical world, 11–17
Omi, Michael, 197
One Dimensional Man (Marcuse), 63
Ophuls, William, 266, 267, 270
Organismal growth, 236
Orr, David W., 209–210, 227–234, 268, 269
O'Toole, Randal, 247–248

Paehlke, Robert C., 211, 256–260
Paradigm
Milbrath's, 210
for undeveloped world, 11–17
Pareto Optimality, 125
Parfit, Derek, 273
Passmore, J., 268, 270
Pesticides. *See* Chemicals
Phillips, Channing E., quoted, 163
Philosophy, Greek, 15–16
Philosophy of Right (Kant), 289
Physics (Aristotle), 15
Plato, 14, 15
Platonists, on Augustine, 27
Pocock, J.G.A., 122
Pogo, quoted, 164
Political Difficulties Facing Waste-to-Energy Conversion Plant Siting (Cerrell Associates), 199
Political freedom, 113
Political theory, 3–5
and the environment, 265–271
Politics, progressive, 256–260
Pollution, 134, 150, 169, 170, 253
Population Bomb, The (Erlich), 134, 156–160
Population growth, 13, 156–160, 238–239
Hardin on, 174–176
Preservationism, 132, 208
Press, Daniel, 212, 265–271
Procreation, blameless, 276–280
Progress, 11, 13
Marcuse on, 118–119
See also Growth
Progressives, 259
Property
Locke on, 58–59, 76–86
Marx on, 60, 87–95
Rousseau on, 59–60, 64–75
Property rights, 5, 122, 124, 125, 207, 244
Public policy. *See* Government, role of

Racism, 136, 196–202
Radiation, 150–151
Radical, defined, 137n
Radical feminism, 182–183
Ragnarok legend, 185–186
Rawls, John, 58, 62, 104–111, 124–125, 263, 289
Redwood National Park, 133
"Religious Ceremonies and Myths of the Mission Indians" (DuBois), 33
Religious of the American Indians (Hultzkrantz), 36
Republican Party, 258
Resource depletion, 169
Rights
and the future, 273–280
legal, 221–226
See also Property rights
"Rights and the Further Future" (Hudson), 273–280
Riparian rights, 207, 208
Rodman, John, 269
Rostand, Jean, quoted, 155
Roth, William, quoted, 163
Rousseau, Jean-Jacques, 57, 59–60, 284
on private property, 64–75
Russell, Frank, 34

Safe Drinking Water Act, 208
Sandoval, Arturo, quoted, 163
Scarcity, 215–216
Scenic Hudson Preservation Conference v. FPC, 223
Schumpeter, Joseph, 122
Schweitzer, Albert, quoted, 151
Self-interest, 120, 121–125, 245–247, 264
Self-preservation, 59, 64
Sequoia National Forest, 223
Shallow ecology, 135, 167
Shays, Daniel, 121
Shepard, Paul, quoted, 155

Shepard, Thomas Jr., quoted, 164
Should Trees Have Standing? (Stone), 209, 221–226
Sierra Club, 132, 222, 223
Silent Spring (Carson), 133–134, 150–155
Simon, Julian, 243
Smith, Adam, 176
Social ecology, 136
  Bookchin on, 189–192
Socialism, and feminism, 181–182, 183
Soddy, Frederick, quoted, 251, 254
Solutions, technical, 173–174
Sowell, Thomas, 244
Spider Woman. *See* Hopi myth of creation
Steady-state economics, 250–255, 267
Steady-State Economics (Daly), 250–255
Stone, Christopher, 209, 221–226, 286
Storr, Anthony, quoted, 163
Strontium 90, 134, 150
Summers, Lawrence, 200
Sustainable development, 281–290
  defined, 281
Symbiosis, 168–169

Tales of the North American Indians (Thompson), 33
Taxes, 105, 219
Teleology, 15
Theory of Justice, A (Rawls), 62
Thompson, Stith, 33
Thoreau, Henry David, 131–132, 139–146, 284–284
Total-field image, 167–168
Totalitarianism
  Marcuse on, 112–113
  See also Government, role of
Toxic colonialism, 200–201
Toxic Substances Control Act, 208
Tragedy of the Commons (Hardin), 158, 173–178, 216, 219, 237–238, 266
Train, Russell, 133
Truman, Harry S, 132
Truths, shallow vs. deep, 6–7
Turner, Neeley, quoted, 155
Two Treatises of Government (Locke), 58

Udall, Stewart, 132–133
Unions, 260
United States Forest Service, 247
United States Steel Corporation, 223–224
Unruh, Jesse, quoted, 161
Use-value, 60, 87–91

Value, 60, 87–91
Vitousek, Peter M., 239
Vos, Robert O., 281–290

Walden, 285
  See also Thoreau, Henry David
Walt Disney Company, 223
Waste, 165–166, 211
  and racism, 199
Water, 215, 263, 288
Waterman, Thomas, 33
Water Quality Act, 133
Wealth of Nations, The (Smith), 176
Weisner, J.B., 173
Wenz, Peter S., 125, 209, 214–220
Wernette, D.R., 198
Wheeler, William Morton, quoted, 229
White, Lynn, quoted, 163
White, R.C., 31
Wild and Scenic Rivers Act, 133
Wilderness Act, 133
Wiley, George, quoted, 162
Willis, Ellen, on feminism, 179–180
Wilson, Edward O., 136, 193–195
  quoted, 228
Winant, Howard, 197
Wisconsin Nature Conservancy, 244
Wiyot. *See* Luiseño religion
Wood, Gordon, 121
Work. *See* Labor
World Bank, 200–201

Yellowstone National Park, 132, 208
York, H.F., 173
Yosemite Valley, 132, 208

About the Editors

Matthew Alan Cahn is Associate Professor of Public Policy at California State University, Northridge. He has written extensively on environmental issues and public policy. His books include *Environmental Deceptions* (State University of New York Press, 1995), *Public Policy* (with Stella Theodoulou, Prentice Hall, 1995), and *Rethinking California* (with H. Eric Schockman, Prentice Hall, forthcoming). He is currently completing *Building Evaluative Models in Environmental Policy: State Innovations in Environmental Management* (State University of New York Press, forthcoming).

Rory O'Brien is Adjunct Assistant Professor of Environmental Studies at the University of Southern California. He is currently completing work on a project entitled *Just Enough Water? Distributive Justice and Scarce Resource Management*, which focuses on justice and scarce resource management in the western United States.